STOP
WORRYING

Live in the peace
& favor of God

TROY BLACK

INSPIRE
CHRISTIAN BOOKS

TroyBlackVideos.com

TABLE OF CONTENTS

INTRODUCTION

I remember the biting sensation shooting down my neck and into my spine as I unloaded my camera equipment. Normally, weddings thrill me, but all I could focus on this time was the pain. Because of my experience with video production, I had been asked to film my sister-in-law's outdoor ceremony. They had planned an elaborate event. We danced. We ate. We stared into the sun as they said, "I do." Someone sang (not me, thank God). Most importantly, we witnessed the beautiful joining of two fantastic people. Yet, the whole time, the irritation in my head and neck kept me from fully appreciating and celebrating the moment. I also remember dreading the idea of combing through the footage. I knew it wouldn't be my best effort due to my condition—whatever my condition happened to be.

The day after the wedding, my wife and I drove five hours back to our home. By the end of that trip, I had decided to see a doctor about the random pain. Along with the stabbing tingles jolting through my neck, large, red spots began to appear on the back of my head. I hoped the doctor could give me some answers.

After briefly checking over my neck and head, running her fingers along my jaw, and asking me a couple questions about my daily habits, she announced her diagnosis.

"That's shingles. Yes, that's definitely shingles."

Shingles? I had heard the term before, but I couldn't place it. I let her explain how the redness behind and above my ear matched the normal pattern of the rash. I even let her get excited about having never seen the virus in someone my age before. She said she had been a doctor for twenty years, and she had rarely seen shingles in someone younger than fifty-five. I was twenty-five. I couldn't wait any longer to know.

"How serious is this?" I asked.

She altered her excited expression momentarily to further explain her diagnosis and reassure me of my recovery. However, I could tell she viewed me as an anomaly in her profession. It was almost as if she couldn't believe I had really gotten shingles. The more she expounded on the nature of the virus, the more I began to understand its likely cause. She kept talking about how much stress I must have been under. She probed me with questions to find out how anxious I was on a normal basis. I didn't try to conceal anything. I told her about my routine state of worry and stress.

As I left the doctor's office that day, I could no longer conceal the truth from myself either. In many ways, I was a nervous wreck. I struggled with fear of the unknown, the fear of the future, and the inability to deal with life apart from constantly worrying about it. Right there in the parking lot, I made a decision that, years later, I'm seeing the fruitful results of. I decided that I wouldn't live that way any longer. I couldn't.

Pondering over the disappointing, painful wedding weekend I had just experienced, I realized that it was a vivid illustration of my emotional state. The same way I was incapable of fully enjoying the wedding, I was incapable of fully enjoying my life. To appreciate a special moment, I first had to fight off or suppress the worrisome feelings. To let go and relax, I had to wait until the issues I was worrying about were resolved. No wonder I had gotten shingles. Nothing ever seemed to be fully resolved, so I never stopped worrying.

I have a question for you, and I hope you'll be honest with yourself about the answer: Are there areas of your life you would enjoy more if you worried less? If so, I want you to make the same decision I made years ago in that parking lot. Decide to do something about it. You *can* stop worrying, and I'm going to show you how, but it starts with a choice.

I first had the idea for this book the same year I suffered from shingles. I thought, "Worry is a problem (I was smart back then). It's something we all suffer from, so a book focused on winning the war against worry would be generally helpful, right?" Now that I've finally written it, I've lived a little longer, I've bitten my nails a little shorter, and I understand to an even greater degree how destructive worry can be. It is crippling and sinister. You might not have physical shingles like I did, but many of us are suffering from what I would call "emotional shingles." Anxiety is suffocating us. It has attached itself to our system—our core, and it affects everything we do.

Not only do I have a more accurate understanding of the pitfalls of worry, I also have a better solution. I didn't write this book hoping that it might help you. I *know* it can help you. I know this because the truths found in this book have flipped my life upside down. They have helped transform me from a nervous wreck of a soul into a heart at peace.

I started my ministry in 2013, soon before the birth of my first daughter. When I initially got into ministry, I assumed the longer I worked at it, the less worried I would become. I naively thought that diligently working for the Lord would provide a sort of spiritual shield against anxiety. Instead, I found that I'm a target for worry. Three kids, a freelance business, a mortgage, and years of ministry work have worked together to demonstrate to me the dangers of naivety.

Don't we all think similarly at times, though? We put our heads down and work right on through those feelings of stress, frustration, fear, and uneasiness, thinking that eventually they will go away. Or perhaps we're waiting for some big break that's going to turn our life around. Maybe if we finally get that promotion we're aiming for, or maybe if the right person comes along, or maybe if our children start to act right, then we could live worry-free. Whatever it is, we hope something will happen that fixes the way we feel.

You may even be at a stage where you've accepted the way things are, and you've gritted your teeth at the possibility of being on the edge of your seat for the rest of your natural life. If you're at that point or struggling with any kind of anxiety at all, I want to give you a simple word of encouragement: Stop worrying. Stop it. Yes, it's simple to say, but we both know it's not so easy to do.

If you have struggled with anxiety for any considerable amount of time, you may be asking the question, is it really possible to live a life of peace? Is it really possible? The Bible says, *Yes, it is.* In this book, I have three main objectives:

1. to give you Biblical truths which enable you to live a life of peace

2. to encourage you with testimonies of how God has changed my own life with those truths

Yes, I only listed two objectives—good catch. The third objective isn't something I'm going to share with you right now, but don't worry (pun intended), I'll reveal it a little later on.

Though I am boldly making the claim that you can live a life of peace, I don't want to delude you. Living a peaceful life doesn't mean living a perfect life. I cannot honestly say that my life is one hundred percent carefree, because after all, I'm still human. I still have responsibilities, and I still overreact emotionally sometimes. However, I can say that what used to feel like a constant skirmish with anxious thoughts now more closely resembles a victory march.

The clanging of swords and battle cries may still rise around me at times, but there's a song in my heart that rises louder still. Yes, I still walk through challenges, but I'm able to walk in peace. With the Lord as my confidence, I'm consistently taking ground against worry and anxiety. You can too.

- I -

THE ONE THING

A common reaction to an onslaught of negative stress is to buckle down and work through it. The boss is saying, "You had better start being more productive or else you're outta here." So we push ourselves until we feel like we're losing our minds. The family member is sick, and we spend twenty-four seven thinking about all of the treatment options—all of the things we haven't tried yet. Why? Because we feel forced to "do" something. The friend is making poor life choices, so we open our mouths about it every time we see them. We vocalize our thoughts every chance we get because we feel the need to contribute to the solution. We want to fix the problem, and we don't see how the problem can be fixed if we're not working hard to fix it. When we're not busy looking for solutions, we're busy searching out new strategies for generating that feeling of peace.

Maybe you can't relate to all those situations, but I want you to think about how often you respond to anxiety with an attitude that says, "I've just got to work through this. If I just try hard enough, I'll finally feel better."

One mantra of the corporate world is this: Hard work is the price of success. This idea—that the harder we work, the better things turn out—has been engrained throughout many facets of our culture. To an extent, I agree that in many cases hard work delivers results. However, if you want to be free from worry, I'm going to show you why hard work doesn't really work.

In high school, I ran track, and I learned some of the secrets to forcing my body to move at its top speed. The better form I used, the more force I exerted, and the more energy I spent, the faster I could move. This is a similar principle to the work-hard mindset we have when we attempt to battle anxiety. We think that the harder we push ourselves, the more victory over worry we will have. However, the problem we can't see is that some principles only work in certain environments.

My kids seem to run everywhere they go. Unlike my experience with high school track, running is fun to them. I can't imagine what they see in it. They're at that age where they don't care what anyone thinks about them, and so they will often hop up and run out of the room without warning. Most of the time, I don't mind when they run. If they're sprinting across a wet tile floor though, I intervene. I reach out my hand to stop them because I don't want them to slip. In some environments, pushing harder makes us move faster. In other environments, pushing harder causes us to fall sooner.

Some of us are working on our form. We're exerting the effort. We're spending our energy, and we're expecting to win the prize of peace, but we're constantly slipping and falling on the wet floor called anxiety. Maybe we're worried about our health, money, relationships, job, or future. Though they weren't meant to be, the most significant areas of our lives can also be our greatest sources of anxiety. Many of us assume hard work is the price we have to pay to stop worrying about all these areas. I believe God is reaching out His hand to stop us—to tell us to slow down and to start facing anxiety His way instead of our own way.

Let's look at Jesus' response to the hard-work mindset in Luke 10:38-42. As you read this passage, I want you to ask yourself a question: Do I identify more with Mary or Martha?

> *"Now as they were traveling along, He entered a village; and a woman named Martha welcomed Him into her home. She had a sister called Mary, who was seated at the Lord's feet, listening to His word. But Martha was distracted with all her preparations; and she came up to Him and said, 'Lord, do You not care that my sister has left me to do all the serving alone? Then tell her to help me.' But the Lord answered and said to her,*

'Martha, Martha, you are worried and bothered about so many things; but only one thing is necessary, for Mary has chosen the good part, which shall not be taken away from her.'"

The reason many of us identify with Martha is because at some point we've found ourselves asking a similar question to the one she asked Jesus. We say, "If I'm working so hard at this, why isn't it working out?" or "God, I could use a little help here. Have you not noticed how stressed I am about this?"

Jesus' response to Martha's question is full of grace, and that's the same way He wants to respond to us today. First, He acknowledges her struggle. He says, *I see that you're worried—that you're carrying a heavy burden right now.* Then, He lovingly offers her a solution. He points to freedom by telling her about the one thing she missed.

When we are worried, we're doing what Martha did. We're forgetting the one thing that's necessary—the one thing that's most important and the true key to beating worry. The one thing is this: sitting at the feet of Jesus.

I want you to notice the subtle difference between the actions of the two women. Martha's actions were intentional, but they were targeted toward the duties that needed to be done on behalf of Jesus being present. Mary's actions were also intentional, but she was determined to make her focus the very presence of Jesus. There's no way that Mary didn't know how much needed to be done in the kitchen. She knew. Despite the work needed to be done, she made the decision to enjoy Jesus while He was there. In her mind, the food could wait, but she didn't want to miss an opportunity to get closer to her Lord.

Many of us have a hard time allowing the other things to wait. We're willing to do things for God, but we may have a hard time prioritizing His presence. This makes sense with the googazillions (a big number I just made up) of demands life throws at us. Between our jobs, our second jobs, our home, our children, our needy friends, our churches, our stress-relieving yet time-sucking hobbies, our thought life, our hopes and dreams, and our health, it makes sense that we run out of time or energy to sit at Jesus' feet. However, that's the very reason we are so worried about these other things.

The reason many of us can't seem to stop worrying is because we are the Marthas in the kitchen. We're working hard to fix as many issues as we can, but we don't have the peace of mind that Mary is enjoying in the living room with Jesus. When things start getting crazy in the kitchen of life, we look to the person to our left or right and say, "Tell me this is going to be okay." That may be the reason you picked up this book—to find some encouragement to keep going. That's not a bad thing, and I hope to encourage you, but I also want to give you something far better than mere encouragement.

The Marthas are often looking for another person to tell them on behalf of God that it's going to be okay. They're looking for someone to relate to them. A deeper issue plagues them, because even if they receive temporary encouragement, the worries are going to return when the encouragement wears off. They don't realize how good the Marys have it. See, the Marys aren't just receiving a word of encouragement. They have found a constant source of peace. The reason the Marys aren't worried is because they are hearing God speak for Himself, and He is constantly saying, "It's going to be okay."

Through this book, I don't want to just encourage you. I want to show you how to get to that point where you can hear God say, "It's going to be okay," for yourself. You may not believe it's possible right now, but neither did I at one point. For a long time, I thought my relationship with God would always be composed of the duties I performed for Him. I never thought that He could be the close friend He has become.

Because of Mary's position in relation to Jesus, she could receive personal responses from Him. If Mary asked, "Jesus, what about the food preparation?" Jesus could say, "We will get to that. For now, I want to teach you something. I want you to simply rest with Me."

Some of us have been battling the same situation for years, and it doesn't look like it's going to change anytime soon. We can't hear God saying, "Slow down. The reason this hasn't changed yet is because I want to teach you something during this process." We may still be in the middle of the process because we haven't taken the time to wait upon Him. Look at these encouraging words from God in Psalm 46:10.

> *"Cease striving and know that I am God; I will be exalted among the nations, I will be exalted in the earth."*

Sitting at the feet of Jesus means learning to listen to Him. It means listening to the very voice of God. It means ceasing our striving and resting in the knowledge that God is God.

Our ability to hear from God often relies on our willingness to prioritize His presence. If we really believed that God is who He says He is, and if we really believed that He has something to say to us, we would go out of our way to hear what He's saying. We would put the other things on halt, sit at His feet, and wait.

Three months after I married my wife Leslie, we found out she was pregnant. At that time, we were living in a two hundred and fifty square-foot cottage in my boss's backyard. He was a sole proprietor video producer and designer who had hired me on to help keep up with projects, and I relied on him to bring in the work.

In the summer of 2013, with just a few months until our baby was due, the work started to dry up. Due to a tragic death, he lost one of his main sources for video projects and I quickly found myself sitting around twiddling my thumbs. He did the best he could to attract new clients, but it wouldn't be a quick task. After a few weeks of taking a smaller paycheck, I began to feel overwhelmed by desperation and my fear of the unknown. I didn't want to try to raise our child in the cottage. The living space, bed, and mini-kitchen were all packed into one single, little room. That tiny house was part of my wages, and for my wife and I to move into a larger house, we would need a new source of income.

Our ability to hear from God often relies on our willingness to prioritize His presence.

Even before the slump that summer, I had started seeking new business for my boss by marketing my website designing skills as a service offered by his company. When the work went away, I dove into this tactic. I thought, "If I can bring in enough extra work, things are going to be okay." I was essentially saying, *If I can just be smart enough about this. If I can just work hard enough...*

The weeks passed, and I began to lose hope. My boss was trying his hardest. I was trying my hardest. My wife and I were praying daily for new work to come in, but things just weren't working out. Could God have forgotten about us? It felt that way some days.

Take a look at what the psalmist says in Psalm 43:5 when he feels like God has forgotten about him and he is battered with despair.

"Why are you in despair, O my soul?
And why are you disturbed within me?
Hope in God, for I shall again praise Him,
The help of my countenance and my God."

The psalmist asks his soul a critical question. Then he reminds himself where his strength and hope come from. After weeks of wondering, laying nervously on my bed into the late hours, and going for long walks to try to console my anxious heart, the Lord began to urge me to ask myself the same question. I started saying to myself, "Why are you so worried about this? Don't you know who your provider is? Don't you know who your source is? Hope in Him."

For several days after that, I decidedly took time out of my day to wait upon the Lord. Anytime I started feeling anxious about the work or housing situation, I went into that small cottage, shut the door, knelt down, and waited. I prayed. I asked God to provide, but more than that, I began to tell God that I trusted His way above my own. The more I waited upon Him, the more I found peace in the moment.

Then, the real test started. The more I waited upon God, the more I knew He was telling me it was time to start working for myself—to leave my current position and start finding my own work. The idea seemed possible, but it also felt daunting. If my boss, possessing skills and contacts far superior to my own, couldn't find enough work, then how could I manage it? What if it didn't work out? I had no backup plan, no savings, and the baby was coming soon.

I remember telling God, "I don't feel like I'm going to be able to provide for my family. I don't feel like I'm going to be able to do this." However, as I continued to wait for Him, His answer became clear in my spirit. He was saying, *Don't worry. I've got it.*

In my heart I believed Him, but in my mind I battled the

forces of uncertainty. The more I prayed though, the more peace I had. I finally told Him, "God, You're in control. You're our provider. I'm going to trust You with this." I was ready to step out in faith.

The very next day, a former employer contacted me asking if I was interested in signing a contract with their organization. They were offering around 20 hours of design and video projects per week, and I would be able to work remotely. As I considered it, I realized this would be the perfect opportunity to allow me time and flexibility to start generating freelance leads. It was enough work to keep me going as I launched my design business.

I knew that this well-timed answer to prayer had nothing to do with my efforts. It was God's way of providing for me and my wife.

In the moment, I assumed God was opening up doors to make a way for me to start a company. Looking back though, I can now see how He was orchestrating things to give me an opportunity to start my ministry. It was during those beginning months of working as a freelancer that I found time to create my first couple videos and start the process of publishing my first book.

"I wait for the Lord, my soul does wait,
And in His word do I hope.
My soul waits for the Lord
More than the watchmen for the morning;
Indeed, more than the watchmen for the morning.
O Israel, hope in the Lord;
For with the Lord there is lovingkindness,
And with Him is abundant redemption."

Psalm 130:5-7

When we walk through difficult or even impossible circumstances, it often feels like we're sitting in darkness. We're looking for a ray of light—a glimmer of hope—to burst through the clouds of despair, but the psalmist who wrote this passage tells us that we need to be seeking something greater than the solution itself. Finding the answer to our problem is like witnessing the morning sun peek over the horizon and dispel the darkness. However, these verses show us that there's something we ought to be waiting for with more expectancy than the morning: the Lord Himself.

I've never been a night watchman, but I'm sure it can be a tedious job. I had a friend who was a night guard though. One time I asked him about his duties. "What do you do as a night guard?" He said, "I can't tell you. It's classified." That answer made me a little nervous. My guess is that he didn't want to admit he mostly stood around waiting for the night to be over.

Similarly, the struggles we face can also feel like they just keep continuing, like the dark path we're walking down is unending. The psalmist lets us know that we can live a life of hope right now, even though the dark shroud has yet to pass. There are two things we're told we can consistently find hope in: the Lord and His word. As I waited upon the Lord during that season of uncertainty about my work, I found rest in His presence, and I gained strength through His words.

I believe the relationship with God that is made available to us is a widely understated truth throughout Christianity. One of the worst things we, as Christians, can do for unbelievers is tell them they can have a personal relationship with Jesus Christ; then when they get saved, we imply that they can't really hear from God. The question I can't help but ask is, what kind of relationship is that?

I'm not forgetting about the written word of God, either. The best place to start hearing from God is in the Bible, and every personal word we receive from the Lord needs to be measured up against the Bible as well. God is never going to say something to you or me that goes against His written word. However, the Bible, though it is full of God's truth, is general in its application. God wants us to hear truth through His word, but He also wants to speak to us specifically. He wants a *personal* relationship. As soon as our relationship with God becomes impersonal, it ceases to be a healthy relationship. Jesus says in John 10:27,

"My sheep hear My voice, and I know them, and they follow Me;"

I used to assume that God wanted to speak only to great pastors and missionaries, and I would have to settle for hearing from God through people like them. Think about what Jesus says though. He is using an illustration where He is the shepherd and believers are the sheep. If you are a believer, that means He's talking about you and me. He says, "My sheep hear My voice."

16

So, the big question we're left with is this: How do we hear from God? Paul addresses this question in 1 Corinthians 2:10-12.

"For to us God revealed them through the Spirit; for the Spirit searches all things, even the depths of God. For who among men knows the thoughts of a man except the spirit of the man which is in him? Even so the thoughts of God no one knows except the Spirit of God. Now we have received, not the spirit of the world, but the Spirit who is from God, so that we may know the things freely given to us by God,"

I highly encourage you to go read the entire chapter of 1 Corinthians 2, but I want to focus on the amazing revelation within these few verses. Paul tells us that everything God knows, the Holy Spirit knows. Then He goes on to say that God has freely given the Holy Spirit to those who know Him. The Holy Spirit is given to us "so that..." So that what? Listen to this: "so that we may know." The Holy Spirit knows the thoughts of God, and He desires to share those thoughts with us.

As soon as our relationship with God becomes impersonal, it ceases to be a healthy relationship.

I experienced this personally as I waited upon the Lord while I started my freelance business. It was the Holy Spirit who spoke the words "Don't worry. I've got it." into my spirit.

Though hearing those words comforted me in the moment, I don't have to tell you how fickle we can be as human beings. It wasn't long afterward that I found myself in another worrisome situation.

As Leslie's pregnancy progressed, we searched diligently for other housing options. You can't blame us for not wanting to raise a child in a two hundred and fifty square-foot cottage! Eventually, we found a small rental home where we would start our life as parents.

Around the same time that we moved into the new house, I picked up another client, and I began to expand my ministry. I soon found my schedule full. There's a joke I've heard that says entrepreneurs quit working forty hours a week for someone else so they can start working eighty hours a week for themselves. I related to this. I would often work a full work week for clients and then dedicate evenings and weekends to ministry projects.

Because I had little experience with running a business and keeping up with my own clients and deadlines, I found myself constantly fretting over my work. On top of that, I was spending as much extra time as possible trying to build the ministry. I knew God wanted me to minister on the side, but I was receiving little to no support for my time and effort.

I kept telling God, "I'm not in ministry for the support. I'm doing it because You've asked me to." Nonetheless, I still wound up worried about the finances too. Despite how much effort I extended, we were barely making enough to live off of. Part of the reason for this was that we had just transitioned from paying no rent to paying rent plus a monthly electric and gas bill that were much higher than expected. The little house we were living in must not have been well-insulated, because our electric bill during the cold season that year rose to over half the cost of our rent.

On top of that, we used a midwife for our first child's birth, and because insurance didn't cover this option, we had to pay all the bills out of pocket. We weren't starving, but I felt a constant pressure during that time to work harder and harder in order to provide.

I remember one afternoon in particular that I took a five minute break from my work and started to pray, saying, "God, I'm tired. I'm working all the time. I feel like I need a break, but I don't know what to do."

God replied, "Stop working. I've got it."

As I thought about the prospect of taking off work early that day, I laughed.

"Stop working?" I asked, frustrated. "I can't do that or else there won't be enough. I won't be able to provide."

God again said, "Stop working. I've got it."

It may have been my desperation, or possibly the gentleness in His voice, but the second time He said it, I got it. I caved.

At about four in the afternoon, I shut down my computer and decided to take the rest of the day off. Immediately after standing up from my makeshift dining-room-table desk, I walked out onto the front porch steps and breathed in the refreshing breeze. Walking down the short front walk, I looked in the mailbox and found a hand-marked envelope. I opened it.

One single item slipped out of the envelope: a check for five hundred dollars. Nothing inside me could have predicted this. I stood there in complete shock. A relative's name was signed at the bottom of the check, and they had randomly sent the money because they wanted to bless us. They could not have known what it would mean to us.

Only minutes earlier, God was telling me to stop working, and now He had placed a sign of His divine provision into my hands. As I looked at that check, and thought about His words, I realized that God was working behind the scenes in ways I couldn't control. It wasn't up to me to provide. It was up to God, and He was reminding me of that.

I'm not telling you God doesn't want you to work. I'm telling you He doesn't want you to worry.

To be honest, I still messed up when it came to living a life of peace. At times, I worried myself into a frenzy over our finances that year. However, the moments when I stopped relying on my own effort, and took time to remember the one necessary thing, I found peace. As I listened to the voice of my Lord and responded in faith, I saw His divine hand at work on my behalf.

Jesus tells Martha that only one thing is necessary—just one. When something in our lives gets off track, there are a few reasons we start to worry. One reason is because we think the worst is going to happen. But the worst-case scenario doesn't really occur very often, and I honestly don't believe that is our main source of worry. The main reason I think we worry is because we have lost control. We'll sit at the feet of anything that promises us control again. We'll sit at the feet of striving. We'll sit at the feet of hard work. But one reason we don't sit at the feet of Jesus first is because it means losing that control—it means placing control into His hands. That can be a scary thought.

The reason we don't have to be afraid of placing the outcome into God's hands is because His character is trustworthy and good. We can get to know His character—His heart—through His word and through a consistent friendship with the Holy Spirit. I listened the second time God said, "I've got it," because I had learned to recognize and trust His voice. I had learned to trust *Him*.

Jesus says in John 14:1,

> *"Do not let your heart be troubled; believe in God, believe also in Me."*

Some of us have little trouble believing in God's existence, but we have major doubts when it comes to His character. Jesus lets us know that we can live with a heart at peace. We get to that point by learning to trust God—learning to believe in His character. It's one thing to say we are trusting in God, but it's another thing to base our actions upon the words God has spoken about Himself.

How do you learn to trust a good friend? You spend time with them. The more of your life you go through together, the stronger your trust will be in their character. You'll watch how they respond to good days and bad days, and all the days in between. The same way, we can learn to trust God more by spending time with Him and by growing closer to Him in friendship. The Bible describes God's character in great detail. It says He is good, loving, perfect, and faithful, and that's the truth. However, knowing something as a concept and knowing it in practice are two different things.

The reason we don't have to be afraid of placing the outcome into God's hands is because His character is trustworthy and good.

So, how do we get there? How does friendship with God work? Our nearness to God relies on our interaction with the Holy Spirit. Remember, a relationship with God is not as simple as reading His word. God wants more than a contractual relationship. He wants to be our friend. Jesus confirms this in John 15:15 when He says,

> *"I no longer call you servants, because a servant does not know his master's business. Instead, I have called you friends, for everything that I learned from my Father I have made known to you."*

Jesus made known the Father's business to His friends—to us. The major way He does that now is through the Holy Spirit.

Growing up, I witnessed many representations of the Holy Spirit in various churches or on television. One thing you need to know is that not every representation of the Holy Spirit is a correct one. Not every person who says they are being led by the Holy Spirit is actually listening to His voice. Not every person who says, "I-SHOULD'A-BOUGHT-A-HONDA" is necessarily speaking in tongues. Sometimes, the idea of the Holy Spirit and the concept of God's power are used inappropriately and for selfish reasons. Unfortunately, our misconceptions about the Holy Spirit have caused many believers and non-believers to view Him in a negative light. Many people see Him as weird. After years of walking with Him, I can tell you that He isn't weird. He's a friend. Weird people have sometimes mis-represented Him, but that doesn't change the truth about who He is. Also, He sometimes does things that our natural minds interpret as weird, but that still does not change who He is. To find out more about His character, let's look at how the word of God describes Him.

> *"But to each one is given the manifestation of the Spirit for the common good. For to one is given the word of wisdom through the Spirit, and to another the word of knowledge according to the same Spirit;"*

> 1 Corinthians 12:7-8

When Paul says, "to each one," He is talking about all believers. One way of defining manifestation is *the demonstration of.* You could say it this way: The Spirit is given to every believer and He is visibly demonstrated in their lives. Some people are under the impression that the Holy Spirit is nearly impossible to receive. Others consider the Holy Spirit something that is optional for believers. Paul makes it clear that God gives the Holy Spirit freely to every believer. Beyond that, God provides wisdom and knowledge to believers through the same Spirit. It's through the Holy Spirit that God speaks specifically to His people.

When we are first saved, the Holy Spirit comes to live in our hearts. In the Old Testament, God's Spirit rested in the holy of holies in the temple. Now, because the veil of the temple was torn when Jesus died on the cross, the Holy Spirit lives inside all believers. Our bodies are the new temple. 1 Corinthians 12:3 confirms that every believer receives the Holy Spirit when it says,

> *"Therefore I make known to you that no one speaking by the Spirit of God says, 'Jesus is accursed'; and no one can say, 'Jesus is Lord,' except by the Holy Spirit."*

When we believe and confess Jesus as our Lord, we receive the same Spirit Jesus walked in—the Spirit of God. It was through this same Spirit that I heard God say, "Stop working." It's through His Spirit that we are able to receive the same wisdom and peace that Mary received while sitting at the feet of Jesus.

Though Jesus was in Martha's house, that doesn't mean He was in her presence. Because of her list of priorities, she had missed out on an opportunity to receive what she desperately needed from Jesus. The same applies to believers today. Though all believers have the Holy Spirit living in their house—in their body—that doesn't mean all believers experience the personal interaction of the Holy Spirit on a daily basis.

Just because we have met God, doesn't mean we always treat Him like we know Him. Think of a married couple. Just because someone said "I do" at one point, doesn't mean they are prioritizing their relationship with their spouse now. There's more to being in a relationship with God than going to church, singing songs, and reading the Bible. He wants us to relate to Him the way we would a close friend. He wants to interact with us the way a loving parent would with their children.

Some people have a hard time with the idea of the Holy Spirit because they've been saved a long time and yet haven't seen any evidence of His presence. Jesus addresses this in Luke 11:13.

> *"If you then, being evil, know how to give good gifts to your children, how much more will your heavenly Father give the Holy Spirit to those who ask Him?"*

If the Holy Spirit seems weird to you, or if you doubt that He wants to reveal Himself to you, consider the nature of God. Think about the perfect, loving Father that He is. Ponder His goodness. Jesus says, even imperfect, earthly parents know how to give good things to their children. He essentially asks us to reason through God's nature with Him. God is a perfect parent, and He only desires good things for His children. Because of His nature, God desires to give the Holy Spirit to those who ask.

We receive the Spirit at the moment of conversion, but we can also receive a greater filling when we choose to believe what Jesus is saying and we ask. A greater filling is simply another way of describing a closer relationship. None of us have arrived yet. If we are being honest, we can all work on our relationship with God. We can all get closer to Him. The question I'm asking is: Do you want to? Do you want to sit at the feet of Jesus and listen? Are the kitchen duties really that important that they steal your opportunity to draw closer to the God of the universe—the God who loves you? Martha and Mary were both given the same chance, but they responded in different ways. Because of their responses, one worried and one found peace. You can trade your worry in for peace today. You can respond like Mary.

- 2 -

THE GOSPEL WORKS

One of my wife's favorite ways of teasing me is to joke about my childhood. She's heard the stories about my obsessively diligent habits. In order to earn our weekly chore money (or allowance, really), my siblings and I were given a list of chores to complete Monday through Friday. Being driven by a compulsion for keeping things in order as well as the possession of an achievement-focused mindset, I worked hard to always finish my chores. More than that, I kept up on which siblings completed their chores too. If a given task remained undone by Friday, I would complain to my mom, saying something like, "It's not fair. Why do they still get paid when they didn't sweep the kitchen floor like they were supposed to?" The fact is, I regularly did more chores around the house than any of my siblings, but I got paid the same rate.

My wife likes to laugh about how annoying my holier-than-thou behavior must have been. Since then, I've had to apologize to my siblings for always being on their case. The truth is, even though I begrudged having to do more work for the same pay, I had no ground to stand on because it wasn't my money that my siblings were receiving. If my Mom wanted to still give one of my brothers or sisters their money even if they didn't check off their list, that really wasn't my business. She had a right to do what she wanted with what was hers. However, I think most of us can relate to the feeling of unfairness that comes with not getting what we feel like we deserve.

Imagine for a second that you've been hired onto a job where you work long hours in difficult conditions. Maybe you know what it's like to work a job like that. After working for a few weeks, you start to notice that one of your coworkers is slacking off. Anytime the boss isn't around, they sit on their phone, playing games and chatting with friends. Don't you think you would feel cheated by your coworker? I would. If your extra sweat was making up for their laziness, you would want to see them fired, or at least demoted. It just wouldn't feel fair for them to be receiving the same benefits if they weren't willing to put in the work. Why? Because they didn't deserve it. You did.

Many of us have this same feeling when it comes to our relationship with God and the condition of our lives. We consider ourselves diligent workers. We feel like God owes us something. We look at the way we've lived our lives and we consider that we deserve for God to bless us. It seems unfair that God constantly blesses others but never treats us with the favor we've earned.

There are others of us who would have to admit we're more like the lazy coworker. We look at the way we've lived and we know that we don't deserve anything good from God. We think we've let Him down, and because of that, we don't deserve the good treatment that other, better Christians deserve.

No matter which side you identify with more, I want to ask you to look past those feelings as you read this chapter. The reason I say this is because the truth differs from what we might naturally assume. The same way that my mother had the right to do what she wished with her own things, God has the same right. God created us along with the entire universe, and He doesn't owe us anything. He doesn't owe us. However, because He is loving, He orchestrated an opportunity for us to receive everything. Let's take another look at our busy friend, Martha, as I explain what I mean.

The picture I painted of the diligent worker resembles the character of Martha. In the mind of this assiduous, devoted woman, she and Mary both have a responsibility to fulfill. They both have tasks to complete, and yet Martha is treated unfairly by her sister. Mary leaves her with the short end of the stick, and she feels like she deserves more.

I had someone tell me that this story irritated them because it seems like Jesus doesn't appreciate the work Martha is doing for Him. I can understand why it irked them, too. I'm sure Martha also wanted to spend time with Jesus. After the preparations were complete, she probably would have sat down with Jesus and engaged with Him. What was so negative about finishing the chores before enjoying time with the Lord? After all, her efforts were based on devotion to Him, right? Didn't her devotion give her a right to be worried and upset?

The reason Jesus' response to Martha is not insensitive and misplaced is because He can see something you and I can't see. He can see Martha's heart. He looks past the exterior performance and straight at the interior motivations. He can see the motivating fears, anxieties, and stresses, yet He also sees that she is missing the one thing that's most important. Jesus lovingly corrects Martha by showing her a reflection of her own heart. He knows that, if she gets the one thing right, the other things will cease to worry her.

When Jesus looks at the hearts of the people of Jerusalem in Matthew chapter 23, He sees a similar problem. Many of the people and religious leaders want to please God, yet many of them are also unwilling to come to Jesus. Jesus laments over the people of Jerusalem as He speaks these words in Matthew 23:37,

> *"Jerusalem, Jerusalem, who kills the prophets and stones those who are sent to her! How often I wanted to gather your children together, the way a hen gathers her chicks under her wings, and you were unwilling."*

Jesus talks about how strongly He desires to protect and provide for the people of Jerusalem, but even though they are doing things for God, He knows that many refuse to accept the gift of life He offers them free of charge.

They must have felt like they were earning God's favor based on what they were doing, yet they couldn't see that the real problem was in their hearts. They possessed a desire to please God, yet they were unwilling to do things His way.

As He looks at Martha in Luke 10, He feels the same love in His heart for her, and His words are meant to point her to the protection and provision He knows she needs.

When a name is repeated twice in the Bible, it denotes importance. Jesus' choice to say, "Martha, Martha" reveals His passion. He is expressing similar feelings when He says, "Jerusalem, Jerusalem." He cares about Martha, and He wants her to understand a specific truth that she is missing: We can only have the peace *of* God when we first have peace *with* God. Winning the war against worry starts with us admitting that God's way of doing things is better than our own.

When I said before that God doesn't owe us anything, that wasn't completely true. I should instead say that He doesn't owe us anything good. Because of our sinful lives, what He really owes us is death. However, because of His love, He has offered us life through His Son, Jesus.

God created us to know Him—to be in relationship with Him. When humankind sinned in the Garden of Eden, we said "no" to that relationship. We rejected God's way of doing things. We were unwilling to let Him be our protector and provider, and we took those roles upon ourselves as we listened to a lie over God's truth. When that happened, we lost the peace we had with God. The peace that existed between our Creator and us was destroyed. Why? Because God is perfect, and when we sinned we became less-than-perfect people. I probably don't have to tell you how dirty sin can make you feel. The reason we feel ashamed when we sin is because we were created by God for good works, and sin is a perversion of what God created us to do.

Sin is anything that goes against God's will. When we, as a human race, chose to follow our own will above God's, we were doing what Jerusalem did to Jesus. We were saying, *I can make this work on my own. I don't need You to rule over me.* In God's will for us, there is life, freedom, and blessing. Outside of God's will, there is the opposite. So, when we rejected God's way of doing things and chose sin instead, we accepted a fate of death, captivity, and curses. It's no wonder we tend to worry so much.

Despite all this, I have really good news. God has provided a way to restore the purity, peace, and fellowship we lost. You may have picked up this book hoping to find a better way to receive God's favor. You need to understand that we can never receive God's favor unless we are first a part of His family. In the introduction,

I told you I had three objectives in writing this book, but I only gave you the first two. The third objective is this: If you have never accepted the invitation to belong to God's family, I want to give you an opportunity to do that.

You may be thinking, "Well, I've lived a pretty good life. I think I deserve for God to let me into His family." This idea is similar to what the people of Jerusalem were thinking. The problem with this thinking is that we can never live a good enough life to undo what we've done. We have all sinned—every one of us. Any sin at all makes us unworthy of knowing God because God is perfect. He has a perfect standard. None of us can ever work hard enough to please Him—to be at peace with Him.

However! Yes, I just wrote a one-word, fragment sentence. The reason I say "however" in such a prominent and obtrusive way is because of what God chose to do despite the fact that we rejected Him. If you read the Bible all the way through, it's almost as if God states one great, cosmic "however" in the middle of the book. The first half of the Bible depicts man's fall away from God, God's laws given to man, and man's failure to follow those laws. The first half can feel like a sad story; *however,* the second half tells the beautiful story of redemption. We all rejected and failed God; however, God still loves us. God still loves you.

We can only have the peace *of* God when we first have peace *with* God.

Despite how undeserving we all are, God still loves us. He still chose to love us. In His perfection, He loves us perfectly. Because He is perfect though, He could not just ignore our sin and bring us back into His family. God knew that the punishment for our sin would need to be paid. The debt we owed would need to be wiped out before He could bring us back into a relationship with Him. In His love, He sent Jesus to pay the debt on our behalf.

The gospel means "good news." We all know the bad news. We can all look at our lives and see where we've messed up. Jesus came so that we could receive the good news of God's love and grace. Jesus is the Son of God—He is God and man. Because of this, He was able to live a perfect life on earth. Then, He was tortured and killed by crucifixion on a cross. When He did this, He took the punishment we deserved upon Himself. Jesus' body was laid in a tomb, but on the third day after His death, His Spirit entered His body and He rose again.

Because of His perfection, Jesus deserved life, favor, and blessing from God. Instead, He received death, punishment, and curses. Jesus was essentially offering us a trade. He was willing to take what we deserved and give us what He deserved.

> *"But God demonstrates His own love toward us, in that while we were yet sinners, Christ died for us."*

Romans 5:8

The gospel message is clearly stated in John 3:16-18. You may have heard John 3:16 a thousand times, but I want you to read this is the newest light possible. I want you to think about the meaning behind these words of Jesus.

> *"For God so loved the world, that He gave His only begotten Son, that whoever believes in Him shall not perish, but have eternal life. For God did not send the Son into the world to judge the world, but that the world might be saved through Him. He who believes in Him is not judged; he who does not believe has been judged already, because he has not believed in the name of the only begotten Son of God."*

Yes, this book is still about learning to defeat worry. The reason I'm talking about the gospel so much is because some of us are unable to sit at the feet of Jesus. This inability is not because we're busy in the kitchen, but because we haven't yet invited Him into our house. Like I said, before we can have the peace *of* God, we must first have peace *with* God. Surrendering your life to Jesus is the first step.

Many people desire to know God, but they are unwilling to go through Jesus to get to Him. I believe this is because we often want what God can give us, but we don't always want Him. The problem is this: If you only come to God to get what you want, you'll never find what you need. We must come to God with a heart that is willing to change. We must be willing to say, "God, I don't want to live my life my way anymore. I need You to save me."

I know this isn't easy. It's the hardest thing you might ever do, but it's worth it.

Think about the story of Mary and Martha again. In that moment, which of the two women were more interested in God's way of doing things? Mary wanted to know what Jesus really had to say. But Martha's motivations were fixed on doing things her own way, and she was worried sick because of it. Once she took the time to seek Jesus out—to ask Him for help—she discovered that He wanted to be her source of peace. In fact, He wanted to give her peace that she couldn't earn no matter how hard she worked.

Peace with God isn't something you or I can earn. It's a free gift. It's a gift Jesus paid for on the cross.

I want to share an illustration with you that may help you visualize this gift. I'm going to get a little creative with the analogy, so bear with me.

When I was a child, my mother was very strict about the shows and movies my siblings and I could watch. We consumed most of our entertainment through VHS tapes that we would play on a VHS player hooked up to our TV. If you're too young to know what VHS tapes are, say a prayer of thanks right now. Unlike streaming services or movies on disc today, you had to physically take the VHS tape out of the player, insert it into the rewinder, and wait for it to rewind before putting it away. If you had a fancy model, you could rewind it directly in the player.

Most of the VHS tapes we owned were G-rated, Christian cartoons and shows. When it came to watching those, my mom would essentially say, "Knock yourself out." However, a few of the movies we owned on VHS contained minor scenes of violence, gore, or other content my mom preferred for us not to see. She had a solution to this problem. We didn't just have a VHS player; we also had a VCR, which allowed us to record directly over the tape.

When my mom would come across a questionable scene in a movie, she would put the tape in the VCR, fast forward to that scene, hit record, and switch the TV input over to a Christian television station. So, the next time my siblings and I popped that tape into the player, we were in for a surprise. I remember sitting on the edge of my seat, awaiting the violent or scary moment in the film. Right before we reached the scary part, the screen would suddenly flash with static, and then it would switch over to a Christian pastor on stage, preaching away.

"What! Noooooo! Mom recorded over the good part!" we would all shout. My siblings and I considered many great films ruined due to that dreaded VCR.

Now, I love my mom, and I appreciate the efforts she put forth to protect our innocence. But the reason I'm telling you about this is because I want to paint a picture of the end of your life. I want you to imagine with me for a moment that you've just died and are awaiting judgement. You stand before God, knowing it's your turn to give an account for the way you lived your life.

Peace with God isn't something you or I can earn. It's a free gift. It's a gift Jesus paid for on the cross.

For the sake of this illustration, let's say that God records everyone's lives on a nearly endless collection of VHS tapes. As you stand there waiting for His judgement, you watch Him open the doors of that gargantuan cabinet. His fingers run down one of the shelves. Finding the tape marked with your name, He pulls it out and places it into His heavenly VHS player. He hits play.

On a screen, you begin to see the images of your life flash by. It starts with your life in the womb, and then you watch your infancy and young childhood. You're thinking, "I was so cute as a toddler."

But then, you reach that point in your life when you made your first big mistake. It's the first time you willingly sinned. You're awaiting the look of disappointment on God's face. You're wondering how mad He might get. Then, you start thinking about the rest of the sinful acts you're about to have to watch together with your Creator.

Just before you get to that first sinful moment though, something happens. A sudden flash of static bursts across the screen. Then, before you know what has happened, the image switches over to a recording of Jesus on the cross.

You say, "Wait a minute! That's not how it happened. That's not what happened that day!" Grabbing the remote, you fast forward to that terrible year of your life when you made all those mistakes you thought you would never forget. As you hit play, you only see more footage of Jesus hanging on the cross.

"I don't understand. I don't get it," you say, turning to God. "That's not what my life looked like."

He kneels down, and you can see the tears in His eyes as He says, "When you believed in Jesus, you got a new life. The old things have been washed away. It has all been covered over by the blood of My Son."

This is just an illustration, but it's a picture of a very real truth. When we choose to put our faith in Jesus, believing that He paid the full price for all our sins through His death on the cross, our sins are completely forgiven. We're made new in Him. God says in Hebrews 8:12,

"For I will be merciful to their iniquities, and I will remember their sins no more."

If you know you need to accept God's free gift of salvation, don't wait. Don't wait any longer. Nail it down right now. The most important decision you will ever make is to allow Jesus to be your Savior—to make Him the Lord of your life. I want to give you the chance to do it right now. I wrote this book to help people deal with worry, but I also wrote it so that I could give you an opportunity to know Jesus. This is the reason behind everything I do. I used to live under a weight of doubt, fear, shame, and hopelessness. Then, one day God broke through the darkness in my heart and He pointed me to the cross. It changed everything.

I believe God is reaching out His hand to you right now, and He's saying, *Accept My gift of forgiveness and grace. Accept My Son.* If you know you need this, then I want you to pray with me. This is not a magical prayer or anything like that. The prayer doesn't save you by itself. Instead, it's a prayer acknowledging a change that's happening in your heart. Romans 10:9 says,

> *"...if you confess with your mouth Jesus as Lord, and believe in your heart that God raised Him from the dead, you will be saved;"*

Pray with me: *Jesus, I confess that I am a sinner and I need You to save me. I confess that I've tried living life my own way, and I don't want to do that anymore. I want You to come into my heart and change me. Make me new. Jesus, I believe You are the Son of God. You came to earth as a man, You lived a perfect life, and You died on the cross to accept the punishment for my sins. On the third day, You rose again, and now You are seated at the right hand of God. I'm joining Your family today, Lord. Thank you for dying for me. Thank You for saving me. Amen.*

If you just prayed this prayer, you need to know how proud I am of you. Please do me a favor. Reach out to me and let me know. I want to celebrate with you!

There are Benefits to Knowing God

Whether you just prayed with me or if you've been a believer for a while, salvation doesn't just provide you with forgiveness of your sins. It also opens up the opportunity for you to begin a loving relationship with God through faith. Just like any good relationship, there are benefits to knowing God. Now, relationships do come with challenges. I'm not ignoring that fact. Knowing God personally doesn't mean life will be perfect. However, a healthy friendship with God is the foundation for living a peaceful life.

Overcoming worry starts with knowing God and understanding His benefits. The greatest benefit is that we'll spend eternity with our Savior. However, the Bible informs us that the list of benefits doesn't stop there.

We all feel like God has let us down at times. We must keep in mind the truth that feelings come and go. They don't define reality;

they only attempt to help us respond to it. Many of the long-term effects of the disappointing moments in life rely on our response to that disappointment. When nothing is going our way, we must remember the destructive path we were on and consider the lengths God went to in order to lead us in a better way. We must learn to place our complete hope in the gospel. When God seems to let us down, we have to keep this basic concept in mind: We are owed nothing, but we are given everything through Christ.

In fact, all of God's promises (or benefits) are made available to us when we are abiding in Christ. Look at what Paul says about those who know Christ in 2 Corinthians 1:18-20.

> *"But as God is faithful, our word to you is not yes and no. For the Son of God, Christ Jesus, who was preached among you by us—by me and Silvanus and Timothy—was not yes and no, but is yes in Him. For as many as are the promises of God, in Him they are yes; therefore also through Him is our Amen to the glory of God through us."*

He is basically saying, *Look at the many promises of God in His word. See them? Those are all yours in Jesus.* In Jesus, God's promises are "yes." They aren't no, yes, and maybe. They are simply yes.

Ponder a moment on the benefits of being a son or daughter. Imagine a millionaire oil tycoon sitting at the kitchen bar in his mansion one Saturday morning. He peers over to witness one of his secretaries helping himself to the breakfast spread. The young man is piling a plate high with blue cheese quiche, egg and cheese soufflé, basque potato, lobster salad, shaved truffle, and fruit. As he sits at one of the breakfast tables, the millionaire notices the puddles of water trailing behind his secretary. It's obvious that the man has just been going for a pre-breakfast dip in the patio pool. A single question forces itself to the front of the millionaire's bewildered mind.

"What are you doing in my house?" he asks.

"I work for you," the secretary responds, unaware of his intrusive behavior.

"Yes, but that's work. This is my house. I'll see you Monday morning at the office, but this is not acceptable. You need to leave."

Maybe the millionaire would be a little more upset than that. I can see him kicking over the coffee table. But you get the picture. Just because the secretary works for the millionaire doesn't mean he has access to the millionaire's private resources. Now, picture the same thing happening, but replace the secretary with the millionaire's daughter. If his daughter walked in from taking a morning swim and helped herself to breakfast, he wouldn't think twice about it. Why? Because she is his family.

Those who haven't entered His family don't know what it's like to receive the benefits of being close to Him. Others of us have entered His family, but we think that the only thing God wants from us is work. The millionaire's daughter might work for the millionaire during the week, but when she gets home, she says, "Lets relax. Let's talk. Let's go play a round of golf together." She understands who she is, in relation to her parent. Some of us know God, but we are not consistently receiving the benefits of knowing Him. We're acting like a secretary when in reality we're His child. I want to show you how to change that.

One occurrence in the Bible of people receiving the position but not the benefits is the case of the Israelites after they left Egypt. When Moses led the Israelite people out of slavery in Egypt, they accepted the saving hand of God in their lives. God was delivering them in order to have a relationship with them. He wanted them to be His people and He wanted to be their God. However, although the Israelites wanted to receive the benefits of knowing God, they often refused to trust in His salvation. They often forgot the position they had been given.

Let me show you what I'm talking about in Psalm 78. I hope you'll read the whole chapter, but I'm going to focus on a few key verses. The psalmist, Asaph, starts out by describing the wondrous works God has done for Israel. Then he encourages the reader to pass on the message of God's goodness to their children. Verse 7 tells us that He wants them to do this so "that they should put their confidence in God..." He warns them not to be like their ancestors who lived during the time soon after Israel had left Egypt. He describes their ancestors in verse 11, saying, "They forgot His deeds and His miracles that He had shown them."

Asaph doesn't just leave the reader there though. He gives a semi-detailed account of what God did for those who left Egypt. He reminds the reader of God's blessings. In verses 13 through 16, he says about God,

> *"He divided the sea and caused them to pass through, and He made the waters stand up like a heap. Then He led them with the cloud by day and all the night with a light of fire. He split the rocks in the wilderness and gave them abundant drink like the ocean depths. He brought forth streams also from the rock and caused waters to run down like rivers."*

God blessed the Israelites with miraculous deliverance, direction and guidance, as well as physical protection and provision. The Israelites looked at all of God's blessings and essentially said, *This isn't enough.* They were happy for a few moments when God would provide something new for them, but they quickly reverted back into an attitude of frustration and complaint. They wanted everything up front, but God wanted them to learn how to trust in and rely on Him.

As soon as the trials in the desert began, the Israelites doubted God's willingness to provide. Verse 18 says,

> *"And in their heart they put God to the test by asking food according to their desire."*

God had plans to give them everything they needed, but because of their unbelief, they unwillingly rejected God's blessing. Verse 19 says,

> *"Then they spoke against God; They said, 'Can God prepare a table in the wilderness?'"*

The answer to their question is simple: absolutely. The reason they doubted, though, wasn't because of their impossible circumstance. God had already delivered them from an impossible situation in Egypt. So He could easily do it again. The reason they doubted was because they had forgotten the salvation they received. Verse 22 confirms this when it says,

"Because they did not believe in God and did not trust in His salvation."

God's greatest desire for us is for us to know Him. We get to know Him by simply choosing to believe what He's done for us. When we are walking in belief and living in a close relationship with Him, we then get to receive His benefits (blessings) with a grateful heart.

My basis for this book is simple: As believers, we worry because we're not receiving the benefits of a close relationship with God. We've been given the gift, but we're not treasuring the gift, and therefore not enjoying the value of the gift.

For the remainder of this book, I'm going to show you how to stop worrying and start receiving the benefits God has promised to those who know Him. Each chapter is going to focus on a specific area of our lives we have the propensity to worry about. Some chapters may apply to you more than others, but what may not apply now may apply at some point in your life. I'm going to discuss anxiety about the future, work, health, money, and relationships. As we move forward, I'm going to open up about my own struggle with worrying about these things, and I'm going to show the progression of moving from a place of doubt to a place where we can receive God's benefits with joy. The key to finding peace in each of these areas is the same. The answer to beating worry is to learn how to apply the gospel—the salvation of God—to every area of life.

If that answer doesn't sound great to you right now, my goal is to help you see it from a different perspective by the end of this book. Remember that Jesus Himself said we must become like children to enter the kingdom of God. The deep, life-changing truths of God's word are not the ones that intrigue our intellect, but rather the ones that feel foolish at first glance. To move forward with God, we have to learn how to examine His word through the mind of a child. The reason is because God knows our tendency to want control. He knows how badly we seek to hold everything together in our own little worlds. When Jesus said we must become like children, He was basically saying, *Learn to give Me control. Learn to trust Me the way an innocent child trusts their loving parent.*

One of my children's favorite movies is *The Emperor's New Groove*, an animated comedy about a selfish ruler who is unwittingly turned into a llama. Because of the oddities in the plot, it's hilarious to listen to my children attempt to explain the story. I remember one night as I was leaving the house, I overheard two of my young daughters giving my wife Leslie the rundown of the movie. I laughed at the funny way they attempted to explain the storyline. Many of the twists in the movie were obviously over their heads. They attempted to recite some of their favorite lines, but they misquoted each one.

If I had attempted to explain the plot of the movie to my wife, I could have easily presented her with an accurate retelling of the tale. The older we get, the more we have experienced, the better we are at learning (in some ways), and the more understanding we have. Because of this natural progression, adults rarely value the opinion of young children. School boards don't often invite the students in the school to chime in at the meetings. Because intelligence is so highly valued in our world, it only feels natural for us to attempt to apply the same principle to the kingdom of God, but God warns us against this. One of these warnings is found in 2 Corinthians 11:3, which says,

The answer to beating worry is to learn how to apply the gospel—the salvation of God—to every area of life.

> *"But I am afraid that, as the serpent deceived Eve by his craftiness, your minds will be led astray from the simplicity and purity of devotion to Christ."*

The world values human intelligence above most qualities, but the gospel works the opposite way. The world measures people by their intellect; God measures those same people by their faith. We have to become like adults to understand more in the natural world, but we have to become like children to more fully comprehend the kingdom of God.

When we understand and admit the reality of our sinful state, it becomes the greatest problem we could ever face. Our natural brains tell us that the most difficult challenge we could ever face is going to be incredibly, if not impossibly, hard to overcome. Some of us resolve to simply live with shame and regret because we eventually understand that to fix the problem, we would have to reverse time and completely undo what we've done. Either that, or we decide to try to reject the idea of God because we know we can't live up to His standard. Our intelligence tells us that the problem is impossible to fix. Here's that cosmic "however" again. *However*, God tells us that our problem is the easiest thing in the world to fix. He tells us that He's already done the work for us, and all we need to do is to accept His generous gift of forgiveness by believing in Christ Jesus as our Lord and Savior.

The lies of worry will never be able to stand up against the truth of the gospel.

When people get new things in life, like an expensive, classic car, at first they are fascinated and thrilled. Over time though, they forget to enjoy the benefits of those things. The car sits in the garage, and they use their modern vehicle to get to work and back. When they really think about that classic car, they realize it's still there and they can take it for a drive anytime they want. When they don't dwell on it though, they forget to enjoy the benefits of having it.

We do the same thing with the gospel. When we are not dwelling on the gospel daily—keeping it at the center of our minds, we cannot experience its full benefits. Because of this, some of us are living in a perpetual state of worry and fear. As you keep reading, I encourage you to pull the classic car out of the garage. What I mean is, remember the love of God you experienced when you first got saved. Remember the hope His grace produced in your heart. The lies of worry will never be able to stand up against the truth of the gospel.

When we decide to constantly put our hope in what Jesus has done for us, that's when we wake up in the morning with peace in our hearts. When our hope is in the gospel, that's when we start singing the words of God over ourselves during our morning routine. It's when we sit in traffic with a smile on our faces, thinking about how good God has been. It's when we carry a constant expectation with us even through the disappointments of the day. It's when the joy of the Lord washes away those thoughts of depression and frustration as we settle in for bed at night.

You *can* live a life of peace. Remember, I'm not saying a peaceful life is a perfect life. It's a life in which our strength is being supplied by a source of hope greater than what we can see. It's a life where worry doesn't have the final say. It's a life where worry doesn't hold a position of influence at all.

- 3 -

STOP WORRYING ABOUT THE FUTURE

Have you ever experienced that fearful thought that says, "Today is going to be a bad day?" Have you ever worried about what the next week, month, or year might bring? Some people might consider these irrational fears, but the truth is we can't say for certain what the future will hold. Tomorrow is not guaranteed. Even if tomorrow comes, the state in which it comes is not guaranteed either.

Worrying about the future isn't just a joy-stealer. It also robs us of our energy, time, and fingernails. Worry affects the way we live, the way we relate to people, and the decisions we make. The good news is that, if worry has been able to rob you, it doesn't get to anymore.

The reason worrying about the future steals our time is because we assume (consciously or not) that if we invest enough time into figuring out how to make the future work, we'll be able to stop worrying about it. We want to see how all the pieces of the puzzle are going to fall. We want to know how the story ends.

One thing I want you to know about me is this: I don't have to know the future in order to stop worrying about it. I'm not claiming to be smarter, wiser, or more experienced than anyone else. I'm not saying this because I think God loves me anymore than anyone else either. The reason I can stop worrying about the future is simply because I know God, God knows the future, and I trust Him.

My brother Reese told me about a time when he attempted to help his friend Caleb construct a 40,000 piece puzzle. Not surprisingly, he eventually gave up. The puzzle of life is a lot like that, except there are an endless number of pieces. As humans, we don't have the ability to figure out where all the pieces go, but God does. What seems impossible to us is not difficult for God.

One person in the Bible who had to trust God with his future was King David. For years, David had no knowledge that he would one day be king. Born the youngest son in his father's house, his main job involved tending to the sheep out in the field. David may have been tempted to worry about whether or not he would ever be anything other than a shepherd, but he chose not to. Instead, he employed his time in a passionate pursuit of his Creator. To David, having extra time on his hands equalled an opportunity to know God in a deeper way.

Many years after his sheep-herding days were over, David wrote a psalm as the King of Israel, and in it he shares some of the major benefits he experienced because of his personal relationship with the Lord. These benefits are listed in Psalm 103:2-5.

> *"Bless the Lord, O my soul,*
> *And forget none of His benefits;*
> *Who pardons all your iniquities,*
> *Who heals all your diseases;*
> *Who redeems your life from the pit,*
> *Who crowns you with lovingkindness and compassion;*
> *Who satisfies your years with good things,*
> *So that your youth is renewed like the eagle."*

I've briefly mentioned a couple of these benefits, and I'll cover a few more in later chapters. For now, I want to look at verse 5, which tells us that the Lord satisfies our years with good things. Some translations actually say that *He satisfies your mouth with good things* (I'm guessing ice cream is included here). This verse implies that God has the responsibility of taking care of your future—of giving you what you need to live a full, abundant life. Here's one way of saying it: It's not our job to satisfy ourselves. It's not our job to work the future out in our minds. God wants to be the one planning and providing for our future.

I get it. It's not as if our worries about the future are unfounded. Because when we honestly consider the many random turns life can make, it's easy to assume things are going to go wrong. If you send a boat adrift by itself in the ocean, it's likely that it's going to eventually sink. Some of us feel like that boat, and we're trying to see over the next wave. We're being tossed and turned, and we grow more nervous by the second because we know that any old situation could be the one that tips us over. I'm not trying to frighten you by saying this. I'm simply pointing out the fact that we are limited in our ability to control the future. We can fret and plan all we want, but no amount of worrying can force things to go our way. That's the very reason we need someone in our lives who can control the waves. Not only can God see the future, He can manage it as well.

The reason I can stop worrying about the future is simply because I know God, God knows the future, and I trust Him.

Psalm 103 begins by listing some blessings of knowing God, but a little further down it begins to address the finite, limitedness of mankind. It points out our frailty, reminding us of our great need for God.

> *"As for man, his days are like grass;*
> *As a flower of the field, so he flourishes.*
> *When the wind has passed over it, it is no more,*
> *And its place acknowledges it no longer."*

Psalm 103:15-16

Depressing? It's not meant to be. I don't think David is trying to scare his listeners. He's painting an accurate picture of what life is really like. If you consider the span of history, and then measure your life against it, you'll see that we don't get much time on this earth. In fact, we aren't even guaranteed the time we think we have.

None of us are guaranteed 120 years, 100 years, 80 years, or even 60 years. Despite our best efforts to extend it, the future is uncertain. Here's my point: Since we're really not in control, isn't it time we stop pretending to be? Why are we trying to carry a weight we can't possibly lift? Attempting to pick up a weight that's too heavy to lift can still take a lot of effort. The good news is, when you give control over to God, you get to release the anxiety associated with acting like you actually had things under control.

When we give control of our lives to God, we can rest in the fact that we know the one who controls the future. We can find certainty in our relationship with Him. We won't be sure of every little thing that's going to happen, but we can be sure of the promises He has made us.

Jesus utilizes a similar metaphor to the one David uses when He talks about the grass and flowers in the book of Matthew. He relates the fragility of the lilies to the unpredictability of the future and the fleetingness of life. However, despite the nature of the illustration, He concludes by instructing us not to worry.

> *"And who of you by being worried can add a single hour to his life? And why are you worried about clothing? Observe how the lilies of the field grow; they do not toil nor do they spin, yet I say to you that not even Solomon in all his glory clothed himself like one of these. But if God so clothes the grass of the field, which is alive today and tomorrow is thrown into the furnace, will He not much more clothe you? You of little faith! Do not worry then, saying, 'What will we eat?' or 'What will we drink?' or 'What will we wear for clothing?' For the Gentiles eagerly seek all these things; for your heavenly Father knows that you need all these things. But seek first His kingdom and His righteousness, and all these things will be added to you. So do not worry about tomorrow; for tomorrow will care for itself. Each day has enough trouble of its own."*

> Matthew 6:27-34

Jesus doesn't deny our basic needs or even the common question of how they will be met. He doesn't say tomorrow will be perfect either. Instead, He says, "Do not worry about tomorrow."

Don't worry about tomorrow? That's easy for you to say, Jesus! You're the Son of God. Don't forget that Jesus had opportunities to worry, too. I want you to consider for a moment the fact that at some point Jesus knew where His life was headed. Scholars will argue about when He knew about the inevitability of the cross, but the exact time is not important in this case. What I want you to see is that, at some point, He understood that His life was headed to utter ruin. Yet He says, "Don't worry about tomorrow." Jesus would not have told us or His disciples to do this if He was unwilling to do it Himself, even in the middle of hardship. He was, after all, our perfect example.

How then do we apply Jesus' word's practically and actually stop worrying? Look at what Jesus says right before He tells us to stop worrying. He says, "Seek first His kingdom and His righteousness, and all these things will be added to you." If we are seeking first God's kingdom and seeking first His righteousness, we don't have to worry. When these two things are first in our hearts, God personally takes responsibility for our future. When Jesus mentions "all these things," He's referring to the things in our life we're worried sick about. They are the uncertainties we wrestle with in our beds at night. They're the puzzles we try to solve in our minds. Jesus is saying, God wants to give you "all these things," so you can sit back, rest, and stop trying to figure out a way to get them yourself.

The good news is, when you give control over to God, you get to release the anxiety associated with acting like you actually had things under control.

I'm not saying God will necessarily make everything go our way. One way God fulfills Jesus' promise is that He begins to shift our desires. Sometimes, we worry about things we don't actually need, and God wants to adjust those desires so that the unnecessary things don't matter as much anymore. It's not wrong for us to desire nice things, but God wants our desire for temporary blessings to be overcome by our desire for eternal rewards. He wants us to take our focus off of our own kingdoms and put our focus on His. We will still be disappointed by life at times. I'm not denying that, but when we are seeking first His kingdom, temporary disappointments are not going to faze us the way they used to.

I'll admit, temporary disappointments don't always feel temporary at the time. Sometimes, the downward spiral of circumstances will appear permanent. Emotionally, we may feel like we'll never be able to climb out of that pit we've sunk into. When you feel this way, look at the greatest temporary disappointment of all time. The disciples had high hopes that Jesus would be their new king. Little did they know that He desired to be the king of their hearts more than He desired to be their literal king on earth. When He was murdered on the cross, all their hopes were dashed. However, there was one person who had faith until the end. That was Jesus Himself.

Did Jesus really have to have faith? Having faith means putting your complete trust and confidence in who God is and what He says. The Bible even tells us that the righteous will live by faith (see Romans 1:17). Jesus was God, but He was also a man. Jesus was the only human who lived a perfectly righteous life and never sinned. Putting His complete hope in God, He even trusted so deeply that He allowed God's plan for His life to lead Him to His own death. Jesus had the same truth in mind as David—that God could be trusted.

Before David, there was another man in the Bible who had to make a similar choice. God promised Abraham that he would be the father of many nations. He promised him an heir, and then He made Abraham wait decades before giving him his son Isaac through his wife, Sarah. Then, surprisingly enough, God told Abraham to sacrifice his only son and heir. He told him to destroy the promise! Look at the thoughts that ran through Abraham's mind as he journeyed with Issac to the mountain on which he would sacrifice his son.

> *"He considered that God was able even to raise him from the dead, from which, figuratively speaking, he did receive him back."*
>
> Hebrews 11:19 (ESV)

As crazy as this sounds, Abraham looked at the death of his son as a temporary disappointment. He held his own plan in one hand, and He held the plan of God in another. He did this figuratively and literally. God's plan was the knife with which he would kill his son. He considered both plans, and He decided that God's plan was better despite how bad it sounded at that moment. He decided to believe that God could be trusted. He decided to give up control. As God intervened with a substitute sacrifice, Abraham found that God did not let Him down.

I don't believe we are given insight into Abraham's thoughts simply so that we could know more about why Abraham did what He did. Abraham's decision to walk in faith mirrored Jesus' decision centuries later. Jesus looked at the cross and believed the same thing Abraham believed, that God is able to raise people from the dead. Despite the agony of the cross, Jesus believed it would be a temporary setback. He believed God would come through for Him. He believed it enough to release control of His own life. He is the same one that has told us, "Do not worry about tomorrow."

The reason I'm talking about God being able to be trusted is because seeking God's kingdom first requires us to have the correct motivation. The Bible makes a promise in Psalm 37:4-5 saying,

> *"Delight yourself in the Lord;*
> *And He will give you the desires of your heart.*
> *Commit your way to the Lord,*
> *Trust also in Him, and He will do it."*

It's tempting to interpret this verse to mean that, as long as we do the right thing, God will give us anything we want. When we look at this verse through the lens of the rest of Scripture though, we can see how that's actually a misinterpretation.

Seeking first God's kingdom is not a trick. It's not a simple formula for success. If we're trying to seek His kingdom simply because we want to get the things He has promised, then we're still not seeking His kingdom first. We're seeking those things first. The moment we start seeking God's kingdom first is the moment when we start seeking it to get *Him*. It's when we decide to seek His kingdom and His righteousness no matter what we lose in the process. When we are seeking His kingdom in this way, the way Abraham and Jesus did, that is when He promises to give us what we need.

We can't manipulate God into giving us what we want. However, when we allow Him to change what we want—to change the desires of our hearts, He then promises to provide for us.

I experienced this truth at work in the first few years of growing my ministry. I told you about some of the financial struggles my wife and I had when we were first married. Less than a year after our first daughter, Mirabelle, was born, my wife became pregnant again. As excited as we were about another baby entering our lives, I began to worry about money once more. We were planning on having our second daughter at home, and our insurance still wasn't going to help pay for the expenses of the birth.

The moment we start seeking God's kingdom first is the moment when we start seeking it to get *Him*.

I was attempting to use my time to do what I believed God was calling me to do. I had aspirations for a business, and I worked diligently at the freelance projects I picked up, but I also knew God wanted me to dedicate some of my schedule to building an online ministry. I could have been using more of my time to earn money for the family, but I knew the online ministry was one way God was telling me to practically prioritize His kingdom.

I'm not pretending like I was doing everything God wanted me to do all the time. I wasn't perfectly seeking His kingdom every day. I was still human, after all. However, my heart was in a place where God could mold it, shape it, and continue to lead it. When I sat down to work on ministry content that wouldn't help pay the bills, I had to choose to believe God could be trusted.

Because we didn't anticipate all the expenses of raising our first child, we were already having some consistent financial problems. I guess I didn't read enough of those parenting 101 books! On top of that, I was looking ahead at the future. I looked at the direction our finances were headed. I considered the cost of having another child, and the fear of the future hit me like a punch to the gut. We would need to make large midwife payments every few months, and I knew we didn't have the money to do it.

I kept asking myself and God the question, "How are we going to pay for these things? Where are we going to get the money from?" Despite my doubts, I remember the very day when I began to look at the situation the way Abraham did. I had been praying about the fears and uncertainties that faced me, and I remember God encouraging me through His written word that He was our provider. I prayed on my own and told God that I was firmly deciding to trust Him. Then, I went into the kitchen where my wife was cooking dinner like a pro and I told her the same thing. We both agreed we were going to trust God with the future despite what we could see. We knew we were doing what He had been leading us to do, and we believed He would provide.

That same week, my wife came up with an idea. Our respective parents had gifted us both a vehicle when we got married. My parents let me have a Mitsubishi Outlander they owned, and her parents let her keep the Ford Explorer she had been driving. My wife pointed out the fact that I worked from home and she stayed home with our daughter, so we really only needed one vehicle between the two of us. It would be a minute inconvenience for us to share a car. If we sold one of the two vehicles, we would have money to make the payments we needed to make.

At first, it sounded like she had had a great idea, but I quickly remembered that we didn't possess the titles to either vehicle. Both cars were still registered in the name of our parents, so we couldn't sell either of them. So, in her ingenuity, my wife came up with a revised idea.

She said, "My parents still have the title to my car, so we could try to sell it back to my parents." I remember thinking, "Wow. That sounds like a bad idea." I'll admit, part of the reason I didn't jump at the idea was because of some pride on my part. As difficult as our financial situation felt, I didn't want to have to tell my in-laws that we were struggling. Also, I felt like trying to sell the car back to them would essentially be rejecting the gift they had given us. The car was a wedding present, and to try to sell it back would be basically saying,

"Thanks, but no thanks. We'll take some cash instead." I couldn't bring myself to do that.

I told my wife, "I can't do that. I'm sorry. The only way I could possibly do that is if they came to us and offered it first." They didn't know we were having financial issues at the time, and I told my wife not to say anything about it. I reminded her that we were both believing God was going to provide—that with His help, we would find a way to make it work.

We were living in Bastrop, Texas at the time, and Leslie's parents lived about 5 hours away. The weekend after Leslie had the idea of selling the car, her parents drove down for a quick visit. At the end of their visit, right as they were walking out the door, her dad looked at me and said, "Before I go, I feel like there's something God wants me to ask you. I want to ask if you want to sell the car back to us."

At that moment, I remembered exactly what I had said earlier that week. I said, "The only way I could possibly do that is if they came to us and offered it first." I had been standing next to a chair between our kitchen and living room, and I immediately had to sit down. I looked at Leslie's dad, Dennis, and it was all I could do to keep myself from crying. I knew that God was providing for us.

At the end of that year, I reviewed our income and expenses. It was clear that the money from the car exactly covered the payments we had needed to make.

Did you know God knows what we need before we ever ask? He cares about the little, daily things, but He also desires to meet our deepest needs. In Matthew 6:8, Jesus says, "Your Father knows what you need before you ask Him."

Think about the story of Jesus feeding the four thousand in Matthew 15. Miraculously multiplying a few fish and a couple pieces of bread, Jesus provides for the physical needs of thousands of people. Shortly after that, when a crowd seeks Him asking for a similar sign, He refuses. In Matthew 15:32, Jesus explains His willingness to provide for one crowd and not another.

> *"And Jesus called His disciples to Him, and said, 'I feel compassion for the people, because they have remained with Me now three days and have nothing to eat; and I do not want to send them away hungry, for they might faint on the way.'"*

One crowd sought Him for Him. The other sought Him for the food He could give them. When He saw the hearts of the crowd that was there to hear His words—to know Him—He had compassion on them and met their needs in a practical way. The question Jesus could have asked both crowds (though He already knew the answer) was this: What are you really after? I want to ask you that same question today. What are you after? Why are you seeking God? Is it because He has the power to give you what you want, or is it because you realize He alone is what you really need?

Before God will revolutionize your life and transform you from a worrier to a person at peace, He wants to see the motivation of your heart align with His will. If you're at that place already, great. If not, that's okay too. My prayer is that, by the end of this book, you'll see a genuine, lasting change occur in your heart. Another prayer I pray nearly every day is that God would continue changing my heart as well.

When our hearts are centered on God's kingdom—on what He wants to do in our lives—He promises to carry the burden we call the future. He promises to take responsibility so that we can stop worrying.

How to Receive the Benefits

As I've said, there are benefits to knowing God. We looked at Psalm 103, which lists some of these benefits. Even though the Psalms were written under the old covenant, and the way you approached God and knew God was different then, the underlying principle still applies: When we know God, we receive the benefits of knowing God.

Jesus demonstrated this when feeding the four thousand. He was essentially saying, *Because you're following Me with the right motives, I see your needs, and I'm taking steps to meet them.* The crowds were seeking to know Him, and because of this they received the benefits of being friends with Him.

If we're going to learn to stop worrying about the many areas of our lives, we first need to be able to do three things: understand the benefits of knowing God, believe we will receive those benefits, and then actually begin to receive them. The question I want to answer right now is: *What can we practically do to start receiving the benefits?*

You may think back to Jesus' words from Matthew chapter 6 where Jesus tells us to seek first His kingdom and His righteousness. When we do those two things, He promises to meet our needs, right? I want to throw a loop into this idea that may rattle your perspective.

Maybe you've thought like this at one point: "I'm trying to seek His kingdom and His righteousness as much as possible, but I keep failing. Maybe that's why God isn't coming through for me." Seeking God's kingdom first means prioritizing His will, and I think most of us understand that idea. When we respond to the call of Jesus to share the gospel and build up the body of Christ, we are really building God's kingdom. It's not a difficult concept. However, seeking His righteousness first is where I believe the hang up usually occurs.

When Jesus tells us to seek His righteousness first, the first thought that often comes to mind is that we must attempt to live righteously. We assume God wants us to strive to be good all the time. Believe it or not, that's not what Jesus means by this phrase at all.

Consider for a moment that you have a friend named Hal. Hal is a nice guy. He attends church. He shares his groceries with the struggling widow who lives next door. He prays sometimes, and he even attempts to follow the commands of God. What if Hal comes to you one day and initiates a serious conversation about salvation? He admits, "I know a lot about Christianity, but I just don't feel like my sins are forgiven. I constantly live with shame and guilt, no matter how much good I do. I work so hard to please God, but no matter what I sacrifice, I don't ever feel like it's enough. I feel like I'm missing something, but I don't know what it is."

You might reply with a simple question, "Have you believed that Jesus paid the price for your sins? Have you trusted Him as your Savior, or are you trying to save yourself through your actions?"

The reason I mention our friend Hal is because I want to paint a picture of the only way in which we attain God's righteousness. No matter how many good works we do, we can never be perfect—we can never do enough good to make up for the bad, because God's standard is absolute perfection. In order to be considered righteous before God, He must see us as being morally blameless—as having done everything right. So, to be righteous in God's eyes, we are left with only one solution: complete reliance on the sacrifice of Jesus on the cross. Here's my point: If we must rely on Jesus in order to receive God's righteousness in the first place, then we cannot continue to seek His righteousness through our imperfect works.

How do you find precious stones or metals in nature? You go to the source. When you are seeking gold, you either pan for it or your mine for it. You don't climb a tree and start chipping away at the bark looking for gold. If you did that, people would talk you down and take you straight to a neurologist. You seek gold in the way it can be found. It's the same with God's righteousness. Jesus doesn't want us to seek His righteousness presumptuously. Even after we've already received salvation, we must seek it in the only way it can actually be found.

Think about Abraham again. Look at the way James says Abraham received God's righteousness in James 2:23.

> *"and the Scripture was fulfilled which says, 'And Abraham believed God, and it was reckoned to him as righteousness,' and he was called the friend of God."*

James reveals the way in which righteousness can be found by us: belief. When Abraham chose to believe God, the righteousness of God was credited to him. Consequently, God considered Abraham a friend.

Think back to the first chapter in this book for a moment. I'm going to use my own story as an example again, but please keep in mind that I don't always get this right either. I'm not trying to hold myself up as the shining example, because I'm not. However, there are many times when I've seen the benefits of knowing God at work in my life. When I needed God to come through for me financially, I received a comforting word from God through the Holy Spirit. In my hour of need, God used His voice to communicate His providential plan.

The reason I bring this up is because I want to remind you of the connection between the benefits and the personal relationship. The way I knew God was providing was because I was in communication with Him. I was close enough to Him to hear His voice when He spoke. I'm not saying this to make you feel like God's provision is out of your reach if you don't hear from the Holy Spirit. I'm saying this because you need to know that an intimate relationship with God through the fellowship of the Holy Spirit is closer than you think.

Many of us have a picture of the Christian walk in our minds that resembles a progression chart hanging on a wall. We look at the "steps" of Christianity, like being filled with the Spirit, learning to hear from God, or receiving a spiritual gift, and we think that each step is connected by hard work. We assume that, to reach the next level of "spiritual maturity," we're going to have to be better than we've been in the past. The truth is, that's a lie from the devil that is actually meant to keep us from taking the next step. A relationship with God is not fueled by hard work; it's fueled by faith. As we continue choosing to believe His words, we continue to grow closer and closer to Him. Our nearness to God is not determined predominantly by our works, but by our faith.

I want to show you the progression of righteousness by faith as the Bible describes it. Consider again the question, "What can I do practically to start receiving the benefits of knowing God?" This progression answers that question.

Belief → Grace → Righteousness → Fellowship

Paul writes about this progression in Titus 3:4-7.

> *"But when the kindness of God our Savior and His love for mankind appeared, He saved us, not on the basis of deeds which we have done in righteousness, but according to His mercy, by the washing of regeneration and renewing by the Holy Spirit, whom He poured out upon us richly through Jesus Christ our Savior, so that being justified by His grace we would be made heirs according to the hope of eternal life."*

Belief: We believe in the sacrifice Jesus made for our sins on the cross.

Grace: Because of our belief, we receive God's mercy and grace. Our sins are covered.

Righteousness: When our sins are covered, God sees us as righteous. He attributes the righteousness of Christ to us.

Fellowship: When we are seen as righteous, we have the right to a relationship with God. We have fellowship with Him and grow deeper in this relationship through the Holy Spirit.

One more verse I feel compelled to share is Philippians 3:8-9, where Paul again describes the way in which we are able to attain righteousness.

"More than that, I count all things to be loss in view of the surpassing value of knowing Christ Jesus my Lord, for whom I have suffered the loss of all things, and count them but rubbish so that I may gain Christ, and may be found in Him, not having a righteousness of my own derived from the Law, but that which is through faith in Christ, the righteousness which comes from God on the basis of faith."

A relationship with God is not fueled by hard work; it's fueled by faith.

Paul gives us the key to God's righteousness once more: faith in Jesus—a real belief in who He is, what He has done for us, and what He wants to do in us. Opening up about his intentions, Paul also reveals the object of his pursuit. He says, "so that I may gain Christ." Paul admits to seeking God for the same reason the first crowd sought God—for the same reason Mary sat at the feet of Jesus—to know Jesus.

You may be wondering why I'm going into such great detail about knowing God personally. *How does that relate to my worry?* Consider for a moment how often most loved children worry compared to some adults. Some grown men and women live life with the weight of the world on their shoulders. Most children don't. Some adults worry about how they're going to afford groceries.

Children get hungry and simply ask mom or dad for something to eat. Some adults fixate on the opportunities their children are going to have in life. Most children aren't concerned with their future at all.

The reason I've spent so much time talking about the relationship God wants to have with us is because God wants us to be His children. He wants to be our loving Father. He wants us to be able to bring every worry and care to Him (see 1 Peter 5:7), lay it down at His feet and wait expectantly for an answer. We obviously can't do this if we don't have a real relationship with Him, and we won't be doing it as often as we should if our relationship has been damaged. When your relationship with God is right, God becomes your source of peace and security.

Many people never experienced a good relationship with their father growing up, and I understand that. It's not easy for every person to accept the idea that God wants to be our Father, but I can give you two truths that may help. First, you need to understand that God is not like earthly fathers or mothers. In all the ways your earthly parents came through for you, God comes through for you too, and in all the ways your earthly parents let you down, God still comes through for you. He is a perfect parent, and His actions are always motivated by His love for you.

The Bible says that God is love—He is the very definition of real love. That means that, even when God does something we don't understand, He still acts in love because He cannot change who He is. However, we also need to keep in mind that God is not bound by our human description of what is loving. God will not always do what we consider to be loving. Instead, He will always do what truly is loving, despite what we think. Think about a child screaming because their parent won't let them play in the street. From the kid's point of view, the parent isn't acting in love. However, the only thing on the parent's mind is the loving protection of their child.

The same way a child is reliant on a parent, we can rely on God. Unlike the parents, role models, or guardians in our lives who have disappointed us, God never disappoints those who are trusting in Him (see Isaiah 49:23). We will still feel emotionally disappointed at times, because we are still human. God isn't going to simply hand us everything we want either. However, God has an endless store of foresight, wisdom, and strength that we can always count on. When we're willing to put our trust in His better judgement—in His truth—we will never end up with anything less than the promises He has made to us.

The second truth that will help you accept God as a loving Father is to understand that He is also a friend. The same way that He is a perfect parent, He is a perfect friend to those who know Him. When you're in the presence of a business associate, employer, mentor, or stranger, your demeanor can be closed off and guarded. You don't want to say or do anything to embarrass yourself. When you're in the presence of a friend, you can truly relax, rest, and enjoy their friendship. God wants you to enjoy His friendship. You don't have to strive all the time—He wants you to enjoy His gifts. You don't have to do everything yourself—He wants you to ask for His help. You don't have to appear perfect in front of Him—He wants you to be honest with Him and accept His grace.

God is a perfect parent, and His actions are always motivated by His love for you.

The more we learn to walk in a healthy, intimate relationship with our good Father and best Friend, the less shaken we'll be by life's twists and turns. When the future casts those unanticipated waves our way, we can confidently say, "I'm not worried because I have a strong anchor holding me in place. His name is Jesus Christ."

Your Eternal Future is Secure

One of the most common questions I've heard in ministry is: *How can I be sure I'm saved? How can I know for certain God has forgiven my sin?* When you have a personal relationship with God through faith in Jesus, and when you are abiding in Christ through the fellowship of the Holy Spirit, you have an assurance that nothing in this earth can take away. God doesn't want us to worry about our earthly future, but He doesn't want us to wonder about our eternal future either.

I grew up in church, and I prayed the "sinner's prayer" countless times, always hoping that God heard me that time. As a child, I possessed a healthy fear of God (as well as an unhealthy one), and my dread of not pleasing God constantly led me back to that anxious thought: *What if I'm not really saved?* If you've ever faced that worry, or if you know someone who worries about this, you need to know that God has provided an assurance of salvation that surpasses our fears and doubts, leaving us with a supernatural peace regarding our eternity. Knowing God comes with benefits, and the first and most important benefit is salvation. Jesus' words in John 6:27 confirm the importance of eternal security through salvation.

> *"Do not work for the food which perishes, but for the food which endures to eternal life, which the Son of Man will give to you, for on Him the Father, God, has set His seal."*

There are some benefits believers never experience here on earth, but this is the one benefit all believers share in common. Whether because of unbelief or continual disobedience, some believers never get around to receiving all the spiritual gifts God wants to give them here and now, but every person who is truly saved will spend eternity with God. There's no in-between when it comes to this benefit. Some religions claim that there's a half-way point for those who almost make it to heaven, but the Bible doesn't teach that. The Bible tells us that there will be two judgements: one for those who believe in Jesus, and one for those who disbelieve. It also tells us that we can be certain about which judgement we will attend.

> *"By this, love is perfected with us, so that we may have confidence in the day of judgment; because as He is, so also are we in this world."*
>
> 1 John 4:17

I want to share a story from the gospels with you that in many ways parallels the story of Jesus at the house of Mary and Martha. Reading the account of the rich young ruler, the similarities may not jump out at first glance, but they are there. As we observe this young man's questions for Jesus, keep in mind Martha's approach as well.

The story of the rich young ruler is found in Matthew, Mark, and Luke, and I'm going to be focusing on the telling from Mark. I encourage you to go read the whole passage in Mark 10:17-31, but I'm going to pull out a few key verses starting with verse 17.

> *"As He was setting out on a journey, a man ran up to Him and knelt before Him, and asked Him, 'Good Teacher, what shall I do to inherit eternal life?'"*

Notice the man's passion. Running up to Jesus, he falls down on his knees, and then he asks Jesus about the requirements for salvation. He says, "What shall I do?" This isn't a flippant question; it is a direct, thought-through concern that plagues the man. Jesus is about to set out on a journey when the young man sprints up to him. The man doesn't want to miss his chance to ask this important question. How many nights had he stayed up wondering if he had truly found favor with God? How many times had he swallowed those doubts and tried to move on with his day?

Jesus replies by listing off some of God's commandments. He reminds him not to murder and not to commit adultery. He tells him not to steal, lie, or cheat. Look at the man's response in verse 20:

> *"And he said to Him, 'Teacher, I have kept all these things from my youth up.'"*

There are two thoughts that could be running through the rich man's head at this point. He could be saying through his answer, "Well, I've gotten it right then. I've done all those things so I should be good." The other more likely option is for him to be unsatisfied with Jesus' answer. I believe his answer really gives us insight into an internal monologue that is screaming out, "I've done all those things, but I still don't feel assured!" I believe this phrase reflects his thoughts because of what Jesus says next. Keep in mind, Jesus knows more than the man is willing to share.

"Looking at him, Jesus felt a love for him and said to him, 'One thing you lack: go and sell all you possess and give to the poor, and you will have treasure in heaven; and come, follow Me.'"

Mark 10:21

Jesus responds to Martha with compassion, and he responds to the rich young ruler the same way. He also cuts straight to the heart of the issue. The man followed the commandments outwardly, but his heart was not following God inwardly. Jesus does not disapprove of the man's actions, but instead he points out the man's single flaw: The man wants to add God to his life but he does not want to allow God into His heart. The place in his heart where God wants to dwell is filled with a love of money, and Jesus knows this.

In a way, the man is a lot like Martha. Notice how Jesus uses the exact same words here that he uses when responding to the worried hostess. He says, "one thing." Jesus says to Martha, "You are worried and bothered about so many things; but only one thing is necessary." He tells the rich young ruler, "One thing you lack." The one thing the rich young ruler lacks is the same thing Mary finds at the feet of Jesus: a personal relationship.

The man wants to keep his pursuit of God impersonal by following all the rules—by checking off the boxes. Jesus immediately makes it personal by saying, "Come, follow Me."

We do the same thing the man in the story does, don't we? We depersonalize our relationship with God. Yet, God is always leading us back to a personal interaction with Him. Look at these common phrases I've heard from people when asking them how their relationship with God is going:

"I'm trying my best not to sin", or "I'm trying my best to do what's right."

"I really need to study the Scripture some more."

"I just don't feel like I can talk to God about the issues I'm facing."

We may not fully realize it, but when we say things like this, we're focusing on what we're doing for God instead of focusing on what God has already done for us. We're making our relationship with God about rules instead of about relationship. We all do this at times, so I'm not saying I'm better at this than you. However, I want you to see how passionate God is about a personal relationship. Look at God's responses to our striving in Scripture. He's always trying to make it personal:

> *"you have left your first love"*
>
> Revelation 2:4

> *"you will be My people, and I will be your God"*
>
> Ezekiel 36:28

> *"I have called you by name; you are Mine!"*
>
> Isaiah 43:1

> *"You search the Scriptures because you think that in them you have eternal life; it is these that testify about Me; and you are unwilling to come to Me so that you may have life."*
>
> John 5:39-40

The rich young ruler's perspective mirrors the attitude of Martha. He relates to God in an impersonal way. Yet, the disciples' perspectives mirror that of Mary. Like her, they choose to relate to God in a personal way.

The rich young ruler leaves, saddened by the words of Jesus. After he walks away, the disciples ask Jesus who can be saved. Jesus' interaction with the rich young ruler has suddenly brought up some doubts in their own hearts about how salvation is obtained. Jesus calms their fears with His answer.

> *"With people it is impossible, but not with God; for all things are possible with God."*
>
> Mark 10:27

He lets them know that, when we are willing to come to God on God's terms, God does the saving work for us. Without Him, no work we do will ever be enough. Paul's words in Romans 9:31-32 sum up the story of the rich young ruler.

> *"...but Israel, pursuing a law of righteousness, did not arrive at that law. Why? Because they did not pursue it by faith, but as though it were by works. They stumbled over the stumbling stone."*

The stumbling stone is Jesus, and the way we stumble over it is by rejecting a personal relationship with Him. Following commandments is not the way to salvation. Instead, obedience is a demonstration of the faith that we have when we say yes to Jesus' invitation to follow Him. Salvation by grace leads to obedience, not the other way around.

When you're worried about something, who do you go to for help? When you need help with something, do you first go to an employer you barely know with your troubles? Probably not. Most of us run to our family or our friends first. We tell the people we know—the people who really know us. When you are resting in the certainty of your relationship with God, you can always run to Him first. When you're worried about something, your first instinct will be to ask God for help. I bet the disciples said something like this a lot when dealing with the worries and cares of life: "Just go ask Jesus. He always seems to know. He always seems to have the answer." Listen to me. God has the answer, and that answer is available because of grace.

One thing I believe many believers do is wait until they feel worthy before running to God for help. This doubtful way of thinking causes us to attempt to impress God before we can ask for help. You're not going to always feel worthy at first, but thankfully God doesn't ask you to feel your way into His presence. Instead, He says you can come boldly before Him through faith—by believing in Jesus' finished work. The same way obedience follows grace, our feelings follow our faith. Be willing to invest in your relationship with Him, but don't try running to Him through works. Run to Him through faith. The good news is this: The faster you run to God when you start worrying, the faster your worries will run from you.

I want to expand on the subject of assurance for a little while because I believe this subject is too weighty to speed through. It's also a strategy the devil uses to try to shake our faith at times. If the devil can get us to doubt our position in God's family, he can get us to doubt that God can really change us or use us. He can get us to doubt God's promises.

The antidote for doubt is belief. I want to ask you a simple question, and I want you to consider your true feelings about the answer. Do you believe God *wants* a personal relationship with you? He says He does. God is not pursuing you out of obligation; He is pursuing you out of a deep, passionate desire for you to know Him intimately. Everything we receive from God starts with us choosing to believe what He says. Belief is the key to the best relationship you've ever been in.

Another question I want you to ponder is this: Do you approach God with an expectation based on His words? Look at these amazing words of expectation in Psalm 86:6-7.

> *"Give ear, O Lord, to my prayer; and give heed to the voice of my supplications! In the day of my trouble I shall call upon You, for You will answer me."*

King David could have said, "You might answer me." He could have said, "I hope You answer me." Instead, he says, "You *will* answer me." How does he have such a great expectation? The answer is that he knows God personally—not impersonally. He believes God's words about who He is and what He wants. His prayer is based in real relationship and real belief.

Where does King David's expectation meet our own? If you don't know much about David, one defining characteristic about him is that he often wrote prophetically. Many of the lyrics in David's psalms describe the coming of the Messiah, who would be born into his lineage. David wrote about the birth of Jesus, who would deliver to humankind the greatest gift anyone has ever given. Our expectation about what God is going to do can be solidified when we look at what God has already done. People like Abraham and David looked ahead with expectation at the coming of Christ, and now we can look back at the fulfillment of that promise.

We can even look ahead at the completion of the fulfillment as we await the second coming of Christ and the eternal life God has given us through His Son. Listen to the mind-blowing level of expectation found in the words of Peter:

> *"Blessed be the God and Father of our Lord Jesus Christ, who according to His great mercy has caused us to be born again to a living hope through the resurrection of Jesus Christ from the dead, to obtain an inheritance which is imperishable and undefiled and will not fade away, reserved in heaven for you, who are protected by the power of God through faith for a salvation ready to be revealed in the last time."*

1 Peter 1:3-5

Everything we receive from God starts with us choosing to believe what He says.

We can read words like those written by Peter or David and have a hope that is unshakable—a belief that is unmovable—an assurance that is complete. The way the words in Scripture can be solidified in our hearts is through our relationship with *the Word*. Jesus is called "the Word made flesh" by the Apostle John. The reason "the Word" is used to describe Jesus is because God's power is wrapped up in His word. In the beginning, He spoke and created the world. He then spoke a promise to Abraham that He would bless the nations of the earth through him. It was a word from God that was eventually fulfilled by the birth of Christ. After Jesus left, He told the disciples to preach the gospel, which means *good news*. News is a communicated word—a message. Then, in 1 Corinthians 1:18 Paul explains the power behind the word of the gospel and how it is intricately connected to the saving power of God through Jesus Christ.

> *"For the word of the cross is foolishness to those who are perishing, but to us who are being saved it is the power of God."*

He says that the word is the power. For God to powerfully show up in our lives—to powerfully assure us that He is holding us securely in His hands now and for eternity—we have to know *the Word*. Our expectation must be wrapped up in our intimate friendship with Jesus.

I used to put a lot of stock in what I did *for* God. Maybe I assumed one day I would be standing before Him at the gates of heaven and He would ask, "Why do you deserve to be allowed in here?" At one point in my life, I would have pointed to the things I've done. I would have said, "Do you remember that one time I gave that single mom that money so she could buy groceries?" or "Don't you remember the lonely kid I befriended in junior high?" But now I know there's only one thing I will be able to say: "I know Your Son. He paid the price for me to come in."

Whether you prayed to make Jesus the Lord of your life while reading this book, or whether you've been saved for years, the devil will attempt to raise doubts in your mind if he can (he is the devil, after all). He will attempt to direct your line of sight away from God's truth about who you are in Christ. He can't undo what Jesus has done for you, but the devil will still try to get you to question your salvation.

You might ask, *Shouldn't we question our salvation? Shouldn't we want to make sure that we belong to Christ and are on our way to heaven?* Yes, we should want to be sure. However, there's a difference between Satan speaking doubts into our minds and a healthy desire for assurance. We can see the evidence of that difference clearly in the way we worry. If we're battling spiritual warfare, meant to attack our faith, the questions that are raised in our minds are going to be questions that cause anxiety. You may have heard questions like these racing through your mind before:

Have I really done enough to be saved?

What if God doesn't really love me as much as He says He does?

What if God wouldn't choose to save me?

These questions all have their basis in a lie—an assumption or thought that goes against Scripture. Doubts like these are not meant to lead us toward assurance. They are meant to torture us mentally and emotionally. They are meant to keep us in a cycle of works-based righteousness and fear.

The question God wants us to ask about our salvation is not like that. The question God wants us to ask is grounded in a healthy fear of God, and it sounds more like this:

God, if I'm not consistently allowing You to be the Lord of my life, will You show me how to do that?

Jesus, if I haven't fully understood Your love and grace, will you continue revealing it to me?

Holy Spirit, if I haven't truly repented of sin in my life, can You help me do that?

Now, to our natural minds, questions like these may sound as if they would produce the same level of worry and fear, but there's a Biblical reason why they don't. The reason is found in passages like Psalm 34:18, Acts 17:27 (ESV), and Psalm 145:18.

"The Lord is near to the brokenhearted and saves those who are crushed in spirit."

"that they should seek God, and perhaps feel their way toward him and find him. Yet he is actually not far from each one of us,"

"The Lord is near to all who call upon Him, to all who call upon Him in truth."

The reason we can ask for assurance of salvation without worry is because God wants to answer us personally. When we reject the lies we've been believing and call out to Him in truth, He *Himself* assures us. That's what friendship looks like. When we allow our spirits to be broken and we cry out to Him for real answers, He reveals just how near to us He really is. When we get real with God, He gets personal with us.

Getting Practical About Assurance

The way God gets the most personal with us is through the voice of the Holy Spirit. There are benefits to knowing God, and the number one benefit is eternal life with God. The Holy Spirit is the one who assures us that we've received that benefit, and I believe this is one of the most important things the Holy Spirit does for us. In Matthew 7:21-23, Jesus talks about those who will think they are believers on the last day but will not be allowed into heaven. He gives us the reason in verse 23: "I never knew you." How do we know that we know God? We talk with Him and He talks with us. There's a real relationship there, and that relationship is walked out in our day-to-day lives through fellowship—intimacy—with the Holy Spirit.

Now, I'm going to be honest with you. This section is difficult for me to write because though I want to paint an accurate picture of what it looks like to be saved, I also don't want to be a source of condemnation for those who really are saved. Here is the first question that may have gone through your mind as you read that last paragraph: If I don't hear from the Holy Spirit daily, does that mean I'm not really saved? Not necessarily. The truth is that you might not have learned to hear Him clearly yet. However, my encouragement to you is that you would ask God the questions I listed as you continue reading this chapter. Let God know that you're serious about this. Lay your heart bare before Him. Let Him change anything that needs to be changed, and I believe you will begin to receive an unshakable assurance.

If you go read Matthew 7:21-23, you'll see that Jesus also talks about two other pieces of evidence in that same passage: faith and works. I want to mention these first two, but I want to focus on the third assurance, which is the Holy Spirit. The reason I want to focus on the Holy Spirit is because the people in that passage had deceived themselves into thinking they were saved based on false evidence of the first two assurances.

The first practical step to have a healthy assurance of salvation is to examine our faith. Ask yourself the question: *Have I truly turned from sin and believed in Jesus as my Lord and Savior? Am I really trusting in Him to save me?* If you have, you can be sure that God has written your name in the Lamb's book of life. If you know you have believed, and yet you still wonder if God has taken you seriously, remind yourself of verses like Romans 10:13, which says, "for 'whoever will call on the name of the Lord will be saved.'"

The second practical step to being sure of your salvation is to consider the fruit in your life. Look at the evidence. You should be able to think back to the person you were before you got saved and see a difference between yourself then and yourself now. If your heart has been changed, your actions will reflect that change. I'm not talking about being perfect—we all still make mistakes. I'm talking about an obvious change. 1 John 2:1-11 gives us a clear picture of the transformed Christian life. If you read passages like this and recognize that you are bearing fruit, yet you still worry if you make too many mistakes, look at the first few verses in the chapter. John says, "My little children, I am writing these things to you so that you may not sin. And if anyone sins, we have an Advocate with the Father, Jesus Christ the righteous; and He Himself is the propitiation for our sins…" Anytime the condemning voice of the devil tries to tell you that you've made one too many mistakes, you take out verses like this and shout them back at him (or whisper if you happen to be in a library or on a public tram). Every time we mess up, the grace of God is available through Jesus Christ.

The third practical step to knowing you are saved is the one on which I want to spend the most time. The reason I'm going to focus on this answer is because I want you to understand that you can be completely certain of your salvation. The key to a genuine, peaceful assurance is found in the nature of faith.

> *"Now faith is the assurance of things hoped for, the conviction of things not seen."*
>
> Hebrews 11:1

God desires us to have a faith so strong that it acts as a doubt-free assurance—an unwavering conviction in our hearts of the truth. I'm telling you right now, that kind of faith is not impossible to possess. In fact, it's a lot closer than you think. The obvious question is *how do I get there? How do I get that kind of faith?* Romans 10:17 gives us a simple answer to a hard question.

"So faith comes from hearing, and hearing by the word of Christ."

Faith comes from hearing the words of Christ. Does that mean reading the Bible all day long is the only thing that can increase our faith? It definitely does build our faith, but that's not what this verse is focusing on. If you look at the original Greek behind the phrase "word of Christ," the original language uses the root word *rhema* instead of *logos*. Logos refers to a written word, but rhema refers to a living word, a spoken word, or an utterance. It's specifically saying that the *spoken* word of God builds our faith.

Some people say that this verse means we need to read the Bible out loud, but I want you to think about the Pharisees for a moment. The Pharisees habitually read the word of God out loud all the time, and yet when Jesus showed up, they had no faith. Jesus Himself points out where they fell short in their attempt to find salvation in John 5:39-40.

"You search the Scriptures because you think that in them you have eternal life; it is these that testify about Me; and you are unwilling to come to Me so that you may have life."

Jesus is talking about an assurance of salvation, and He points out the fact that the Pharisees were putting more trust in the printed words on the page than they were in the God who wanted to use His word to speak to their hearts.

We've talked about how God wants to share His thoughts with us through the Holy Spirit. Jesus confirms this in John 10:27 when He says that His sheep hear His voice. When we apply this truth to the assurance of our salvation, we find the third practical way that we can know we are saved. It is simply this: The Holy Spirit personally assures us that we belong to Christ. When we are hearing His voice clearly, He speaks into our hearts and lets us know that we no longer have to worry about whether we're saved or not. 1 John 3:23-24 confirms this as it speaks of all three methods of assurance.

"This is His commandment, that we believe in the name of His Son Jesus Christ, and love one another, just as He commanded us.

The one who keeps His commandments abides in Him, and He in him. We know by this that He abides in us, by the Spirit whom He has given us."

You may still be thinking, "If I don't hear from the Holy Spirit on a regular basis, does that mean I'm not saved?" Like I said before, remember the first two steps to assurance. If you have truly believed in Jesus as your Lord and Savior, you are His. Also, examine the evidence—look at the fruit God has grown in your life.

If hearing God's voice is an area you need to grow in, remember that we all need to work on our relationship with God. Being filled with the Spirit is the best way we can develop a better and deeper relationship with God than we've ever had. Every relationship takes time. The same applies to our friendship with Jesus. None of us have gotten this perfect. However, today can be the day when things change. You can learn to identify God's voice right now.

If you've been taught against the works of the Holy Spirit, I encourage you to look back at verses like the one we just read from 1 John 3. We know we are in Jesus because of the Holy Spirit within us. The voice of the Holy Spirit is a blessing too good for you to miss out on.

In the first chapter of this book, I asked you a question. Do you want to get closer to God? Do you want to sit at the feet of Jesus and listen? If the answer is yes, I want to give you an opportunity to ask for a greater filling of the Holy Spirit right now.

Remember that the Holy Spirit lives inside every believer from the moment they are saved. As I said earlier, Jesus teaches us in Luke 11:9-13 that, even if we are saved, we can ask to be filled with the Holy Spirit to a greater degree. Any relationship you want to develop you invest in. This is one of the main ways we invest in our relationship with God: We ask and we wait in faith. When you believe the words of Jesus and choose to ask, God hears you, and He loves to give good gifts to His children.

If you know you need this, I encourage you to pray with me right now. After you pray, sit and wait for Him. Take some time to let go of any distracting thoughts and concentrate on His goodness and grace. Think about what Jesus did for you on the cross. Pray with me.

Dear Jesus, You said, "Ask, and it will be given to you; seek, and you will find." I believe You mean what You say. I'm asking that You fill me with the Holy Spirit right now. I recognize my need for a deeper relationship with You. I want to be closer to You. Open my ears so that I can hear Your voice. Open my heart so that I will listen to Your truth. Open my eyes so that I will see Your hand at work in my life. I believe You are God the Father, God the Son, and God the Holy Spirit. Fill me with Your Spirit, Lord Jesus!

I wrote a detailed account of when I heard from the Holy Spirit for the first time in my testimony book, *My Mess*. However, I want to share it briefly here.

During my freshman year in college, I developed a slew of addictions and habitual sins that left me feeling empty, depressed, and dirty. All my life, I had worried about whether I was saved or not. Throughout that year, I often stayed awake all night long due to my fretful emotions. Worrying over God's wrath and judgement consistently kept me up while everyone else enjoyed their sleep. I would lay on the lobby couch, wishing I could somehow forget my anxious thoughts.

At the end of that year, I repented of my sins. I told God I wanted to be free, but I still didn't understand His love and grace. About half a year later, I began to seek Him. I wanted to know Him personally, even though in my mind that meant working hard to earn His favor. After weeks of reading the Bible late at night, praying, and laying on the common room floor of my dorm suite, the Holy Spirit began to speak to me. His words echoed the truths I had been reading and beginning to believe. When He spoke the words in my spirit though, I finally got it.

He essentially spoke two truths to me: He told me that He loved me and that Jesus died for me. In that moment, a transference of peace occurred. As I truly believed the gospel for the first time, God took my worry and fear and He handed me peace. Excitement overwhelmed me. All the time, I thought I would have to make myself God's servant through hard work. God wanted to make me His child through belief in Jesus.

Since that defining moment, I've never doubted my salvation. Every time someone else tells me that they wonder if they are really saved or not, I think back to what the Holy Spirit said to me. I'm not saying you'll never experience fearful thoughts if you hear from the Holy Spirit. I'm saying that you'll have an assurance that will cut through the worry like a knife through soft butter.

If you're thinking, "I want that!", here's one final practical step you can take right now: Start finding assurance in God's word. Find a collection of verses and passages that clearly spell out the gospel message and meditate on them. Read them every day and remind yourself that you have really believed in Jesus. Then, pray and ask the Holy Spirit to speak a confirmation of those verses to you personally.

> *"You will seek Me and find Me when you search for Me with all your heart."*

Jeremiah 29:13

God isn't hiding Himself from you. He's simply waiting for you to lay your heart out before Him. Seek Him and you will find Him. You will find an assurance that nothing—the devil, your own mind, your family or friends, or anything else—will ever be able to shake. While you're looking for verses, Romans 8:38-39 is a good one to start with.

> *"For I am convinced that neither death, nor life, nor angels, nor principalities, nor things present, nor things to come, nor powers, nor height, nor depth, nor any other created thing, will be able to separate us from the love of God, which is in Christ Jesus our Lord."*

The exact route the future will take may feel uncertain, but you can always be certain of God's love for you. The cross was a once-and-for-all demonstration of that love. Now, not only does God hold the future in His hands, He holds you in His hands as well. You can face the future with a confident assurance that, no matter what happens, God wants to walk with you every step of the way, and His love will never fail you.

- 4 -

STOP WORRYING ABOUT YOUR WORK

Especially if you live in the United States of America, like I do, your work may be one of the main causes of your worry. I know there are many other cultures that face a similar problem. When I start talking to young men around my age, the first subject I try to cover is the topic of work. I know that, if I don't let them get their frustrations about their work off their chest, they're not really going to be engaged in a conversation with me because they're going to be thinking about that stressful project or upcoming due date the whole time instead of what we're talking about. The reason I know this happens to others is because it happens to me, too! I worry and stress over either the amount of work I'm doing, the quality of my work, or the pressures that come with the work.

Have you ever seen one of those egg-carrying competitions? Perhaps you participated in one as a child. I'm not sure what maniacal person thought up that game. Essentially, you grab a spoon, balance an egg on it, hold it out in front of you, and then run toward the finish line. The whole time you worry about that dumb egg slipping off the spoon and cracking.

Many of us see our work like that egg on that spoon. We're running, trying not to twist our ankle in divots in the ground, and balancing that egg in front of us like our life depended on it. Our hands are shaking, and our heart is beating, but somehow we're keeping that egg on the spoon. We keep telling ourselves that if we just make it a little further, the anxiety will pass. No matter how far we get though, we never stop worrying. Here's what you need to know about that egg: God doesn't want you to be constantly worrying about it. God created us to work, but He did not create us to worry about our work. He has a better design in mind than that.

I know not everyone works a traditional, 9-to-5 job. That's okay. Even if you're a stay-at-home parent (which counts as a full-time job in my mind), retired, or unemployed for any other reason, there is a lot of groundwork in this chapter that we will need later on. Each chapter in this book focuses on a different area of life that may be a source of worry, but I've also taken the building blocks of peace and laid them evenly throughout. So, if you see a chapter heading who's topic doesn't really interest you, don't skip it because you'll be skipping some of these building blocks of peace.

This next block may be the one which is most overlooked and ignored, even by those who have been Christians for a long time. We may have received salvation, and we may have even heard from the Holy Spirit at some point, but if we don't get this next block in place, worry will always be a personal struggle.

The groundwork I want to talk about is the idea of *principles*. As we discussed, there are benefits to knowing God, but there are also principles found in God's word through which we receive some of those benefits. I know what you might be thinking right now: *I thought we got all the benefits purely through having a relationship with God.* The answer is yes. However, truly knowing God means choosing to accept the way He is. What I mean is, our relationship with God cannot be based on what *we* think a good relationship with God looks like. It must be based on *His* idea of a good relationship. His ideas, after all, are perfect. Ours are not. Just look at the egg game some strange person came up with. That was definitely not from God.

Many books and sermons have been written on the idea of promises and premises. Many Christian teachers will say, "For every promise, there's a premise." They mean, if we want to receive the promise of God, we must be fulfilling the requirement God has set up in order for us to receive that promise. When I'm talking about principles, I'm talking about something similar to that idea, but very different in a few major ways.

Not always, but sometimes, the idea of promises and premises can quickly lead us to operate in a works-based mindset. We start focusing on the promises—what we want to receive from God—and we try to work really hard in order to do enough to receive them. We're less focused on God and more focused on what He can give us. I'm going to do my best to present the principles of God from a relational, grace-based perspective in this book, because it's really all about a relationship and not a set of rules.

Think about a loving parent who has a set of principles they live by. Because they love their children, they expect their children to also adhere to these principles to an extent. The principles are there not to stop the children from enjoying life, but instead to help give the children their best chance at a fulfilling life. When a child is born into a family, they receive all the benefits of being a part of that family immediately. Nothing is restricted from them. However, as they grow older and begin to know this parent better, they learn the principles the parent expects them to live by—principles that are set in place for the child's good. If the child decides not to live by those principles, the parent may restrict some of the benefits of being a part of the family.

Take this example: A parent may ask a teenager and remind them several times that they want the teen to be home at a reasonable hour on weeknights. Yet, when a teenager repeatedly takes the car and stays out past midnight, a parent may come to the son or daughter and say, "I want to give you the benefit of being able to take my car when you want, but I can't give you that benefit right now because I want what's best for you more than I want you to be happy."

When we enter God's family, we receive all the benefits. Through faith in Jesus, we are given the righteousness of God. We get all the benefits of being a loved child of God. However, as we get to know God more through His word and through fellowship with the Holy Spirit, we also learn about His principles—what He wants for us. When we choose not to abide by His principles, we are essentially restricting our own access to some of the benefits. We're saying, "I know You said You want me to live this way, but I don't believe that's what is best for me." And God, because of His love for us, takes the car keys away in one area of our lives.

Here's another example: If a husband cheats on his wife, there is still a relationship between them, but it's going to be severely affected by the actions of the husband. The actions of that man cause a separation to occur in the relationship. The same is true with us and God. If we are saved, we are in a relationship with Him. But when we allow something to bring separation in that relationship, we are not able to receive the same benefits as if the relationship were going great.

Look at the subject of Paul's prayer for His fellow believers in Ephesians 1:17-19a.

> *"that the God of our Lord Jesus Christ, the Father of glory, may give to you a spirit of wisdom and of revelation in the knowledge of Him. I pray that the eyes of your heart may be enlightened, so that you will know what is the hope of His calling, what are the riches of the glory of His inheritance in the saints, and what is the surpassing greatness of His power toward us who believe."*

He prays specifically that those who are saved would have a greater revelation of the knowledge of God—that they would know God better than ever before. This includes the idea of principles I've been talking about. When we read the Bible and allow the Holy Spirit to teach us, He gives us a greater revelation of God's character, desires, and expectations. Paul goes on to talk about the inheritance of the saints, and this is where the benefits come into play. An inheritance isn't earned. It's received. We don't earn benefits through our actions, but we can restrict those benefits when we separate ourselves from the Benefit-giver. Then, Paul gives us the key—the glue that holds everything together. He says the phrase, "toward us who believe." We live by God's principles and receive His benefits, both through belief. If God gives us a principle to live by, and then lets us know that it's directly connected to one of His benefits, the only reasons we wouldn't live by that principle is if we did not believe Him or if we did not want the benefit. We either doubt that He *can* fulfill the promise or we doubt that He *will* fulfill the promise.

If this still sounds like it's based on your efforts, there's two more truths I need to briefly expound upon. The first is this: Living by God's principles, truth, and commands is not something we can do on our own. No matter how hard we try, we'll never be good enough to make it work. We need His help. Galatians 5:16 states this plainly:

> *"But I say, walk by the Spirit, and you will not carry out the desire of the flesh."*

When our nature is being transformed into the nature of Christ, the principles are not a list of rules. They are what we are going to be doing naturally (through our new nature) as we walk in the Spirit—as we abide in Christ. Receiving God's benefits is not a result of trying really hard to keep His principles. Instead, both keeping the principles and receiving the benefits are results of trusting the God you know.

The second truth is this: God's grace is always available to us when we mess up. Unlike earthly relationships, God is always ready to forgive. His love is always reaching out to us. That's the power of grace. God doesn't make us work our way back into fellowship with Him. When we turn away from our mess and toward Him, He offers us the same forgiveness and grace we received when we first got saved.

If you are saved and you truly know God, the one benefit you can never lose is your eternal salvation. Jesus says in John 10:28, "No one will snatch them out of My hand." (So, I guess Jesus would be good at an egg and spoon race.) Even though nothing can separate us from the love of Christ, when we choose to run from God or seek other things above Him, our relationship with Him is damaged, and we need to turn back to Him and receive His grace in order to continue receiving His benefits in that area.

For the rest of this book, I'm going to list several benefits we get to receive when we know God. As I talk about different benefits, I want you to ask yourself the question: If I'm not receiving this benefit, is it because I've let my priorities get off track in this area? Have I sought after something other than God? Or, have I believed a lie that opposes one of His principles?

The Benefit of Wisdom

Think about that egg-carrying competition in the context of work again. If someone hoped to win a contest where they have to run to the finish line without dropping an egg off their spoon, they would need to use a little wisdom to do it. If you simply rode the emotional high of competing, you might run too fast and trip or lose balance. If you listened to wisdom in that moment, you would move at a steady pace, increasing your chance of finishing.

Receiving God's benefits is not a result of trying really hard to keep His principles. Instead, both keeping the principles and receiving the benefits are results of trusting the God you know.

If you've ever worked in a fast-paced, high-intensity environment, you know the emotional roller coaster a workplace can be. Wouldn't it be great if, instead of making decisions based on our emotions, we were able to make decisions based securely in the wisdom of God? Well, it is possible, and it's also a benefit.

I remember standing at a railway crossing one hot summer morning with foolish thoughts running through my head. I had one more year of college ahead of me, and I had taken a summer job to try to help pay some expenses during the following semester. Between my parents' generosity, a few scholarships, work-study, and a loan, my college tuition would be covered. I hoped to earn enough to alleviate my parents of the burden of also paying my living expenses while I was away at school. A local media firm in my hometown had hired me as an intern the previous summer, and they had offered me the same temporary position again. The first summer had been a pleasant work experience. The second summer...not so much.

As I watched that passing train, I remember examining all the reasons in my mind why I was about to jump aboard. The company struggled financially due to a grand slump in incoming marketing projects. Two employees who worked in the web development department had sparked hope in the owner's mind by initiating some new client relationships. Every day, the owner would come talk to me about the poor situation he was in (maybe he needed someone to vent to), and then he would always conclude our chats by looking hopefully ahead at the new web business.

Weeks later, his conversation changed. The web projects were no longer a safe bet, according to him, and now he thought the video department would save the business. Then one day, he walked through the office handing out pink slips. He fired about half the staff, and I thought I would be on that list. For some reason, I wasn't.

You would think I would be happy about not losing my job, but it simply caused the internal stress I was already feeling to grow. The anxiety-ridden environment made me want to leave, but I was also worried about what my parents would think if I quit. Would they see me as irresponsible and selfish? At the time, I thought they would.

Fast forward two weeks, and you'll find an even more stressed-out me. I had only received one paycheck that whole summer, and I kept putting off asking about it. My employer talked to me so often about the struggling business that I couldn't work myself up to say anything about it. I figured that when we landed a high-end project, I would finally get paid. On top of that, my plate was full. Project after project continued to be handed to me, and I worked to complete them as fast as possible. I felt like I was doing a good job, but I received little feedback.

Then, my boss started giving me more information about the situation. While I was alone with him on a video shoot one day, he told me about the two employees in the web department. They had been sending me a lot of projects, and I thought it was just because I was the intern and was there to help in any way possible. My boss informed me that they had stopped working, and that I was doing their work. At first I thought he should just fire them, and then he told me he felt stuck between a rock and hard place. They had mostly dealt with the web clients themselves, and he was afraid if he fired them, they would attempt to steal a large majority of the firm's clients and start their own business. A year before I first worked there, two other employees had broken his trust and done something similar, and now fear gripped him that the same thing would happen all over again.

My boss was a nice guy. I don't believe he understood what level of drama he was dragging me through. I think he just needed someplace to talk it out, but it was starting to worry me sick. The more I considered the facts, and the more I tried to decide what to do, the more I worried. I didn't want to disappoint my parents, and I knew I needed the extra funds for my next semester, but I also didn't know how to handle the situation. I needed some wisdom. I should have read Proverbs 3:13,17-18, which says,

> *"How blessed is the man who finds wisdom*
> *And the man who gains understanding."*

> *"Her ways are pleasant ways*
> *And all her paths are peace.*
> *She is a tree of life to those who take hold of her,*
> *And happy are all who hold her fast."*

I kept assuming that peace and happiness would be a result of the situation getting fixed. At that time, I didn't understand that they are a result of finding wisdom. And I had also forgotten that wisdom was a benefit of knowing God. Look at how James says we can get wisdom:

> *"But if any of you lacks wisdom, let him ask of God, who gives to all generously and without reproach, and it will be given to him."*

James 1:5

The reason we can ask and receive is because we're in relationship with the Provider of wisdom. The same way we enter into relationship with God is the way we continue to grow closer to Him: by faith. So, when James tells us that we can receive wisdom simply by asking, it seems like the only thing stopping us from doing that must be unbelief, right? The truth is, there's one other reason we would hesitate to ask. Even if we believed this verse from James, we would never get around to asking if we thought we simply didn't need wisdom.

Pride stops us from asking for and receiving wisdom. When we consider our thoughts are higher than God's thoughts, we miss out on the divine wisdom He is freely offering to all those who know Him.

Principle: Humility
Benefit: Wisdom

The principle behind the benefit of wisdom that I'm talking about is humility. Humility allows us to run to God for supernatural wisdom instead of merely diving deep into our own catalog of knowledge and experience to search for a sufficient answer. Look at what Proverbs 11:2 has to say about gaining wisdom.

"When pride comes, then comes dishonor, But with the humble is wisdom."

So, because of the worry, I stood there considering jumping on that train. I wanted to run away, even if I didn't know where I was going. Would it have been a foolish thing to do? Absolutely. That's what stressful situations can drive us to do if we don't lay them at the feet of Jesus—foolish things.

Watching those slow moving hand rails, I waited for the perfect timing to hitch a ride. Then, I began to remember who my Counselor was. There appeared to be no way out, but I knew if I took it to the Lord, I could find hope in His counsel.

I watched the train roll by and I walked the final block to my workplace. After that, I began to pray for wisdom every time an anxious thought would arise, and I quickly started noticing an overwhelming sense of peace. I specifically had a lot more peace about surrendering the job.

A few days after that, my boss interrupted my progress on a small video project to have a few words with me. We stepped outside, and I sat on a city bench in front of the firm. He started filling in some of the gaps in the narrative, and I learned a little more about the recent behaviors of my coworkers. Then, I chimed in with a solution.

"What if I quit? Would that help? It would at least force them to make a choice."

It wasn't an easy thing to say, but the Lord gave me the confidence I needed to say it. As the words left my mouth, his face changed. Where anxiety had dwelt, now he showed signs of relief. I knew his stress levels were dropping. Mine were too.

Up to that point, I had been afraid of what my parents would say if I quit. I arrived home early that day and explained the situation to them, and they were supportive of my decision.

> **Humility allows us to run to God for supernatural wisdom instead of merely diving deep into our own catalog of knowledge and experience to search for a sufficient answer.**

That day, I understood that God had made His wisdom available to me simply because I was His child. Unbelief and pride could keep me from choosing to accept His wisdom, but it had been available the whole time. Colossians 2:3 tells us that all wisdom and knowledge are actually found in Christ. Through our faith in Jesus, we start a relationship with God, and through leaning into our relationship with Him, we gain wisdom.

Can people who don't know God learn from their experiences and gain worldly wisdom? Sure, but it's not always accompanied by peace. Colossians is referring to what God considers real, eternal wisdom. Apart from Him, there is no wisdom worth possessing; because if we reject Jesus, we reject the very truths of God. This understanding leads us to a simple reality: When we find that we haven't been trusting God with a specific principle, the answer is not to try really hard to fix it in our own strength. For example, if you lack wisdom, the answer is not to beat yourself down emotionally until you feel humble. The answer is to look at the cross and allow the sacrifice of Jesus to humble you. To walk in the wisdom of Christ, we first must learn to walk in the humility He modeled. That humility is available because of His grace.

Remember, God doesn't make us work our way back into His presence through trying hard to follow all the principles. When we prioritize our relationship with Him and allow the Holy Spirit to remind us of the life-changing truth of the gospel, He helps us get both the principles and benefits right. When we remember how much Jesus has done for us—how much love God poured out for us on the cross—we are called back into step with Him. We see Him walking along the road, our hearts yearn to be near Him, and we sprint for a few steps in order to be at His side again. Guess what, He even stops to wait for us.

If overcoming worry can be narrowed down to a single key step, this is it. We will live a life of peace when we start walking single-mindedly toward our Savior, taking His desires as our own, and making Him our goal. Like Mary, we simply walk out of the kitchen, and we sit down at His feet.

The Benefit of Favor

When you think about favor, one of the Bible characters that might come to mind is King Solomon. Solomon experienced such an incredible blessing of favor from God it's recorded that during his time silver and gold were as common as stones. For every endeavor Solomon set his mind to, favor followed. Though Solomon is an example of someone who experienced God's favor, I'm mentioning him only to point out the principle behind the favor, and then I'm actually going to move on to a less-known passage in the Old Testament about favor.

Principle: Wisdom
Benefit: Favor

If you're wondering if "wisdom" is a typo, it's not. The principle behind favor I'm focusing on happens to be wisdom. Not every blessing from God listed in the Bible follows a cookie-cutter formula. Remember, the key is relationship. In this case, wisdom can be a benefit of knowing God as well as a principle that helps us know Him better. When God grants us the *benefit* of wisdom, He gives us supernatural ability to learn from experiences and apply knowledge, and He gives us divine truth and direction. Wisdom becomes a *principle* when you and I choose to act on those divine truths.

If you read the story of Solomon, you will see him asking for wisdom and gaining favor in the process. Directly after worshiping the Lord in one of the largest worship services of all time, King Solomon had a heart-to-heart talk with God—He got intimate with His Creator—and God blessed Him with divine wisdom. The more Solomon continued to use that wisdom throughout his life, the more favor he experienced. There were some areas of his life where he acted foolishly though, such as the area of romance and marriage (he had over 700 wives—what on earth?), and this foolishness became the chink in his armor. Despite this, the favor of God rested on nearly everything he did.

> *"How blessed is the man who finds wisdom*
> *And the man who gains understanding."*

Proverbs 3:13

As I mentioned, all wisdom is found in Jesus Christ. Anyone can know God's principles, but only those who are living in the Spirit can walk them out. We can't expect to follow God's wisdom apart from engaging with Him on a day-to-day basis. The blessing of divine favor rests on those who are intimately acquainted with Jesus and allowing His wisdom to lead them.

We see a picture of God's desire for real relationship in The Book of Haggai, in the Old Testament. Haggai acted as God's prophet during a time when the Israelites had recently returned from a long exile in Babylon. They began to rebuild God's temple, yet discouragement and opposition brought them to a halt.

Haggai's major message in his short book is one of exhortation and conviction. He passionately pleads with God's chosen people to live up to their name. Amazingly, they listen to the prophet and they turn back to God, which was a rare occurrence in the Old Testament. If you've ever tried naming a child after a Bible character, you know what I'm talking about. ("Here's a good name, Honey. Oh, wait. Nope. He was an evil king, too. We could name this one Joshua too, right?") My point is, the book of Haggai is unique.

I want to take a look at the specific appeal Haggai makes in verses 4 through 6 of chapter 1.

> *"'Is it time for you yourselves to dwell in your paneled houses while this house lies desolate?' Now therefore, thus says the Lord of hosts, 'Consider your ways! You have sown much, but harvest little; you eat, but there is not enough to be satisfied; you drink, but there is not enough to become drunk; you put on clothing, but no one is warm enough; and he who earns, earns wages to put into a purse with holes.'"*

Haggai doesn't pull his punches. Have you ever met someone who just seemed to have the worst luck? It's not something you would necessarily bring up in conversation because it's embarrassing, but Haggai doesn't care. He basically says, *Everything is going wrong for y'all,* and he isn't about to blame their situation on an imaginary force called "luck." Haggai's message points to one simple truth: The people had lost God's favor, and they were suffering because of it. If these

The blessing of divine favor rests on those who are intimately acquainted with Jesus and allowing His wisdom to lead them.

were God's chosen people, why weren't they receiving His favor in their work? We might ask that same question today at times. "If I'm a Christian, why don't my endeavors seem to pan out? Why does it seem like God is fighting against me?" There's a reason why, and Haggai reveals it in verse 9. This is spoken from God's perspective.

> *"'You look for much, but behold, it comes to little; when you bring it home, I blow it away. Why?' declares the Lord of hosts, 'Because of My house which lies desolate, while each of you runs to his own house.'"*

God wasn't simply holding back an extra blessing from the people; He was actually frustrating their work. He was blowing away the rewards of their hard work. This is a hard truth to admit, but it's possible that God is the instigator of the very situations we're praying He will fix.

Have you ever raked a pile of leaves only to have them blown around the yard again by a gust of wind? In college, I worked on the grounds crew. I remember wielding an industrial-grade leaf blower one windy day. I clocked in, ran in circles chasing leaves for two hours, and then I clocked out. When I finished, I could see the fruit of my labors: nothing. The leaves were all in the same places they were when I had started. Leaves don't normally have faces, but that day they did. I could see their smug little grins. Their crackling sounded a lot more like laughter than it usually does. This is essentially what God was doing to His people. They were running in circles trying to make their lives work, but God was not blessing their efforts. In fact, He was restricting the blessing. Why? Because the house of God was nothing more than a heap of rubble. The people had prioritized the construction of their own houses while allowing God's house to stay in ruin. God had delivered them out of exile, and yet upon their return to their homeland, they had forgotten how good His deliverance really was.

Don't we do the same thing? God saves us from the chains of sin and death, and for a little while we're pumped up about prioritizing God's will, but shortly after, we get distracted by our own desires. Many Christians expend themselves in the area of business, and yet their efforts are fruitless. I've personally had friends and family who attended church, seemed to be seeking God, talked about God, prayed to God, and even attempted to commit their work to Him, and yet their businesses still failed. Where was God? When it comes down to it, I really can't judge anyone else in this area, but I can judge my own heart. There have been times when I've worked really hard at things God didn't bless. I don't know about you, but I don't want to waste any more of my life doing that. I want to know I have His favor.

So, what's the answer, then? Let's look at the Israelites' response to Haggai's words. We see in verses 12-13 that the people...

> *"obeyed the voice of the Lord their God and the words of Haggai the prophet, as the Lord their God had sent him. And the people showed reverence for the Lord. Then Haggai, the messenger of the Lord, spoke by the commission of the Lord to the people saying, 'I am with you,' declares the Lord."*

Look at that first phrase. It says they "obeyed the voice of the Lord their God." The people chose to reject foolishness and use wisdom, but not just any wisdom—they made sure they were listening to the wisdom God was actually giving them. When they did this, God let them know that He would bless their work.

There's a problem here that I believe is huge in the Christian church in general. We read about the principles of God, but we don't always listen to the specific wisdom of the Holy Spirit before attempting to apply those principles. We learn God's truth and then try to apply it like you would use a formula—a math equation. The problem is that math is void of relationship (unless you're writing love notes in the margins of your textbook during Algebra class—I'm not saying I did that...well, maybe...). My point is we can't apply God's principles in a purely formulaic way. When we skip a real interaction with God through the Holy Spirit, and we try to live by His principles in our own strength, our own selfish desires get mixed in. We end up trying to fit God's principles into our own mold for our lives instead of fitting our lives into God's mold. This problem can be narrowed down to one specific truth: God wants our hearts, not robotic compliance.

I have a difficult question to ask you, and I hope you take time to really answer it. If God never allowed you to fulfill any of your career goals or dreams for your life, would you still serve Him? Would you still love Him?

God wants our hearts, not robotic compliance.

I'm reminded of the life of Jesus. Many people have never thought that Jesus may have had dreams and desires for His life. He was fully human, after all, and there's nothing wrong with having dreams. Yet, though He would have had similar desires (excluding sinful desires) to an average young man of that day and age, He never saw many of those dreams fulfilled. He gave up His career for the sake of His ministry. He never married, He never had children, He never had many possessions, and He may not have owned His own house. If that was the story of you or me at the end of our lives, we might think we had lived an unsuccessful life. Despite this, Jesus was the greatest success of all time. He was looking ahead to a better promise, and He was listening to a wise Father.

Jesus had God's complete favor in His life. Think about that. His life didn't look the way we would assume someone's life would look if they had all of God's favor. Now, I know Jesus had a different destiny than us. He came to die for the sins of the world, something that no one else could do. However, Jesus Himself told us that our lives would mirror His in some ways. He says in Matthew 16:25,

"For whoever wishes to save his life will lose it; but whoever loses his life for My sake will find it."

One thing we do as Christians is focus on theology and expect it to fix the favor problem. We think, "If I just get my theology correct in my mind, then God will bless the work of my hands, and I will finally start to see some of my dreams fulfilled." That's the reason why the "prosperity gospel" sounds appealing to some. We think, "Now that I know this, God will make everything

90

I do succeed." The problem is, when we think like that, we're still viewing God as if He were a genie in a bottle. We're still focused on us—our works (or in this case, our knowledge).

What we forget is that, when we're walking in a close friendship with Jesus, He may ask us to give up some of our dreams. He may say, "Start that business," or He may say, "Don't start that business." You don't know the reason God gave you specific desires and dreams. He does know the reason though, and it may be that God has a different purpose for your dreams than you first assumed. The only way to find out is to lay those desires down, sit at the feet of Jesus, and listen.

When we try to make God's principles work within the scope of our dreams, we aren't losing our lives for Christ's sake. We are attempting to hold onto God's promises and our lives at the same time, and it just doesn't work that way. When we try to fit God's principles into our own plans, we walk around as pious yet powerless people. I personally believe this is part of the reason some people "try out" Christianity for a time and eventually quit. It's because they were attracted to the benefits of knowing God, but they didn't understand what it means to actually know *Him*. We are all guilty of this at times. We attempt to manipulate God through His own words because we're seeking His blessing over His presence.

It's when we choose to give up our own expectations and desires, lay those at the foot of the cross, and ask God to lead us with His wise counsel that we find the straight-and-narrow path He has in store for us. That's when He doesn't just point us in the right direction; He personally leads the way. The successful Christian isn't the one who walks the furthest or fastest; it's the one who walks next to Jesus.

Yes, God does call some Christians to be business leaders. He calls some to be entrepreneurs. He leads some into politics and others into the medical field. He asks some (some of the bravest of us in my opinion) to be teachers. His plan, for some, is to be stay-at-home parents. No matter what specific work He calls us into, He also wants to show us His overwhelming favor in that work, but His favor is a benefit we can limit depending on whether we're listening to and abiding by His word and His voice—the source of true wisdom.

In the book of Haggai, when the Israelites choose to cease prioritizing their own dreams and begin to prioritize God's vision, this is what God says to them in response.

> *"'all you people of the land take courage,' declares the Lord, 'and work; for I am with you,' declares the Lord of hosts. 'As for the promise which I made you when you came out of Egypt, My Spirit is abiding in your midst; do not fear!'"*

Haggai 2:4b-5

> **When we try to fit God's principles into our own plans, we walk around as pious yet powerless people.**

Look how personal God makes it. He says, "I am with you," and "My Spirit is abiding in your midst." This is what God's favor looks like. It's not all about return on investment or promotion. It's about having His Spirit abiding with you and intimately leading you.

The Israelites could relate to the concerns of the working class. Think about how worried they must have been before they received God's word through Haggai. Anxiety and stress must have surrounded their conversations about where the next meal was coming from, about how to water the dying crops, or about how they could afford to fix their broken houses. What's amazing is that when you receive God's favor, you also experience His peace in a new way.

> *"'The silver is Mine and the gold is Mine,' declares the Lord of hosts. 'The latter glory of this house will be greater than the former,' says the Lord of hosts, 'and in this place I will give peace,' declares the Lord of hosts."*

Haggai 2:8-9

God is saying, *I want to replace your anxiety with My peace. Everything you've been striving for, I hold in My hand. The very work you've been worrying about is something I want to bless, but first I want you to return to Me.*

God takes it a step further and reminds the Israelites of why He's been withholding His favor in verse 17.

"I smote you and every work of your hands with blasting wind, mildew and hail; yet you did not come back to Me,' declares the Lord."

If you've been anxiously chasing career, or even life dreams, for years wondering why God hasn't come through for you yet, I want to make a loving appeal the same way Haggai did. This won't be true for everyone who reads this, but perhaps God has not been blessing your endeavors in order to get your attention. My encouragement to you right now is to make it right. Run back to Him. Make it personal again. Give Him your whole heart and leave those worldly desires at the foot of the cross. He has a better way, a better plan, and a better future in mind. As you do this (I'm having to do it right now as I'm writing this), I believe God will say the same thing to you that He says to the Israelites in verse 19b.

"Yet from this day on I will bless you."

When I first graduated college, I immediately started busily applying for jobs, praying and hoping God would send the right one my way. I prayed for favor with my interviewers and potential employers, but no one offered me a position.

By the time I finally walked into the LeTourneau University Advertising Department, I felt desperate for work in my field of study. I sat through a refreshingly uncomplicated interview process, during which I felt peace from the Lord about being there. I started feeling like this was where I would like to work.

I received a phone call informing me that I could have the job if I wanted it. I had developed a habit of praying prior to making big decisions, so I asked for a few days to pray and think about the offer. I knew in my mind that I was going to say yes, or so I thought. The position was in my field, which is the kind of job many of my friends from school couldn't boast about having found. This probably wasn't the best thought for me to have, but hey, I'm not pretending to be perfect. The position offered me the potential for valuable experience and growth. Also, the campus location sat less than half an hour from my parents' house, and I was excited about being able to save money on rent. I'm sure they were *just* as ecstatic about that fact as I was. *Why won't this kid leave!?*

In nearly every way, the job looked like a gift from God, until He said *no*. Laying on my bedroom floor, my heart nearly jumped out of my chest in raw desire. "Lord, I really want and need this job. I've been praying constantly—like, every single day—for an opportunity like this. Isn't this from You?" *No*.

I laid there in silence. I had a choice to make. I could either chase the dream in my heart or I could use the supernatural wisdom God was extending to me in that moment of prayer. I knew the Holy Spirit was giving me a thumbs down about the job, but I didn't want to miss out on something good. Thankfully, I remembered a few times from my past where He had said the same thing and I had failed to listen. I didn't want to do this the hard way. I wanted to trust Him.

The successful Christian isn't the one who walks the furthest or fastest; it's the one who walks next to Jesus.

"Okay, Lord," I said. I called the department head and told him that I had prayed about the position and felt like God had other plans for me. I wanted desperately to know what those other plans were.

A week later, the Lord told me to move to Arlington, Texas. I moved with only a month's rent in my bank account, and I went in for a random job interview two days after arriving. I had no idea that the organization I had walked into was the National Broadcast Ministry of Dr. Tony Evans, a preacher I had listened to on the radio when I was a young child. The job they offered me was clearly a better opportunity in nearly every way. In fact, I still do some work for the same organization during the time that I'm writing this book. Over the years, God has used the challenges of the job, the rewards of the work, and even the teaching of Dr. Evans as a blessing in my life and in my family. God knew the plans He had for me. He stretched out His hand to give me favor when I needed it, but I could have rejected His favor by choosing not to listen to the wisdom of the Holy Spirit.

The fact that God wants us to have His favor is good news. The other good news is that there's still grace available to us if we've rejected that favor. If you know you need grace in this area to help you get back on track, I encourage you to call out to God right now. He's always listening and He's waiting to lead you down straight paths.

The Benefit of Rest

At the start of this book, I mentioned that anxiety is something I've personally struggled with to a great degree at times. One of the biggest worry pitfalls I've had to learn how to leap over is the stress that comes from working too much or working with the wrong motives.

When my wife and I were first married, I worked anytime I had work I could do. As a freelancer, I could make more money by simply getting projects done faster. I also thought that, the more I got done, the more I would enjoy life. At that time, I willingly worked over the weekends and, sometimes, late into the night on weeknights. Eventually, I started seeing the negative effects of my propensity for working so many hours, and so I started asking God to help me take more time off. Over time, I got to the point where I would consistently take at least one day off on the weekend, and my mental and emotional health greatly improved. I had learned an important principle found in God's word.

Principle: The Sabbath
Benefit: Rest

If you're thinking, *Well, that was easy,* just hang on. I should have said I *thought* I learned this principle. Even though, for years, I faithfully kept at least one day during my weekends free from work, I still wound up burnt out.

During a specific stint of months, I began to recognize a pattern in my stress levels. My most stressful time each week would be Friday evening as I settled into the weekend. The idea of taking time off stressed my mind to the point of breakdown some weeks. I was taking time off, sure, but I was having to force myself to do it. Consequently, my "rest time" wasn't at all restful. I would crawl, broken and beat up, into Monday morning and finally have some peace.

The whole time, I thought that as long as I was keeping the Sabbath in practicality, God would give me the rest He promised. I finally got to the point where I started asking God for help. I finally got personal about it.

God began to graciously reveal to me where I made my blunder. I had technically been attempting to keep the Sabbath, but I hadn't allowed God into that area of my heart. I hadn't surrendered my way of doing things to Him. I was still trying to keep the Sabbath in my own strength.

During my prayer times, the Holy Spirit began to explain what I had missed. He started to show me how there's actually a principle behind the principle. So, I'm going to slightly revise the principle I'm focusing on during this section.

Principle: Trust
Benefit: Rest

During all those weekends when I was forcing myself to take a Sabbath, I wasn't resting. I was waiting. I was waiting for the week to start again so that I could take the reins of provision back into my own hands. The Sabbath is first and foremost an act of trust. When we choose to take time off because God asks us to, we are choosing to trust that He is telling the truth. I was essentially saying in my heart, "I'm going to do this because it's the right thing to do, but I'm not going to trust that You will provide when I'm not working."

> *"Remember the sabbath day, to keep it holy. Six days you shall labor and do all your work, but the seventh day is a sabbath of the Lord your God; in it you shall not do any work, you or your*

son or your daughter, your male or your female servant or your cattle or your sojourner who stays with you. For in six days the Lord made the heavens and the earth, the sea and all that is in them, and rested on the seventh day; therefore the Lord blessed the sabbath day and made it holy."

Exodus 20:8-11

This commandment from the law of Moses not only helps to establish the principle of taking a "Sabbath" rest, it also directly refers to God's own Sabbath rest on the seventh day of creation. Why did God, an all-powerful being who never gets tired or needs sleep, decide to take a rest after working six days? I believe God rested for two reasons: to enjoy His creation and as an example to us because He knew we would need rest.

Do you ever have difficulty resting? Have you ever found yourself overcome with anxiety due to a hectic or crammed work schedule? You may need to institute a consistent Sabbath day into your week. The reason I say "may" is because of the

The Sabbath is first and foremost an act of trust.

difference in nature between the old and new covenants in the Bible. The old covenant, which includes the law of Moses, was essentially a covenant of bondage. The people of God had to obey God's commandments in order to stay in fellowship with Him. The new covenant is a covenant of freedom. When we stay in fellowship with God through the grace of Jesus Christ and the presence of the Holy Spirit, God Himself helps us to obey Him. Look at what Paul says about the new-covenant Sabbath in Romans 14:5.

"One person regards one day above another, another regards every day alike. Each person must be fully convinced in his own mind."

Some Christians argue over whether the Sabbath should be observed on Saturday or Sunday, but I don't think Paul would join in on that discussion. In this verse, he makes the statement that the Sabbath is meant to be a matter between us and God. Which day we take off, or even how long we take off are decisions God wants us to base on our relationship with Him, not on duty or fear. If you need more Biblical evidence for this idea, look at what Paul says in Colossians 2:16-17.

> *"Therefore no one is to act as your judge in regard to food or drink or in respect to a festival or a new moon or a Sabbath day—things which are a mere shadow of what is to come; but the substance belongs to Christ."*

He's saying, don't let any other believer tell you what your day of rest is supposed to look like. That's why I said you "may" need to take a Sabbath. I believe every believer should take a Sabbath, but I also don't want to give you a formula to follow. I want you to sit down with Jesus and figure out your Sabbath schedule with Him. Our Sabbath should stem from the rest we receive through our relationship with our Savior. Jesus Himself tells us that He is the Lord of the Sabbath in Matthew 12:8. Back in Romans 14, Paul confirms this shortly after telling us we should be convinced in our own minds what the Sabbath should look like.

> *"So then each one of us will give an account of himself to God."*
>
> Romans 14:12

The way we become convinced in our own mind is not simply through asking ourselves what we prefer. It's through asking God what He wants us to do.

In the Old Testament, there were harvest times and rest times in the form of festivals and religious holidays. These times were set up by God. However, under the new covenant, we don't have those same designated times of rest. The principle of taking a rest still applies though. How do I know? Well, one way I know is that God never changes. The other way I know is through listening to the Holy Spirit myself and allowing Him to speak to me about the Sabbath. If you've never done that, I encourage you to do it now. Ask Him what your time of rest should look like.

The same way there was a designated harvest season in the Old Testament, there is a time to buckle down and work now. The problem is that some of us are harvesting during a non-harvest season (spiritually speaking) because we aren't listening to the gentle, caring voice of the Holy Spirit in this area of life. When we are resting appropriately, peace and joy will overflow out of those times of rest and into our work. Paul continues his teaching in Romans 14 with this statement:

> *"Therefore do not let what is for you a good thing be spoken of as evil; for the kingdom of God is not eating and drinking, but righteousness and peace and joy in the Holy Spirit."*

Romans 14:16-17

Some people choose to take Sabbath rests from things like social media, eating certain foods, drinking coffee, or other potentially addictive behaviors. There's nothing wrong with taking rests from habits like these because the Sabbath is meant to be holy; however, the Sabbath is meant to also be a joyful time. As we just read, one of the benefits of being a part of God's kingdom is joy in the Holy Spirit. This is a truth that's not always mentioned when someone teaches on the Sabbath, but it's important. If your Sabbath is a holy time but not a joyous time, something's wrong, and you aren't experiencing the rest God wants you to experience.

When we are resting appropriately, peace and joy will overflow out of those times of rest and into our work.

Remember, I don't want you to get too caught up with any of the particulars. If you read about taking a rest from social media and that isn't something you choose to do, you don't have to feel bad about that choice. Every believer needs to make decisions about the Sabbath based on the word of God, on their own conscience, and on what the Holy Spirit is saying to them.

You may be asking the question right now, "How can I know what my Sabbath should look like if I don't know how to hear specifically from the Holy Spirit?" I know I've talked a lot about hearing God's voice in this book, and if you have doubts or questions about hearing Him, you need to know that His voice is much more accessible than you think. The reason I waited for the section on rest to talk in detail about this is because it's in the still and quiet that He speaks. Some of us can't hear Him clearly or consistently because we're so busy with life. God isn't waiting for us to reach some heightened level of spiritual maturity before He will speak clearly to us. He's just waiting for us to set some time aside and learn to wait for Him.

Think back to Martha and Mary for a moment. Martha had the exact same opportunity as Mary to hear from Jesus, but she missed out on His voice because she couldn't take her mind off the distractions of the kitchen. If you want to learn how to hear the voice of the Holy Spirit, you need to decide to do one simple thing: Prioritize His voice. When you make the decision that you need God's voice in your life more than you need to control all your free time, and when you act on that decision, you will start to hear from Him personally.

God isn't waiting for us to reach some heightened level of spiritual maturity before He will speak clearly to us. He's just waiting for us to set some time aside and learn to wait for Him.

I want to give you 5 keys to help you hear from God. Since this book is not specifically focused on hearing from the Holy Spirit, I'm just going to briefly cover these. If you want a less-condensed version of these keys, go to my website, troyblackvideos.com, and read a blog post I've written called *How to Hear God's Voice*.

I encourage you, as you read through the following list, to examine your heart. If you find that there is something here you need to work on, don't get discouraged. Instead, ask God to help you. He's listening.

5 Keys to Hearing the Holy Spirit

I. Humble yourself.

Pride isn't an uncommon enemy. Every single person struggles with it at times. If it is any assurance to you, I still struggle with pride—almost every day. The key to hearing from God is not to never experience pride. The key is to reject pride every time it shows itself.

> *"Or do you think that the Scripture speaks to no purpose: 'He jealously desires the Spirit which He has made to dwell in us'? But He gives a greater grace. Therefore it says, 'God is opposed to the proud, but gives grace to the humble.'"*
>
> James 4:5-6

James directly connects humility with being filled with the Holy Spirit. When we choose to walk in humility, we are in a sense reaching out our hands to take the hand of the Lord. We're like a young child who has finally realized they can't pick themselves up. In their humble state, they reach out to one of their parents for help.

2. Ask to be filled with the Holy Spirit. Seek and wait.

I believe the reason many people never hear from God is that they don't ask to be filled with the Spirit. I love my children dearly, but one thing I have to remind them of all the time is to "ask." I can be sitting on the floor playing with my daughters for half an hour when suddenly one of them bursts out in tears crying, "Daddy, I'm hungry!" Astonished, I'll say, "If you were hungry, you could have asked me for food at any point. Why did you wait until you were desperate?" Jesus uses a similar illustration in Luke 11:9-13 when he instructs us to ask for the Holy Spirit.

> *"So I say to you, ask, and it will be given to you; seek, and you will find; knock, and it will be opened to you. For everyone who asks, receives; and he who seeks, finds; and to him who knocks,*

it will be opened. Now suppose one of you fathers is asked by his son for a fish; he will not give him a snake instead of a fish, will he? Or if he is asked for an egg, he will not give him a scorpion, will he? If you then, being evil, know how to give good gifts to your children, how much more will your heavenly Father give the Holy Spirit to those who ask Him?"

The truth found in this passage is ground level—it's basic, but it's essential. If we want to hear from God, we need to ask for the Holy Spirit. The promise found in this passage is greatly encouraging, too. When we ask, we can be sure that God hears us and will respond.

3. Don't treat His voice like a formula. Treat it like a relationship.

We must treat God's voice the way we treat the voice of a friend. God could have made the decision to completely fill every believer with the Holy Spirit the minute they believe, but He didn't. Every believer possesses the Holy Spirit, but we aren't all experiencing a fullness of the Spirit on a regular basis. One reason is because we're not prioritizing the relational aspect of our Christianity.

God knows what we need before we ask, but He still wants us to ask. Why? Remember that He wants to get personal with us. He doesn't want us to treat him like a robot, and he doesn't want to treat us like robots.

One characteristic of relationships is that they are all unique. I have three children, and I love all of them. Yet, I don't relate to them all the same way. I have a unique relationship with each of them. Similarly, God loves all His children, but He has a unique relationship with each one. Because of the uniqueness of our relationships with God, not every person hears from the Holy Spirit the same way. His voice doesn't sound the same to every person. To begin to hear His voice clearly, we must be willing to get personal with Him every day.

4. Test everything you hear with God's written Word.

Not only can God speak to us through the Bible, but we can also confirm specific words from the Holy Spirit by comparing them to the written Word. Anything the Holy Spirit speaks to us should always agree with Scripture. If it denies or discounts the written Word, it's not from Him.

Here's an example: If you hear a word in your mind that you think is the Holy Spirit that says, "Small sins are really okay," you can be certain that is not from God. It's a lie from the devil. We know this by examining it against verses like Romans 12:2, which says:

"And do not be conformed to this world, but be transformed by the renewing of your mind, so that you may prove what the will of God is, that which is good and acceptable and perfect."

As you grow more familiar with God's written Word, you will be able to confirm the Holy Spirit's voice as soon as you hear.

5. Choose to obey before you hear.

This final key to hearing from God may be the hardest to do. God doesn't just desire us to hear from Him; He also wants us to decide to obey before we ever hear. Remember, God looks at the heart. He knows our intentions better than we do. The reason our desire to obey matters so much to God is because our obedience demonstrates the level at which we are willing to trust Him.

God isn't just interested in Christians doing "Christian things" and trying real hard not to sin. He wants something deeper than that. He wants faith—belief in the words He has spoken. It is faith that pleases God, and our obedience shows whether we have faith or not. You can't have one without seeing the other. Our willingness to act is the paint with which we create a visible portrait of our faith.

When it comes to hearing from the Holy Spirit, God is looking for our hearts to be turned to Him—to be trusting Him no matter how crazy His words seem to our human minds. Some of us want to hear from God simply for the experience of it. Others want to hear from Him so they can appear to reach some high level of spiritual maturity, but God wants us to hear from Him so that we can know Him better. Knowing and trusting Him on an intimate level means we're willing to accept anything He asks us to do or change.

There are a few practical things I sometimes do while waiting upon the Lord. I like to go into a quiet room all by myself. I'll often sing a praise song to God, or at least tell Him how grateful I am for all He has done.

I specifically remind myself of God's love that was demonstrated to me through Jesus' sacrifice on the cross. I remind myself that God is pleased with my faith. Then, I examine my heart to see if I'm actually believing God's words in that moment. If I'm not, I meditate on the truth of the gospel, and I allow God's word to infiltrate and replace my carnal thoughts. Paul says it like this:,

> *"Therefore let us draw near with confidence to the throne of grace, so that we may receive mercy and find grace to help in time of need."*

> Hebrews 4:16

A righteous person can walk right into God's throne without fear, and Jesus' righteousness is gifted to believers by grace and through faith. If I'm not approaching God confidently, I fix my eyes upon Jesus Christ. I remember His blood that was spilled on my behalf, and I remember that God sees me as righteous because of my belief in His precious Son.

I also normally read the Bible, pray, ask God to speak, and then simply wait. If other things come to mind, I tell myself that I'll think about them later, and I attempt to concentrate on what God wants to do with that time. I might lay face down on the floor, or I might just stand there with my hands open. These are just a few ways one could seek the Lord. While we're seeking God, the posture of our hearts is far more important than our physical posture. The important thing is that we're seeking Him based on a firm belief in what Jesus has done for us.

God isn't hiding Himself from you. He isn't muffling His

voice. He hasn't made Himself impossible to hear. He wants to get personal with you and speak to you in a real way. You might not hear an audible voice—I never have. It might take you some time to learn to recognize His voice too, and that's okay.

I don't always hear God perfectly clearly, but the first time I heard Him was unmistakable. His voice resonated through my spirit, louder and clearer than any thought that I had ever had. Have you ever had an experience where your thoughts sound like they are being broadcasted over a megaphone in your mind? When I hear from the Holy Spirit, it's almost like that. Except, it's obvious that the thoughts are coming from a much deeper place than my own mind. They are coming from His Spirit and being spoken into my spirit.

The first time it happened, it was life-changing. It made me aware of His nearness and comfort in a way I had never known before. I suddenly found a divine source of rest that cut through all my fears, anxiousness, doubts, and even depression.

If you've never heard from the Holy Spirit in that way before or if you want to begin hearing Him more clearly, I want you to do two things. First, I want you to pray the following prayer with me. Second, I want you to take some time to simply wait upon the Lord. You can lay, sit, or stand. You can go for a walk. You can kneel before Him if you like. Your physical posture doesn't matter as much as the posture of your heart. Let Him know that you're waiting for Him to speak—that you're listening. Pray with me.

Father God, I want to hear Your voice. I want to know You're near to me. I believe the words of Jesus in Luke 11:9-13. He said that I could ask and I would receive. He said that, if I asked You for the Holy Spirit, You would respond the way a truly loving Father would. I know You are a perfect Father, and I believe you give Your children good gifts. Fill me with Your Spirit, Lord. Give me the gift of closeness—the gift of comfort. I need You. I need You more than I need to be busy. I need You more than I need anything else in this life. I ask that Your will be done in my heart and in my life. I ask for an awareness of Your presence that I've never experienced before. Help me to learn how to listen to Your voice. Help me to find You in the stillness and quiet as I rest in the knowledge of Your love and the truth of the gospel. Reveal Yourself to me, my Savior and Friend. In Jesus' name, Amen.

When Jesus says that we will receive when we ask, He is telling the truth. The problem is that sometimes it takes us longer to receive than we expect. That's why Jesus also tells us to knock. When you knock at the door of someone's house, the door doesn't always open the first time. That doesn't mean you walk away. If you know they're there, you keep knocking.

If you have asked God for the Holy Spirit but haven't had any response, keep knocking. Keep seeking Him. Keep waiting upon Him. He is a loving Father who gives good gifts, and He wants to give a greater filling of the Holy Spirit to you.

When we learn to hear His voice, and when we are listening at His feet like Mary did, our rest isn't limited to a single day of the week. Through Jesus, we can enter God's eternal rest here and now.

> *"He again fixes a certain day, 'Today,' saying through David after so long a time just as has been said before, 'Today if you hear His voice, Do not harden your hearts.' For if Joshua had given them rest, He would not have spoken of another day after that. So there remains a Sabbath rest for the people of God. For the one who has entered His rest has himself also rested from his works, as God did from His."*

> Hebrews 4:7-10

- 5 -

STOP WORRYING ABOUT YOUR CHRISTIANITY

Have you ever watched runners competing on television, online, or in person? Better yet, have you ever participated in a race? My wife recently ran her second half marathon in our hometown. At seven o'clock Saturday morning she started running, and about two and a half hours later, when my kids and I saw her round the corner and begin nearing the finish line next to the downtown coffee shop, the first thing I noticed was that she was still running. Because the race organizers misjudged the distance of the course, she had run almost fourteen miles.

I remember feeling a sense of excitement about running in that moment. Had I run at all? No. I had stood around, inhaling coffee and donuts while I waited. But seeing her move steadily toward that finish line after tackling such an impressive distance made me want to get out there and run, too. A fresh love for running momentarily awakened in my soul. In fact, the next time I went for a jog, I ran with a greater vim than usual. I wanted to run further than I had ever run before. Every time I thought about my wife running those fourteen or so miles, my legs were given that extra oomph they needed to pick up the pace. I quickly encountered a problem though. Every time I took off sprinting, my energy levels dropped drastically. I would sprint for about fifty feet, and then I would start walking. My lack of endurance revealed to me this basic fact: If I wanted to run a great distance like my wife had, I would need to change my strategy.

Some of us are treating our walk with God the same way I attempted to run that day. We exert ourselves through sudden bursts of energy, only to find we soon reach a state of burn-out. Maybe we're living in a constant state of fear that we're not really pleasing God with our actions. Maybe we're ashamed of the life we've led, even as a Christian.

Others of us are burning ourselves out working for the Lord, and we're wondering why we don't see more of a reward for our efforts. I organized this book so that this chapter would come directly after the chapter about work because some of us are treating Christianity the same way we treat our daily work. We are wearing ourselves down. You need to know that God doesn't desire the race of faith to look like that.

About a week after my wife ran her second half marathon, my sister Sabrina and her husband Ryan both participated in a race in their hometown. She ran the half marathon and he ran the full marathon. Now, I've met several people who have run marathons before. Leslie's mother Grace has run one full marathon and four half marathons. What struck me as odd about Ryan and Sabrina's race is that they had both given up on preparing for the race after only a few short weeks of training. Despite not having time to properly train, they chose to run it anyway. When I heard about it, I asked Leslie, "How on earth did they do it?" Then, I heard the story of the race.

The race they ran is famous for drawing out a huge population of the city with its festivities. People gather around every street along the route and basically have a party. There's food, drinks, dancing, music, entertainment, and did I say food? When Sabrina began to relate that day to me, she said that at almost any moment they could stop and have people shower them with sustenance. At one point, she looked around to find that Ryan had disappeared. After a quick scan of the crowds, she noticed him on a stage, dancing away.

When I consider the differences between my own jog and the marathon my brother-in-law ran, I see a few factors that would give him the needed strength to keep going. Though he ran a much greater distance than I've ever tried to run, he made it to the end. Because I kept running out of energy, I probably didn't beat my personal record that day. I got excited about running again. First, I noticed that he got to take breaks (sometimes just to eat or drink something, but they were breaks nonetheless). Second, I noticed that he found joy in the process.

In your Christian walk, you're not in an endless sprint. You're in a marathon, and there are breaks. Even more important than that, you don't have to pull energy out of the depths of your soul in order to keep running. God wants you to find your strength in the joy He provides. Alfred, Lord Tennyson wrote a very long poem called "In Memoriam" that talks about a person rising on stepping stones of their dead self, to higher things. God does not intend for you to get to that point. He wants to be constantly placing the next step in front of you as you seek after Him.

The first principle I want to cover in this chapter is the principle of repentance. I know the idea of repentance may raise some specific ideas in your mind, but I want you to temporarily let go of any previous notions you have about repentance. My hope during this section is to show you how amazingly refreshing repentance is meant to be in our Christian walk.

Principle: Repentance
Benefit: Times of Refreshing

I believe the devil has been able to persuade many Christians to believe a lie that repentance is based in our works. I used to believe this, and it would literally torment me at times. I had been saved for a while, and I knew deep down that I wasn't saved by works. Yet, every time I fell to temptation and sin, I would start this practiced, grueling process of repentance all over again. I knew that Jesus had paid the price for my sins on the cross, but I also knew that I had somewhat separated myself from God's presence through my actions. I had put a stopper in our relationship. In my mind, I would need to prove to God how sorry I was before He would let me come back into full fellowship with Him.

For me, repenting of a sin would look like a variety of things: crying before the Lord in prayer, reading the Bible, simply feeling sorry over my actions for a length of time, or even attempting to do some good work that would make God happy. The problem I kept running into was this: Those things never worked to fix the rift in the relationship. God's presence wouldn't return when I worked hard enough at "repenting." The moment I would begin to be aware of His presence again would always be the moment I heard the gentle voice of the Holy Spirit reminding me of what Jesus had done for me on the cross. Every time I choose to put my hope back in *His* work, not my own, I would find rest from my fears in His presence.

Christianity is not meant to be a shameful, guilt-driven life. It's meant to be a life of freedom through the Holy Spirit. The way we experience that freedom is by whole-heartedly believing in the truth of Jesus Christ. When we choose to consistently believe what He has done for us—that He paid the full price—we can experience the times of refreshing that God wants us to experience.

You might be thinking, *I thought it was repentance, not belief, that leads us into times of refreshing.* Here's a potentially overstated reply: What's the difference? I know that repentance and belief have two separate definitions, but I'm using strong language to lead up to a point. Repentance and belief are often seen as completely separate actions, but I believe they are much more related than we sometimes realize.

> *"Therefore repent and return, so that your sins may be wiped away, in order that times of refreshing may come from the presence of the Lord;"*

> Acts 3:19

To help you see this verse through new eyes, I want you to think about the way Jesus talks about both repentance and belief in Scripture. In some places, Jesus says, "Repent," and other times He says, "Believe." Sometimes He says both. I used to regularly ask God, "Which is it? Do you want me to repent or believe?"

110

The word *repent* implies a return. It literally means to turn-around. It means we're viewing sin the way God views sin, and we're choosing to turn away from it. An exchange of wills is taking place. We're laying our own will down and picking up God's. The lie the devil can trick us with is that repentance also requires certain acts of penitence in order for us to be made right again in God's eyes. This lie leads us into a cycle of shame and fear every time we mess up. Why? Because, no matter how sincere we are, those works won't justify us. They only help to relieve some of the guilt on an intellectual level. Romans 3:28 speaks this truth directly when it says,

"For we maintain that a man is justified by faith apart from works of the Law."

Because we are saved by grace through faith, repentance is not a list of righteous acts you have to do to make up for your sins. It's not even you making yourself look humble enough before God so that He chooses to forgive you (though repentance does involve a humble heart). As soon as we make repentance a work through which we attempt to earn our justification, we've gotten away from the pure and simple truth of the gospel. What I'm saying is this: Repentance is not meant to be tied to works. It's meant to be tied to faith.

Repentance and belief work hand in hand. The truth is that you cannot separate the two. One way to think of it is as a single action. Think about the way physical eyes work. When I'm walking through a store with my children and they see a movie playing on a screen, chances are that they will get distracted and forget to follow me. I know that as long as their eyes are glued to that screen, they won't hear what I have to say. So, instead of telling them, "Let's go," I first say, "Look at me." When their focus shifts to me instead of the movie, they are able to hear and respond.

Our eyes are designed to only focus in one direction at a time. To set your spiritual eyes on Jesus (belief), you have to simultaneously look away from what used to keep your attention (repentance). That's why Jesus was able to often use only one of the two terms depending on what the Holy Spirit was leading Him to say. True belief is always going to be accompanied by a repentant attitude. Likewise, a repentant heart believes the truth upon hearing it.

"...let us also lay aside every encumbrance and the sin which so easily entangles us, and let us run with endurance the race that is set before us, fixing our eyes on Jesus, the author and perfecter of faith..."

Hebrews 12:1b-2a

When we truly receive grace with truth, it becomes the method through which God changes us and makes us more like Jesus. We cannot successfully turn away from sin unless we're willing to turn to Jesus for freedom from that sin. The good news is that, when we truly repent and believe, we receive grace to change. The operative word here is *receive*. Many Christians are stuck in that cycle I talked about because they think the change is up to them, but the book of Hebrews doesn't say that we are the perfecters of faith. It says Jesus is the perfecter of faith. He's the one that, through His Spirit, continues to change us as we continue to look away from sin and to Him. When we're living in that vulnerable, intimate state with our Savior, He is then able to lead us out of sin and into times of refreshing.

You may be familiar with the story of my addiction to pornography and how Jesus gave me the strength to overcome that addiction. Something I haven't talked about as much is the time between initially repenting and finally finding true freedom. The day I decided to stop looking at pornography, I knelt down on my knees and repented. I asked God for forgiveness and for help to quit. For most of that following year, I lived in a constant battle with the addiction. I had attempted to take my focus off of the sin habit, but I had not yet fully set my eyes on Jesus. It was as if I had spiritually crossed my eyes and began walking about in a blurry haze. My eyes weren't focused in any specific direction, and this lack of direction resulted in a constant pull back to the habit. Even when I showed self-control, I battled depression, anger, and self-condemnation.

The day everything changed was when I finally set my eyes on Jesus. I finally began to believe that I didn't have to clean myself up. God saw me as clean based on Jesus' sacrifice for me. That's when I found peace. Times of refreshing came, but not until repentance joined with belief—not till my eyes came to rest on my Savior.

Times of refreshing are in some ways synonymous to the peace of God, and His peace is found in His presence—in His Spirit. I talked about the difference between peace *with* God and the peace *of* God. We receive both of these types of peace through belief, not works. We get peace with God by believing in Jesus for salvation. We get the peace of God when we continue to believe we are covered by grace. If we're really believing His grace is as good as He says it is, we naturally run to Him (repent) when we mess up. Instead of constantly battling anxiety over our mistakes, we run back into His presence through faith. If we think we have to work hard to be pleasing to Him again—that we have to impress Him through grueling acts of repentance before we can ask for help—we'll try anything and everything else to beat this kind of worry before running to Him.

When we truly receive grace with truth, it becomes the method through which God changes us and makes us more like Jesus.

Those who experience this concept of living under the umbrella of God's grace have been given a name in Scripture: the children of God. You see, the gospel doesn't just free us of sin. It changes our position with God. When we are first covered by the blood of Jesus, we enter God's family as children. In a healthy household, young children don't get thrown out of the house when they mess up. They are lovingly corrected, but never thrown out. The same way we become God's child, we can continue to be sure of our position. We can be assured of receiving the benefits of being His children through the Holy Spirit constantly assuring us of our righteousness in Christ.

> *"The Spirit Himself testifies with our spirit that we are children of God, and if children, heirs also, heirs of God and fellow heirs with Christ, if indeed we suffer with Him so that we may also be glorified with Him."*

> Romans 8:16-17

Earlier I said that all God's promises are made available through Jesus Christ. The reason they are available to us is because, as children, we are also heirs with Christ. The blessings of God that Jesus deserves to inherit are also ours when we receive the righteousness Jesus offers to us. We don't deserve it, but Jesus gifted His deservedness to us. That's why we can ask for what we need boldly, without shame or fear. God loves to answer the prayers of His children.

"He who did not spare His own Son, but delivered Him over for us all, how will He not also with Him freely give us all things?"

Romans 8:32

When we ask for forgiveness and help to overcome sin, we receive it fully. God doesn't hold back His Spirit from those who ask in faith. Through His Spirit, God Himself refreshes us with His presence.

One good test to see if we are engaging in Biblical repentance or not is to examine our motivation. Are we repenting out of fear, guilt, and shame? Or are we repenting out of love for God and gratitude for His gift of grace? Romans 2:4 gives us the correct motivation for true repentance.

"Or do you think lightly of the riches of His kindness and tolerance and patience, not knowing that the kindness of God leads you to repentance?"

One of Paul's main focuses in many of his writings, that I don't think is talked about often enough, is motivation. Paul seems to be constantly bringing everything back to the simple but profound idea that correct actions stem from having the correct motivation. When we run back to God based on the extraordinary love of God that was poured out on the cross, we repent in faith, not fear. This kind of repentance is the kind that leads us down the path of real change. Amazingly, when the Holy Spirit is the one changing us, we can stop worrying about it and even be refreshed through the process.

The Benefit of Strength

The second principle I want to pull from the illustration of running a marathon is the principle of gratitude, which I will also refer to as joy. The same way that my brother-in-law Ryan found joy during his marathon, God intends for us to run the race of faith full of joy. Paul says in 1 Corinthians 9:24,

> *"Do you not know that those who run in a race all run, but only one receives the prize? Run in such a way that you may win."*

You've probably heard this verse before, but I want to ask what may appear to be an obvious question: How can we consistently run in such a way that we will win? If I had to ask my nine-year-old self that question, the answer would probably be: cheat! Don't worry nine-year-old me, you'll learn.

Many of us want to run the Christian race right, but I know as well as you that burnout can happen easier than we would like. The second point I want to suggest to you in this chapter is that our strength—our ability to endure through hardship and trials—is tied to our motivation.

Many of us have motivating moments throughout the day, such as a coffee break, a pizza break (if that's a thing), or a bathroom break where we just hide inside the stall and have a healing cry for ten minutes. No, I'm not admitting that I do that. Why would I admit that? These are examples of temporary motivators. However, I'm not talking about temporary motivations. I'm referring to the overarching motivation behind not just our days, but our years. What is it that gives us strength to keep going during the times when it feels like we're running uphill? What is it that compels us to truly live every day for God? To find the correct motivation for our Christian walk, let's look at Paul's motivation found in the verse directly before he tells us to run in a way that we will win.

> *"I do it all for the sake of the gospel, that I may share with them in its blessings."*

1 Corinthians 9:23 (ESV)

I talked about us sharing in the inheritance of Christ in our new position as children of God. Paul is saying here, the same blessings Jesus received because of His work, we can receive as we share in the work of the Lord. Jesus' motivation is clearly defined in Hebrews 12:2.

"fixing our eyes on Jesus, the author and perfecter of faith, who for the joy set before Him endured the cross, despising the shame, and has sat down at the right hand of the throne of God."

Principle: Gratitude or Joy
Benefit: Strength

Jesus endured the cross because of the joy He would receive when united with His bride—the family of God. Paul endured the work God had given Him to do for the same reason: He was sharing in the joy of Christ. God wants us to know that same joy as we run our own race of faith.

When we are attempting to live for God, and yet, we constantly feel burnt out. That means our motivation is probably off. Here's an example: If you're volunteering so much at your church that your home life is out of order and your house is always a stressful environment, have you stopped to ask yourself why you're putting that weight on you or your family? Volunteering is great; don't get me wrong. But stretching something good to an unhealthy level means the motivation is off. If you're volunteering out of obligation or fear instead of out of love for the Lord, then the motivation is wrong, and it's ultimately going to hurt more than it's going to help.

For the sake of the pastors or church leaders reading this, please don't think that I'm attacking the structure of the modern church here. I believe in church volunteering. However, I also know that the best shoes any believer can put on are the ones God has designed specifically for them and not the ones they feel obligated to wear. The strongest position of service and influence any believer can hold is one which is consistently fueled by joy.

1 John 4:19 is short, yet to the point. Condensing our motivation down to a single truth, this verse can help to act as a filter through which all of our Christian efforts should be strained:

"We love, because He first loved us."

When we attempt to serve God's people, share the gospel, or minister in any way out of obligation or fear, we are missing the source of our strength. Jesus found strength to endure the cross through tapping into the joy of the Lord. The joy of the Lord is meant to be our source of strength too, and we can find constant joy in looking intently at the way in which God has loved us.

> *"Therefore be imitators of God, as beloved children; and walk in love, just as Christ also loved you and gave Himself up for us, an offering and a sacrifice to God as a fragrant aroma."*
>
> Ephesians 5:1-2

When examining our motivations, we need to learn to ask questions. What am I trying to do by making myself this busy? Am I trying to ignore feelings of guilt or shame? If so, the cross of Jesus fixes that. Am I trying to work hard enough to earn God's love or favor? If so, the cross of Jesus fixes that, too. God wants our motivation to be a joyful

The strongest position of service and influence any believer can hold is one which is consistently fueled by joy.

response to His love, not a feeling that we have to earn His love. But to get to that point, we have to allow what He's done for us to really sink into our hearts. To live the life of impact God has called us to live, the gospel has to become the source of our life—the root for why we do anything and everything.

When someone hands you a gift, they reach out to you. That's like grace. God purchased the gift, wrapped it, and handed it to you. However, to accept a gift, you have to open your hands and receive it. That's like faith. Faith is believing that the gift of grace is as good as God says it is.

You and I don't have to earn or borrow the gift; it's free. God is one hundred percent pleased with us when we accept the gift of His grace through faith in Jesus Christ. I know I've said this many times in this book already, and here's a spoiler alert: I'll say it again, too. The reason I say it so much is because we need to be reminded of it so often.

Just read Paul's letters in the New Testament. I know I'm not the only one who's noticed that Paul preaches the gospel about three or four times in every single chapter. Preach it, bro! That's short for "brother Paul," by the way. The reason Paul couldn't help himself but to restate the gospel in as many ways as possible is because he understood its power for changing lives and its importance in sustaining changed lives. Satan constantly seeks to bind those who have been set free in Christ. If he can get us to put the shackles of condemnation back on our wrists and the burden of shame back on our shoulders, he will. Thank God the Holy Spirit is also working to keep us walking in freedom.

For us to begin working for the Lord with the correct motivation, a heart transformation must first take place. We must move from a starting point of fear to a starting point of freedom. Someone who doesn't owe anything is working for a different reason than someone who is millions of dollars in debt. We all owed a debt we could not pay. Jesus paid it for us. If you are a believer, don't allow the lies of the enemy to put the weight of that debt back on your shoulders. You get to walk in freedom.

Isn't this teaching just an excuse for Christians to be lazy? Again, let's look at our friend Paul. Through the inspiration of the Holy Spirit, Paul wrote many of the verses I've been presenting; yet, he also potentially worked harder than any other New Testament believer. Some people would try to take the idea of grace and use it to live however they want to live, but that's a good indication that they haven't really received it or that they are taking it for granted. Though we owe nothing to be made right with God, we owe Him everything out of love. The gospel's motivation is one of transformation. When we really see how great a debt has been paid, our heart overflows with gratitude and joy. Our response is one of generosity. We are able to work for God from a place of strength because we have an endless source of joy in our hearts.

Imagine a teenage girl who steals from her father's business and runs away from home. Once her money runs out, she begins working to make enough money to support herself. She has to bear the burdens of adult life long before she was meant to bear it. Out of desperation, she runs home and begs to be able to simply work at her dad's company. Instead of making her an employee, the father gladly welcomes her back into the family and gives her the same honor, the same provision, and the same covering she once possessed.

Though she once carried the weight herself, she now understands that she has someone who is willing to carry the weight for her. Instead of taking advantage and stealing her father's money again, she begins to act responsibly and work hard out of love for her father. Every day she wakes up, she reminds herself that she's been freely given a life she doesn't deserve.

We all allow our motivations to shift at times. I know I do. If you're recognizing some areas right now where your motivation has been off, my encouragement to you is simple. God fixes our motivation when we do what Mary did: sit at the feet of Jesus. Sit at His feet in the figurative living room. Sit at His feet at the foot of the cross. Allow the Holy Spirit to remind you of the lengths God would go to show His love to you. When we let ourselves crumble under the intensity of His love, our hearts melt with joy. That's where we find true strength.

The Benefit of Purpose

I want to discuss an anxiety I believe tends to haunt artistic, creative people most. Poets and romantics, of which I am one at heart, may be old friends with this fear. I'm talking about the fear of never finding purpose. I can't tell you how many nights I used to stay up late worrying about whether or not my life would ever amount to anything. I remember that aching desire to create something or do something people would remember. I wondered if anyone would talk about me after I was gone—whether my life would count for more than just the time I was here on earth.

The bad news is that many people meander through their entire lives looking for their purpose. Other people know something is missing, but they don't even realize what it is. Some people constantly change jobs because the one they are working for isn't meeting this need. Others transition from one relationship to the next, hoping that another person will provide them this sense of satisfaction. Others reach out into the world and attempt to fulfill their longing for meaning with exciting pleasures or over-eccentric living. That's the bad news. The good news is that, when we know God, we get to receive the spiritual benefit of purpose.

Principle: Calling
Benefit: Purpose

The benefit of purpose is different from any of the other benefits of knowing God. It is related to our works more than any of the other benefits, because you cannot experience your purpose without fulfilling your calling. However, even though purpose is realized through a process of work, that doesn't make it any less of a benefit. The truth is, even though you get to enjoy your purpose *through* what you do, you cannot find your purpose *in* what you do. You must find your purpose in *who you know*. This is where motivation comes into play. If we are working hard simply in order to find our purpose, we won't find it. To know our purpose, we have to first know the purpose-Giver. It is through real intimacy with God that we receive our personal calling and accept His purpose for our lives.

I remember praying for a life verse one night. I know we can read the entire Bible and find meaning and direction for our lives; however, I also know that God wants our relationships with Him to be personal—unique to each person. The general calling God gives to every believer is evident in Scripture, but God also calls each person with a specific calling, too. He doesn't command us to walk down a cookie-cutter path. So, I asked the Holy Spirit to give me a verse that summed up my calling. A few weeks later, as I sat on my living room couch one night, the Holy Spirit said, "I'm giving you your life verse."

In a matter of seconds, the Bible that had rested next to me was opened and primed for page-turning. In anticipation, I waited. Then He said, "It's Isaiah 43:10." I thought, "I hope I'm not just hearing my own thoughts right now." That's one of those doubts that likes to occasionally arise when you're listening to the Holy Spirit. A good retort for a doubtful thought is a faith-filled thought. I determined, "No, I'm going to believe that I'm hearing Him clearly. I'm going to hope in faith that this is my life verse." I flipped to the reference He had given me.

"'You are My witnesses,' declares the Lord, 'And My servant whom I have chosen, So that you may know and believe Me and understand that I am He. Before Me there was no God formed, And there will be none after Me.'"

In this verse, God is speaking to the children of Israel, His chosen people. The same way they were His witnesses to the nations of the earth under the old covenant, believers are His witnesses now. Jesus Himself told us to go into all the nations and preach the gospel. No matter who you are, if you are saved, being a witness is part of your calling. You'll never truly experience your purpose apart from it. God doesn't just give us the commission to go, though. He also gives us the Holy Spirit to show us how to go. That's where the specifics behind our calling come into play.

The truth is, even though you get to enjoy your purpose *through* what you do, you cannot find your purpose *in* what you do. You must find your purpose in *who you know.*

When I was a child, I used to mow my parents' yard all the time during the spring months. Being one of the chores I most enjoyed, I often volunteered to do it. However, I enjoyed mowing mostly because we owned a riding lawn mower. During those solitary moments of riding around on that machine, I sang songs, let my thoughts wander into entertaining storylines, and soaked up the sun.

Now, if my parents had looked for volunteers to mow, and then they proceeded to pull out the push mower (or worse, the scythe—yes, we had one), you would have found me hiding in a closet. I would have dreaded it because we lived on three acres. Some of us Christians have our general calling down. We're exerting ourselves for the sake of the gospel. Yet, we're not experiencing the fulfillment of our purpose and we're not enjoying the work very much because we're attempting to cut acres and acres of grass with a push mower. We haven't allowed God to lead us into the specific calling He has for us, so we're doing things the hard way.

Listen to me. No matter how much effort you put into pushing that walk-behind mower, you're not going to find more satisfaction in the task by working harder. You need to upgrade to the riding mower. You need to sit at the feet of Jesus and allow Him to get specific with you about your calling. That's when you're able to start doing what you have been commissioned to do in the way you were designed to do it. That's when you can begin to experience the fulfilling sense of purpose God wants you to receive.

One way to put it is like this: In order to fulfill our purpose, we must respond appropriately to our calling. How does God expect us to respond? Let's take a closer look at Isaiah 43:10, the life verse God gave me. First, God calls His people "witnesses." Then, He calls them "servants." Then, He tells His servant what He wants them to do for Him. You would think this would be the moment when God says, *Now obey all My commandments* or *Work really hard to accomplish all the tasks I've given you to do*. Instead, He simply says, "Know and believe Me."

The three keys to unlocking and fulfilling your purpose are these: know God, believe God, and then obey God. This is how God expects us to respond to our calling. It's easy for us to think that it's all about obedience, but the truth is we cannot obey apart from first knowing and believing in Him. Knowing Him involves hearing what He has to say. It means sitting at His feet and getting intimately acquainted with His wishes, desires, and expectations. When we get to know God in a deeper way, we are then offered a choice. Will we choose to believe His words or not? Our belief or lack of belief will then direct our steps toward or away from obedience. When we attempt to obey God without hearing and receiving specifically from Him, we position ourselves behind that push mower and we start sweating profusely.

The same way that the grace of God gives us strength, it also motivates us to work toward purpose. His grace is like a riding lawn mower which carries us forward into the next part of our calling. The good news is that you don't have to work hard to find His grace. You simply have to wait on Him. The more we sit at Jesus' feet, the more He reveals His grace to us. As we consistently receive it, that grace motivates us. I talked briefly about Paul's motivation to work harder than any other New Testament apostle. He explains this motivation in 1 Corinthians 15:10,

"But by the grace of God I am what I am, and His grace toward me did not prove vain; but I labored even more than all of them, yet not I, but the grace of God with me."

Diligence did not spur Paul on. Self-control, commitment, perseverance, and even purity were all things Paul possessed, but they were not what carried him into his calling. Grace did the work through him.

The reason I'm spending so much time talking about the effects of grace is because, I believe if we get the correct motivation down, our actions will follow. If we start walking in the direction grace is pointing, we'll discover our purpose. When we are working for the kingdom with the wrong motivation (anything other than God's grace working through us by the will of His Spirit), we will always be striving for the benefit of purpose, but we'll never truly find it.

Before being saved and filled with the Spirit, I asked myself nearly every day, "What should I do with my life?" In my anxiousness, I attempted to find a solution. Now, I get to rest in the knowledge that God has a good plan for my life. It's a plan that involves me fulfilling my calling through the working of His Spirit within me.

Think about the reason why we want to find purpose in life. The truth is that many of us want our lives to last beyond us. We hope our actions produce an effect that extends past the short, few years we are here. Many non-profits, charitable trusts, and legacy projects are born out of someone's ambition to make their life last beyond their years. These are all man-made attempts to find purpose, and they cost a lot of effort and money. I'm not bashing non-profits or legacy projects at all, but the comforting truth about living a life that answers God's calling is that it doesn't matter how rich or talented you are, you can make an eternal impact simply by allowing Him to lead you.

If I get to heaven and one person says, "You planted a seed that helped lead me to Christ," then all my worries about finding purpose will become silly. We need to remember that the tiniest eternal impact in heaven is greater than the largest temporary impact on earth.

A few years back, I remember finding myself in a state of indecision. I had been offered a position as a part-time videographer and editor at a local emerging app company. Around the same time, I had been approached to ghost-write a book about an individual's testimony and healing story. For days, I prayed and prayed, and yet a constant nervous strain overshadowed my every thought. I knew I was supposed to reserve enough time to continue working on my ministry on the side, and I wouldn't have time to work on both the book and the part-time job. The job paid well, offered me a nice change of pace, and it promised prolonged income security, but I knew God had asked me to write and I also wanted to develop my skills in that arena. As I prayed, I remembered a few words I had heard from the Holy Spirit several years before.

As I set out to go for a morning run one day during the first year of my marriage, I had asked Him what He wanted me to do with my life. He answered with a simple but clear phrase: *books and videos.* At that moment, I knew He referred to books and videos aimed at ministry. If I took the part-time video job, would I be rejecting His specific call toward ministry? With these thoughts running around in my head, I was in turmoil about potentially making the wrong decision.

For days, I bounced back and forth between which decision would be better. One afternoon, I went for a walk to clear my head. At the time, we lived a few blocks from downtown, so I headed in that direction. I told God that I couldn't make the decision myself. I needed His help. With all my heart, I desired to continue walking down whichever path in life He had called me to walk. I told Him I was willing to give up my selfish desires in order to respond to His call. Then, I walked silently along, waiting for His Spirit to intervene.

As I walked past a bank parking lot, a sudden peace filled my heart, and His gentle voice began to speak. *You're at a fork in the road. Whichever way you choose to go, I'll go with you.*

In my worrisome state, I hadn't once thought that the decision would be left up to me. There had been times when the Holy Spirit had clearly instructed me to take a certain road, but now He offered me the choice. When I looked back a year later, I realized that the decision between writing the book and working for the app company wouldn't have affected my obedience to God's calling on my life. Either way, I would have continued to create the books and videos God asked me to create.

We need to remember that the tiniest eternal impact in heaven is greater than the largest temporary impact on earth.

I decided to turn down the video production job and write the book, and I witnessed God's favor in many unique ways during that next year of writing. The fork in the road turned out to be a blessing. I can't say the same about every choice I've made, though. At times, I've made decisions to use my time and energy in ways that distracted me from the calling of God, and I've always looked back and wished I had consulted God before walking down those paths.

The good news is that, even when we choose to reject or run away from God's calling on our lives, we can always turn around and choose to begin seeking His will.

One person in the Bible who ran from God's calling you probably know well. The story of Jonah is often portrayed as a story of a man learning to obey God, but I believe the story of Jonah is also a beautiful picture of God's gift of grace. Because Jonah hated the idea of preaching repentance to the city of Nineveh, he chose to run away from God instead of obeying His voice. If we consider what Jonah was really running from, the obvious response might be, "He was running from the calling on his life." But I want to show how he was actually running from something more fundamental than that.

"But Jonah rose up to flee to Tarshish from the presence of the Lord. So he went down to Joppa, found a ship which was going to Tarshish, paid the fare and went down into it to go with them to Tarshish from the presence of the Lord."

When we catch up to Jonah in chapter 1, verse 3, Jonah is running from the actual presence of the Lord. Think for a second about how Jonah received God's presence in the first place. It wasn't something he had earned. The same way we receive God's grace and enter into a relationship with Him through faith now, Jonah had a personal relationship with God because of God's grace. Jonah didn't wake up one morning and decide to be God's prophet who would hear personally from his Creator. God chose Jonah to be His prophet. Jonah's status with God was a gift. Jesus offered us a similar gift when He died on the cross. Hearing the voice of God and receiving a personal calling of God on our lives is a result of us accepting His gift of grace.

In order for us to miss God's purpose for our lives, we have to do something more than simply ignore our calling. We have to run from His presence. We have to ignore His voice.

When Jonah ran from God, he essentially pushed God away, saying, *I don't want to be close to You anymore. I would rather live my life my way than live my life with You as my friend.* Amazingly, even when Jonah chose this path, God still offered him the same gift. Because of His mercy, God caused a great storm to overtake the ship in which Jonah slept. When Jonah finally admitted his sin and told the sailors that he was the cause of the storm, they agreed to throw him overboard. Hitting the water, Jonah watched the storm immediately cease. He also watched the enormous jaws of a monster fish close around him. I'm not sure if the fish had real jaws, but it sounds more sinister than enormous lips.

The storm and the monster fish lips may have felt like punishment to Jonah in that moment, but we can read about Jonah in the Bible and see how they were really extensions of God's grace.

Finding himself with a lot of time on his hands in the belly of a sea giant, Jonah began to pray. I want to pull out a few honest lines from Jonah's heartfelt prayer:

> *"I called out of my distress to the Lord, And He answered me."*

> *"So I said, 'I have been expelled from Your sight. Nevertheless I will look again toward Your holy temple.'"*

> *"While I was fainting away, I remembered the Lord, And my prayer came to You, into Your holy temple."*

> *"That which I have vowed I will pay. Salvation is from the Lord."*

Jonah 2:9b

Jonah didn't save himself through his prayer. God saved him because of His grace. Jonah found salvation from the belly of the whale by simply returning to the Giver of grace. When he received forgiveness, he then chose to start walking out God's calling in obedience. If you've been reading this and realizing that you haven't fully responded to the call of God in your life, you need to know that there's grace available to you right now. The storms and the fish that have surfaced in your life may even be signs of that grace. My encouragement to you is not to try to make up for anything in your own strength. Instead, like Jonah, simply return to the Giver who gives good gifts. Go back to the gift of salvation and grace that was offered to you at the cross. Pull out the gift every day and look at it. Meditate on the great salvation the Lord has won for you. Obedience doesn't start with guilt or shame. Obedience starts with grace. It stems from the freedom found only in God's presence.

This idea is so simple but so critical. When we are motivated by the idea that we need to make up for our actions or earn our way into God's good graces, we are always going to be stuck in a cycle of shame. Freedom is found in learning to live in light of the unmerited favor God has granted to those who believe. Paul said it like this,

"And working together with Him, we also urge you not to receive the grace of God in vain—for He says, 'At the acceptable time I listened to you, and on the day of salvation I helped you.'"

2 Corinthians 6:1-2a

Any work we are able to do for God is because of the work Jesus did for us on the cross. Don't take God's grace lightly. Let it inform everything you do. When we choose to make our Christian walk all about what God has done and not about what we think we can do, we experience these three amazing benefits of knowing God: times of refreshing, strength, and purpose.

No one can describe the calling of a disciple of Christ better than Christ Himself.

"At that time Jesus said, 'I praise You, Father, Lord of heaven and earth, that You have hidden these things from the wise and intelligent and have revealed them to infants. Yes, Father, for this way was well-pleasing in Your sight. All things have been handed over to Me by My Father; and no one knows the Son except the Father; nor does anyone know the Father except the Son, and anyone to whom the Son wills to reveal Him. Come to Me, all who are weary and heavy-laden, and I will give you rest. Take My yoke upon you and learn from Me, for I am gentle and humble in heart, and you will find rest for your souls. For My yoke is easy and My burden is light.'"

Matthew 11:25-30

Obedience doesn't start with guilt or shame. Obedience starts with grace.

The Christian walk was never meant to be anxiety riddled. It was never meant to be shame driven. God designed it to be a walk of peace, and we receive His perfect peace by learning to accept His grace with the willingness of a trusting child. Stop worrying about your Christianity. The hard part of the work has already been done.

Through Jesus, God took care of your biggest problem 2,000 years before you were even born. You can trust Him with the rest, too. You can walk a walk of peace.

– 6 –

STOP WORRYING
ABOUT YOUR HEALTH

Some people worry about the health issues they do have, some people worry about the health issues they could have, and others worry about health issues they'll never have. Health crises can be bad enough by themselves, but if the devil can get you to add worry on top of everything else, he will do it. I've had my share of anxiety based on health problems, and one thing I've learned is that worry never helps the situation. Healthy concern and caution can help at times, but anxiety never does.

We've talked about anxiety stealing our peace and joy, but something else it can steal is our health. Many major health issues are brought on by stress and constant, unchecked worry. I opened this book by telling the story of myself contracting stress-initiated shingles at an early age. I'm not exaggerating when I say that worry can affect us physically.

Even if our anxiety isn't so out of control that we lose our physical health, it nearly always affects our emotional health. We can be physically unhealthy, and that might be obvious. It's not always as obvious when we're emotionally, mentally, or spiritually unhealthy. One thing I'm going to discuss in this chapter is the truth that our spiritual health nearly always affects the other three. When something is out of joint in our spirits, it can sometimes show up in our emotions, our thoughts, and even our body. That doesn't mean that every physical ailment, injury, or disease is the result of a personal sin; so please don't get me wrong. However, it can be a factor.

The good news is that, because of the benefits we get to receive through a real relationship with God, we don't have to worry about our health. Do I mean, after reading this chapter, you'll never stress over something happening in your body again? No, because no one is perfect. I still occasionally worry about health related issues myself, but thankfully I know who to turn to when I do start to worry. I know that God doesn't want me to worry, and I also know that He has already provided freedom from that worry.

Some people seem to live for their health. They are what I might call fanatics. You would assume that the fanatics are the ones who worry the least and live the longest, but that's not always true. I've met very healthy people who worry a lot over their health, and I've met unhealthy people who don't seem to worry much at all. I've seen people with great health habits die young, and I've seen people with seemingly bad health habits live a long time.

We could review a multitude of statistics and conjecture a lot of different opinions about health, but instead I want to go straight to the Word of God. How much should we care about the state of our bodies? Paul gives us an answer in 1 Timothy 4:8.

> *"For bodily discipline is only of little profit, but godliness is profitable for all things, since it holds promise for the present life and also for the life to come."*

Paul is actually making the statement here that the importance of our spiritual health far outweighs the importance of our bodily health. However, there is also a subtler truth in this verse I want to focus on. He says, "Bodily discipline is only of little profit." Did you catch that? Though he's making the point that bodily discipline only matters a little in the grand scheme of eternity, he does admit that it matters to a certain extent. We shouldn't oversimplify to the point where we are not taking care of ourselves physically. When we respond to the truth of this verse in a balanced way, we will live life with a healthy amount of prudence, yet we won't worry about our health.

The Bible actually tells us that our bodies are the temple of the Holy Spirit. We read in Haggai earlier in this book about God's plea to His people not to reject the maintenance of His temple. His temple under the new covenant is the body of Christ—believers like you and me.

> *"Or do you not know that your body is a temple of the Holy Spirit who is in you, whom you have from God, and that you are not your own?"*

1 Corinthians 6:19

If our bodies are the temple of God, we should not neglect them. We shouldn't purposefully walk down physically destructive paths. Why? Because the Holy Spirit resides in our bodies, and more than that, He actually owns them. However, since we're using the illustration of the temple, let's also look at Jesus' take on the importance of the temple.

Jesus is speaking to the Pharisees in Matthew 23, and He repeatedly says, "Woe to you" as a warning of the many hypocritical ways in which they lived. I think He says, "Woe" so many times because the truth of His words should have made them say, "Woah!" That's a bad dad joke. He really says, "Woe" in order to warn them, and one of the things He warns them about is the way they viewed the temple of God. Let's pick it up in verses 16-21.

> *"Woe to you, blind guides, who say, 'Whoever swears by the temple, that is nothing; but whoever swears by the gold of the temple is obligated.' You fools and blind men! Which is more important, the gold or the temple that sanctified the gold? And, 'Whoever swears by the altar, that is nothing, but whoever swears by the offering on it, he is obligated.' You blind men, which is more important, the offering, or the altar that sanctifies the offering? Therefore, whoever swears by the altar, swears both by the altar and by everything on it. And whoever swears by the temple, swears both by the temple and by Him who dwells within it."*

Two points I want to show you from this passage can be applied to our bodies. Jesus is talking about the literal temple in Jerusalem, and God uses that temple in the New Testament to represent our bodies. Jesus reveals that it's not the gold that sanctifies (sets apart) the temple, but it's the temple that sets apart the gold. If your body is the temple, then the adornments of your body can be considered the gold. The gold is your physical strength, your good genes, your beautiful features, your body type, and even the clothes you wear. The things about your body that people could potentially consider impressive, Jesus says, are not as important as the body those things are attached to.

The other point Jesus makes is that the offering is not more important than the altar the offering is made upon. The offering is the sacrifices you make in your body. This could be the way you live your life for God's kingdom, but it can also apply to strictly physical choices. Here's an example: I've heard some preachers say, "I decided to start exercising because I want to be able to serve the Lord for a long time." I would consider that a physical sacrifice for the sake of God's kingdom.

I say all this to make a single point: Jesus points us to the most important aspect of the temple. He gives the most weight to the fact that God's Spirit dwells *within* the temple. If you've ever doubted your ability to be used by God because of your body type or a physical disability or condition, you need to know that God's Spirit dwelling in you is what makes the rest of you a worthy vessel. It's His Spirit that makes anyone a worthy vessel. Psalm 84:1 reinforces this idea when it says,

> *"How lovely are Your dwelling places,*
> *O Lord of hosts!"*

It's not the state of your body that makes God want to dwell in you. It is God dwelling in you that makes the rest of you beautiful, usable, and holy. Remember that the altar sanctifies the offering, and His Spirit sanctifies the altar. His Spirit sanctifies you—mind, soul, and body.

What people think about you doesn't matter one ounce compared to what God says about you. Even how you see yourself doesn't matter compared to the way God sees you. I understand that this may not apply to you depending on what issues you are currently dealing with, but please know that I'm taking the topic of health one step at a time. Before we can move forward, my hope is to help you develop an eternal perspective about your body.

Even if you don't suffer from a disease or illness, you are aging. Every person grows old and eventually dies physically. I remember a time when I felt like I was king of the world physically. I'm a little older now and I don't feel the same way anymore. In some places where there was muscle, now there's flab. The hair that used to be full has thinned out. I was a cheerleader in college, and at one point I was able to perform a host of physical feats and tricks as a tumbler. I don't have the same capabilities I once did. Now, I'm not old by any stretch, but I'm at a point where I can see clearly that our physical bodies are headed toward a slow decay.

If we live life too caught up with the state of our earthly bodies, the aging process and the physical issues we deal with will become distractions from the purpose God has put us here to fulfill. Eternity lasts forever, and in comparison, this life is but a short sigh. It comes and goes in a flash. Don't let the temporary steal the joy of the eternal. Does God care about the physical state of your body? Yes, he cares because He loves you, but He cares more about the state of your spirit. Unlike us, He can look forward into eternity and see the new bodies you and I will be given. He can see the joy, the wiped away tears, and the strength and life we will have in Him.

What people think about you doesn't matter one ounce compared to what God says about you.

My hope is to encourage you, but I also understand that encouragement can be hard to accept when experiencing a lot of pain. If you're in pain, and especially if you've been in pain for a long time, I want you to know that Jesus understands your pain. I may not understand it, your friends and family may not understand it, but Jesus does understand it. He has felt it, too. You also need to know that He doesn't want to leave you in a state of confusion or helplessness. As we progress through this chapter, my prayer for you is that you will begin to see the heart that God has for healing and restoration. As you read, ask God to open up your heart and to give you His perspective on your pain. Ask Him to replace the suffering with healing. Ask Him to replace the emotional hurt with love. God is a God of healing. He can heal. He wants to heal, and He cares about the pain you've walked through.

Two Reasons Why God Allows Pain

Some of the biggest questions we can have while experiencing pain are the "why" questions. "God, why would you let this happen? God, why am *I* the one who has to experience this?" Since God is all-powerful, it seems like He could step down and intervene at any moment, right? Yet, believers and unbelievers alike experience pain. I'm going to discuss two main answers to those "why" questions when it comes to pain.

First, God sometimes allows temporary pain for the promotion of His glory. Another way of saying it is this: God can repurpose pain in order to demonstrate His glory. Let's take a look at a story in John 9:1-3 where Jesus reveals a clue that helps us answer the problem of pain.

> *"As He passed by, He saw a man blind from birth. And His disciples asked Him, 'Rabbi, who sinned, this man or his parents, that he would be born blind?' Jesus answered, 'It was neither that this man sinned, nor his parents; but it was so that the works of God might be displayed in him.'"*

Have you ever judged someone based on their physical condition? If I'm being honest, I know I have. I especially did it when I was a child. I used to look at people who were suffering and assume they must have disobeyed God in order to reach such a state. The older I've grown, the more I've discovered that pain doesn't always originate with our own sin. When we choose to live a life that goes against God's principles, we do cause ourselves pain. I'm not disqualifying that truth. However, pain can also be the result of the simple fact that we live in a fallen world. Nature itself has been affected by the fall of man, and every person born on this earth experiences some pain by default.

Jesus tells us that, yes, God saw that pain, and He didn't prevent it. However, He also wants to display His glory through the healing of that pain. He desires to use that pain for His kingdom work. You may have never thought of this before, but God can take something as miserable as your pain and He can use it for good when you choose to respond to His words in faith. This is the same choice the man born blind is given in John chapter 9. Jesus offers him an opportunity to operate in faith in verses 6-7.

> *"...He spat on the ground, and made clay of the spittle, and applied the clay to his eyes, and said to him, 'Go, wash in the pool of Siloam' (which is translated, Sent). So he went away and washed, and came back seeing."*

Jesus reaches out in compassion to the blind man, but the man isn't forced to accept Jesus' help. If he listens to the voice of doubt, the natural reaction is to walk away or even get angry. Instead, he goes in faith to the pool and he washes. It is because of his faith-filled response that we see God's work being done. We get to see God's glory displayed in his life, and the crowds see it, too. Look at the way the Pharisees respond to the man's healing, though:

> *"Then the Pharisees also were asking him again how he received his sight. And he said to them, 'He applied clay to my eyes, and I washed, and I see.' Therefore some of the Pharisees were saying, 'This man is not from God, because He does not keep the Sabbath.' But others were saying, 'How can a man who is a sinner perform such signs?' And there was a division among them."*

John 9:15-16

Jesus uses the healing of the man's pain to testify of Himself to the Pharisees. He uses a man that many of the people would consider an unworthy vessel to speak truth to the religious leaders of that time. Apart from Christ, you and I are unworthy vessels, but with Him living in us, God calls us worthy no matter what state we're in physically. When we choose not to hinder God's work through us—when we move forward in faith despite the pain—God can bring purpose out of the pain.

God can take something as miserable as your pain and He can use it for good when you choose to respond to His words in faith.

The second reason God allows pain is to turn our hearts to Him. God's first desire for all people is that they would know Him. Consider the man born blind again. Because of his condition, he has spent his entire life as a beggar. He's probably had little hope for a better life. As he sits and begs, it's safe to assume he has no real ambition. By the time Jesus walks up to him, what pride can he have left? The Bible doesn't specifically answer this question, but it does tell us that he had been forced to live a life of loneliness. Could it be that, if he had possessed his sight from birth, had worked a good job, had made something of himself, and had married and produced offspring, that he would choose to reject Jesus upon meeting Him?

When Jesus arrives on the scene, the man born blind is very in tune with his own neediness. He relies fully upon the generosity of others just to survive. Could it be that this humble position gives him his best possible chance of accepting the generosity of Jesus? I think it's possible.

My point is that God can see the greater perspective. God is willing to allow us to walk through temporary pain in order to save us from eternal pain. What if God looked ahead in history and saw that the only way that man would ever be saved is if he were born blind? Could it be that God has allowed pain in your life and my life to draw us unto Him as well?

It's also important to consider the cause of the pain. God did not cause pain to enter the world. We did. When humankind sinned, we rejected God's life and health, and death and pain began. God could have potentially said, "I will protect you from all pain until you die," but that wouldn't have been a loving response. Why? Because it would have been similar to giving someone a high dosage of painkiller for a bullet wound without removing the bullet. If we had been spared pain in this life, then we could have lived out our whole lives without ever realizing how serious our condition really was. Genesis actually tells us that God cursed the ground after the fall. If God had not done that, life would have been much easier—a lot more pain-free—than it is. We still would have been heading toward eternal destruction, but it wouldn't have been as obvious. Pain, especially in the life of an unbeliever, can point to that person's need for God. Better yet, the healing of that pain can be a turning point in their heart when they decide to accept Him.

After the Pharisees throw the man out of the synagogue (which would have been a very shameful experience in his culture), Jesus catches up with the man and initiates a proper introduction in verses 35-39.

> *"Jesus heard that they had put him out, and finding him, He said, 'Do you believe in the Son of Man?' He answered, 'Who is He, Lord, that I may believe in Him?' Jesus said to him, 'You have both seen Him, and He is the one who is talking with you.' And he said, 'Lord, I believe.' And he worshiped Him. And Jesus said, 'For judgment I came into this world, so that those who do not see may see, and that those who see may become blind.'"*

Look at this man's willingness to believe whatever Jesus tells Him. He doesn't even know who Jesus is, and yet He essentially says, *Tell me who the Son of God is because I've already determined to believe in Him.* That's not a regular faith. It's an extraordinary faith. What drives this man to walk in an amazing level of faith is not the simple fact that his eyes were healed. It is the fact that a personal God who loved him reached down and pulled him out of a cycle of pain that had lasted for years and years. He experienced a real connection with God, and he didn't even fully realize or understand it. It didn't matter to him, though. He knew he could trust the one who had loved him enough to stoop down into the mud and help him. His choice to respond to God's love in belief opened up amazing opportunities for not just physical healing but spiritual healing as well. His eyes were opened physically and spiritually on the same day.

Jesus stooped down into the mud for the blind man, and He stooped down into the mess of this world for you and me. His willingness to lower Himself to the state of a humble carpenter, to live among us, to feel the pain of life, and to experience the darkness of an undeserved death should spark an extraordinary faith within us. One way to know if we're responding to God's everlasting love with a heart of belief is whether or not the size of our faith can be easily stretched by the size of the miracle we need. When we've decided to act on what God says—no matter what He says—based on what He's already done for us, a bigger problem should simply cause us to expect a greater miracle.

Believing God's words doesn't just mean choosing to trust Jesus as our Savior one time. It's a choice we have to make every time we experience the pain of life. The choice we all have is this: *Am I going to respond to this pain with belief or with doubt? Am I going to allow this pain to push me closer to my Savior or further away from Him?*

No matter what you and I are facing, the first thing that should always cause us to run toward our Savior when we're hurting is His love, and the second thing is the knowledge that He has a heart for healing. Some people say, "I believe God loves me, but I don't believe He necessarily wants to heal me." If you believe that way, I'm not trying to hurt your feelings at all. I get it. I used to believe that very thing, too. However, that belief is theologically wrong, and it keeps a lot of Christians from ever receiving the healing God wants for them. That's why I want to take you through Scripture and show you that, because of God's love for us, He offered us His grace, and His grace makes healing freely available to us.

Principle: Grace
Benefit: Divine Health

Yes, pain can expose our need for God. However, once we believe in Jesus, we get to take on a new perspective. We no longer have to wonder whether God wants to heal us or not. We get to know by faith that He does.

You and I can receive the benefit of divine health through receiving and continuing to receive God's amazing grace through faith in Jesus. You might be thinking, "I thought we received salvation, not healing, by grace through faith…" The truth is, both are made available to us by grace. In Scripture, there is a frequent connection between receiving forgiveness from God and receiving healing from God. I quoted Psalm 103 earlier in this book, but I want to focus on one specific benefit found within that chapter.

> *"Bless the Lord, O my soul,*
> *And forget none of His benefits;*
> *Who pardons all your iniquities,*
> *Who heals all your diseases;"*

Psalm 103:2-3

Divine forgiveness and divine health are connected. Not only are they connected, but they are also promises to those who know God. When you got saved, did you have to believe God forgave all your sins through Jesus' sacrifice, or did you just have to believe He forgave some of your sins? You had to believe that God forgave all your sins, and it's that completeness with which the writer David speaks about both forgiveness and healing in this chapter. Psalm 103 doesn't say, "who pardons some of your iniquities and heals some of your diseases." Instead, David tells us that God "pardons all your iniquities," and that He "heals all your diseases." This is a picture of God's best for us. God's desire for His creation is that it would be fully cleansed, redeemed, and healed.

One way to know if we're responding to God's everlasting love with a heart of belief is whether or not the size of our faith can be easily stretched by the size of the miracle we need.

So, the question I want to ask you is this: How do we receive God's forgiveness? How does God pardon our iniquities? Ephesians 2:8-9 makes it clear that His forgiveness is a result of His grace.

"For by grace you have been saved through faith; and that not of yourselves, it is the gift of God; not as a result of works, so that no one may boast."

We receive God's forgiveness by grace through faith, and we can receive His healing the same way: by grace and through faith. Another verse that shows how divine health is a benefit attached to God's grace is Isaiah 53:5, which is also quoted in 1 Peter 2:24.

"But He was pierced through for our transgressions,
He was crushed for our iniquities;
The chastening for our well-being fell upon Him,
And by His scourging we are healed."

This description of the torture and death of Jesus paints an image of God's desire for His children: Jesus was crushed so that we could be healed. The original language used in this verse for the word "healing" refers to a physician who is curing, healing, repairing, or making someone whole. God is the ultimate physician, and He will eventually make every believer completely whole in eternity. Yet, He is also our loving Father, and He wants us to receive the benefits of knowing Him now by grace through faith.

Let's look at another connection between receiving forgiveness and receiving healing found in Mark 16:20.

"And they went out and preached everywhere, while the Lord worked with them, and confirmed the word by the signs that followed."

Forgiveness and healing are also connected through God's desire to confirm the truth of the gospel (God's message of grace) through signs and wonders. In the Old Testament, God allowed Gideon to ask twice for a sign showing it was really God speaking to him, and God granted his request. Similarly, there are many instances in the New Testament where God uses healing miracles to confirm that His disciples and followers are actually speaking the truth that leads to divine forgiveness.

Some Christians reject the idea that God heals today because they don't want to lessen the effect of the gospel. They are afraid that, if they focus too much on healing, the message of the gospel will be watered down or changed. My heart is not to attack believers who think like this, because we *should* take special care not to water down the gospel. However, I also think they're missing out on a major benefit. When you look at the way the early church apostles and leaders witnessed, you see a picture of God's healing power working hand in hand with the preaching of the gospel. The Bible emphasizes the need to preach an unadulterated version of the gospel, but it also tells us that the preaching of the gospel can and probably should be accompanied by signs and wonders.

> *"For this reason we must pay much closer attention to what we have heard, so that we do not drift away from it. For if the word spoken through angels proved unalterable, and every transgression and disobedience received a just penalty, how will we escape if we neglect so great a salvation? After it was at first spoken through the Lord, it was confirmed to us by those who heard, God also testifying with them, both by signs and wonders and by various miracles and by gifts of the Holy Spirit according to His own will."*
>
> Hebrews 2:1-4

This passage is referring to the message of the gospel, and it's warning us against veering away from the purity of that message. However, at the same time, it confirms the signs and wonders that accompanied the preaching of the truth. God does care more about your eternal salvation than He does your earthly health. It's true. He is looking at your life through the lens of eternity, after all. Yet, He still cares about your health, and He still performs miracles.

I told you about the time when my wife and I lived in South Texas away from our families. A few months after our second daughter was born, we made the return trip to our hometown in East Texas and moved into an old but spacious apartment in the downtown area. During those years, I continued to create ministry videos and I continued to write ministry-focused books in my spare time.

Some of the worries I had felt in South Texas were now gone because of the help of our nearby families, but little did I know new sources of worry were about to emerge. I had put off visiting a dentist for a few years because of financial reasons. We were still taking our daughter Mirabelle in for her checkups, but I didn't want to pay for a checkup for myself, so I stayed away. Every time I considered making an appointment, I would get nervous about the state of my teeth. Finally, I decided I had waited too long and I needed to go in for a visit.

I remember sitting there in that dental chair, waiting anxiously for the report. Six cavities. That's how bad it had gotten. Well, I can tell you I wasn't happy to find that my worries had been well-founded. Because of our inadequate dental insurance, the cost of filling all six cavities made me shake in my boots a little (though, I guess I probably wasn't wearing boots). The point is, I couldn't afford to pay the bill at that time because of the expenses of raising little children. So, again I decided to wait. Whenever I had the money I would get the cavities fixed.

The problem with that plan was that, the longer I waited, the more worried I became. Cavities aren't even close to the worst thing one can suffer through. I know that. They are minuscule compared to some physical ailments. But at the same time I couldn't escape the worry associated with it in my mind. A year passed by, and I began to experience anxiety every time I brushed my teeth. On top of that, my teeth hurt every day. There were a few occasions when I would stay awake at night thinking about when I was going to get around to visiting a dentist, how many more cavities I would have by then, and how much it was going to cost.

Through the entire process, the Holy Spirit had been attempting to calm my fears. He had been saying things like, "Don't worry about it," but I had failed to allow Him to comfort me. Maybe it was just raw doubt, or possibly stubbornness, that kept me from listening to Him, but either way, it took me a little while to start trusting Him in the area of my teeth.

Every night when I brushed my teeth, the Holy Spirit would chip away a little more of my fear. He kept working on my heart until eventually I decided I was going to stop worrying and just place the outcome completely into His hands. Even if I didn't have the funds to fix my teeth right away, God would walk with me through the experience, and if He was with me, I could have peace.

After coming to that realization, anytime I thought about my teeth I would think, "God is in control. He will help me fix this at the right time." Sounds a little dumb and irresponsible, right? Or, could I suggest that it sounds like what a child who trusts their mother or father might think?

When I started trusting God about the health of my teeth, the fear surrounding the problem left, and that helped motivate me to be more practical about finding a solution. I signed up for some better dental insurance at the beginning of the second year, and then I made an appointment.

I remember one night when I was talking to my brother Reese on the phone, and the thought of asking for prayer arose in my mind. I hadn't prayed for God to heal my teeth much at all, probably because it's a lot easier to believe that God will heal a sickness than it is to believe He will heal something like cavities. It's also easier to believe for gradual healing. Instantaneous healing feels like a greater miracle for some reason. However, I remembered two things that helped me begin to have faith for healing. First, I remembered that it's never hard for God to heal. He's the Creator of the universe. It's always easy for Him. Second, I remembered Reese talking about someone in his church who had been healed of something much worse than cavities. At that moment, I stepped out in faith and asked for prayer. He prayed that my teeth would be healed and he even said he would ask his church to pray, too. I felt a strong sense of God's peace that day.

Soon after that, I made a startling realization. The pain had ceased. I no longer felt the sharp sensations I had experienced when drinking cold liquid or brushing my teeth.

On the way to the dentist one Friday morning, out of hope that God was responding to my faith, I asked God again to heal my teeth. Sitting alone in the car, I decided to pray out loud. As I prayed, an image of the three men in the fiery furnace popped into my mind.

In this story, Shadrach, Meshach, and Abednego are threatened with being thrown into the fire for choosing to worship God alone in Daniel 3:17-18. Listen to their response to King Nebuchadnezzar.

"'If it be so, our God whom we serve is able to deliver us from the furnace of blazing fire; and He will deliver us out of your hand, O king. But even if He does not, let it be known to you, O king, that we are not going to serve your gods or worship the golden image that you have set up.'"

As I remembered their prayer, I prayed, "God, I ask that You heal my teeth, but even if You don't, I still want to say thank You. I still trust You. I still want to walk through this process with You."

God wants to get you and me to the place where we can say, "Even if He doesn't deliver me from this, He is still my Deliverer." The reason we can confidently say this is because God has already delivered us from everything we ultimately need to be delivered from.

One thing God reminded me of that morning was that seeking God just to get something from Him is a form of double-mindedness. I'm not saying it's wrong to seek God in prayer and ask for our needs to be met. The Bible encourages us to do this. However, it is wrong to seek God only to get something out of Him. If we're not willing to accept God's answer, even if it differs from what we want or expect, then we're seeking Him with the wrong motives. Look at what James says about double-mindedness.

"But he must ask in faith without any doubting, for the one who doubts is like the surf of the sea, driven and tossed by the wind. For that man ought not to expect that he will receive anything from the Lord, being a double-minded man, unstable in all his ways."

James 1:6-8

I want to apply this verse in two ways. First, I want you to ask yourself a question: *If I begged God to heal me and He didn't, would I still trust Him?* The truth is, if you know you're going to get angry at God if He doesn't respond the way you want Him to, you're already walking in doubt. When we approach God conditionally in our minds, we're doubting His character. Shadrach, Meshach, and Abednego had faith that God would deliver them, but they also had faith in God's character. The Bible tells us that God is good and that He has good plans for us; so if He doesn't heal us or deliver us when we want, He has a good reason. Now, that reason may be that we're rejecting His principles (and that's something we'll cover in a little bit), but sometimes God is simply waiting for us to stop doubting and really begin to believe Him without reservation.

Despite what it may look like in the moment, God hasn't gone against His promises, and He never will. It's when it appears that He has forgotten His promises that our faith is really tested. It's the appearance of God letting us down that reveals whether or not we are a double-minded person. When you know God's word says a specific truth, and yet that truth isn't working for you, are you going to stop believing it? You might say, *How could we not? If it's obvious something doesn't work, why keep putting hope in it?* That may sound like a good reason, but it's not a good reason when it comes to God. Our natural minds tell us to give up when we don't see results, but God wants us to start thinking with our spiritual minds.

James is telling us that, even when it feels like God has completely let us down, we still need to believe or else we're double-minded. That's something the natural mind can't understand. It's a truth we can't grasp if we're only thinking with our brains. Earlier in this book I talked about how, to learn more in the kingdom of God, we've actually got to become like children. In this case, we need to set our natural wisdom aside and allow the wisdom of the Holy Spirit to be our guide. Walking by faith means the thoughts of the natural mind are constantly being overruled by supernatural truths hidden in the heart by the Holy Spirit.

The way we rectify double-mindedness is to remember God's grace and allow it to motivate us. When we are able to look at the unfiltered message of His grace, we see His perfection, His holiness, His love, His compassion, His wisdom, and His desire to walk with us. When we're holding on to His grace, we can confidently say, "Lord, I believe You want to heal me because of Your

> **It's the appearance of God letting us down that reveals whether or not we are a double-minded person.**

compassion and love, but I also believe that even if that healing doesn't happen when or how I want, You are still good and Your decisions are still right."

So, as I drove to the dentist that morning, I prayed for healing, but I also chose to accept God's will above my own. Even more than asking for healing, I asked for God's Spirit to walk with me.

I arrived at the dentist office and checked in for my appointment. After having my teeth cleaned by the dental assistant, I heard her say something odd to the dentist. She said, "His teeth look good. He knows which side of the toothbrush to use." The thought occurred, "She's probably just being nice in front of me." Then I decided I wasn't going to limit what I thought God could do for me, so I added the thought, "Or my teeth are healed."

The dentist sat down, I opened up, and he began to examine my teeth. It didn't take him long. I remember his words verbatim. He said, "If more people like you came in here, we would go bankrupt. You don't have any cavities." Then he said something that really clenched it in my spirit. He said, "You don't even have cavities where you should have cavities."

One of the reasons I tell this story is because I want you to understand something. God didn't heal my cavities because I'm better than anyone else. I'm not. Please don't think, "Of course God shows up and works on your behalf. You have a ministry." God didn't heal me because of what I do. He healed me because of His grace. I need His grace the same as anyone.

Now, if you're thinking, "I do have a good understanding of God's grace and I do feel like I'm receiving it on a regular basis, but I still don't see His hand at work in my life or in my body," then I want you to dive with me a little deeper into the principles behind healing.

I'm about to talk about a principle that may not be easy for you to hear. In fact, you may reject the idea of it completely. If you have trouble with this principle, that's okay. I'm not asking you to simply accept it based on what I say, but I do encourage you to take it to God. The truths in God's word are not always easy for us to hear, and I don't like talking about this principle as much as I like talking about some of the others. However, my goal is to speak the truth in love, so I am going to talk about it. If you have an issue with it, I encourage you to have a conversation with God about it. He knows a lot more about it than I do anyway.

The Benefit of Grace

Now that I've prefaced this next principle, I want to share about the divine principle of forgiveness and the benefit of grace. Yes, I know I've talked about forgiveness being a benefit of knowing God, and I've also talked about God's grace being a principle! But remember that God's principles and benefits don't always follow an exact formula.

Even though we get to receive God's benefits by simply being His friend, we can limit those benefits by choosing to reject His principles. The reason is because when we reject His principles, we are in a sense rejecting part of Him. You aren't going to be experiencing a good relationship with someone when you are actively rejecting them. The same way, our relationship with God always suffers when we choose to reject His principles.

When we believe in Jesus, God is merciful to us and forgives our sins. That forgiveness allows us to live in fellowship with Him and constantly experience His grace. When we are experiencing His grace, we have access to divine healing through faith. Yet, because God so graciously forgave us of our sins, He also asks us to forgive others.

Principle: Forgiveness (and Obedience)
Benefit: Grace

The principle I'm talking about isn't focused on God forgiving us but instead, on us forgiving others. How much or little we choose to forgive can limit the amount of God's grace we experience. You might be thinking, "This is a scary principle." It's not my intention to make you feel bad, but the verse I'm about to share with you is potentially even scarier. Let's take a look at the importance Jesus places on believers choosing to forgive one another.

> *"For if you forgive others for their transgressions, your heavenly Father will also forgive you. But if you do not forgive others, then your Father will not forgive your transgressions."*

> Matthew 6:14-15

This is one of those verses I used to skip over in a heartbeat while reading through the gospels. I never stopped to examine why I would ignore it. I just didn't like the way it read. Then, one day I stopped to think about it. I had to admit to myself how much I disliked and even scorned this verse. If grace comes through faith and not through works, why would Jesus say something like this?

The answer is simple: Jesus is telling believers that they have the ability to limit the flow of God's grace in their lives.

Imagine with me that I died suddenly. Let's say I volunteered to taste test a new series of pudding cups flavors. One of the batches of pudding—an inventive pickle-lime flavor—had rotted and turned to poison. I ate ten cups of pudding and fell over dead. How could I be certain God would allow me into His heavenly kingdom? Because I had received His grace through faith.

Now, let's say I had argued with my wife the morning before the taste test. In the moment I fell over lifeless, full of pickled pudding, I still had not chosen to forgive her. Would I still be welcomed into heaven? Yes. To say otherwise, we would have to be basing salvation upon our works, which the Bible doesn't do. Just because I had messed up that morning doesn't mean I would lose my salvation. When I first accepted Jesus' gift of grace, I received forgiveness for past, present, and future sins. I'm telling you this silly story so that I can ask you a question: If Jesus isn't talking about forgiveness of sins that results in eternal life, then what is He talking about?

When Jesus says that God won't forgive us if we don't forgive, I believe He is speaking two separate warnings. He is warning unbelievers of eternal judgement, and He is warning believers of the consequences of sin here on earth. A heart that is willing to forgive is a heart that has experienced the magnificent forgiveness of our loving Savior. Love, patience, and kindness are three results of the Spirit of God abiding in a believer. If someone is unwilling to forgive, then they are not displaying God's love, patience, and kindness to their fellow sister or brother. If we are able to live life with no desire to forgive, I believe Jesus is telling us that we need to examine our salvation, because receiving His forgiveness should result in a willingness to forgive overflowing out of our hearts.

However, even after we're saved, there are times when we choose not to forgive. When this happens, even if we don't realize it, we are striving against the new nature of Christ within us. God's grace is meant to flow through us, not just to us. When we are unwilling to share His grace with others, we cut off the flow to an extent. Not only will an unforgiving heart cause a believer to live a potentially miserable existence, it will also limit the benefits of God's grace in their life.

There's a subtle distinction I don't want you to miss. God doesn't limit His grace to us. He is still there holding it out to us as a free gift. However, when we choose not to forgive, we limit how much of His grace we experience because we aren't accepting that grace through faith. The Bible tells us that vengeance and justice are God's, and that means that forgiveness is an act of faith. When we let someone off the hook, even when they've wronged us, we are offering them the same love Jesus showed us, and we are believing God will make things right in His own way.

When we choose not to forgive, we essentially put up our hand and say, "No thanks, God. I've got enough grace. I don't need any more." That's why unforgiveness can result in sickness. Remember, divine health is a benefit tied to the principle of grace.

Forgiveness isn't a suggestion. It's a command given to us straight from Jesus. If we choose to live in unforgiveness for a time, yes we will still make it to heaven if we're saved, but God won't be able to treat us like we're fully forgiven here on earth.

I remember a time when I began to take on offense after offense. In my mind, I had been sailing smoothly through life for a while, freely handing out forgiveness left and right. Suddenly, I found myself unable to forgive people for the smallest inappropriate remark. Someone would leave me out of a conversation, and I would get angry and stew over it. I thought I had just turned into this terrible person overnight, but I couldn't see what was happening under the surface.

I normally let offenses roll off my shoulder in a heartbeat, so I went to the Lord in prayer to try to figure out what had caused this sudden shift in attitude. The Holy Spirit pointed out to me that I wasn't hurting from fresh wounds. An old, deep hurt had surfaced, and the recent offenses were simply byproducts of that past offense. I wanted people around me to suffer the same pain I had buried a long time ago. The bitterness reawakening within my heart was subtle, and without the Holy Spirit's help, it might have taken me years to figure out what was really going on.

The Holy Spirit began to reveal that it would be necessary for me to revisit the hurt in my mind in order to deal with the bitterness. I remember telling Him, "I don't want to have to go back to that place for the sake of the people in my life who I'm holding a grudge against." Because of the pain of the experience, I had buried the memories and decided never to bring them up again. Even if it would help me forgive the new offenses I had taken on, I couldn't see how it would be worth it to feel the pain all over again. He gently and lovingly replied, "Jesus went to hell for your sake. You can go back there for the sake of others."

Now, technically, the Bible tells us that Jesus descended into Hades (Sheol), which was possibly the temporary resting place of every person who died under the old covenant. I don't personally believe He went to the place prepared for the devil and his angels, but that is a theological discussion for another book. Still, all that aside, I understood what the Holy Spirit was saying, and He said it in a way that got my attention.

When He said this, I resolved to do whatever was necessary to let go of the bitterness from the past and forgive those who I currently held grudges against. In reality, I wasn't hurting anyone else by holding onto the offenses anyway. I was only hurting myself more.

As you read this, you may find that you need to revisit painful memories from your past. If you've been holding onto bitterness for years, it can be difficult to even know what still needs to be forgiven. The Holy Spirit will walk you through it, even holding your hand and helping to heal the hurts, if you'll allow Him.

Choosing to forgive is an act of faith, but it's also an act of obedience. In Scripture, there is a link between unforgiveness and sickness, but there is a more general link between disobedience and sickness. Thankfully, when you and I are suffering the consequences of unforgiveness or disobedience, the solution is found in embracing our relationship with our loving Father. Don't forget that divine health is a benefit of knowing God.

In Exodus, God leads His chosen people out of Israel for the sake of having a relationship with them. He often uses the phrase, *You will be My people, and I will be your God.* Leading them out from under the tyranny of the Egyptians was an act of salvation, and God saves us in order for us to be able to walk with Him. Remember, salvation is the beginning of a relationship. God's desire for relationship with the Israelites is described in Exodus 15:17.

> *"You will bring them and plant them in the mountain of Your inheritance, the place, O Lord, which You have made for Your dwelling, the sanctuary, O Lord, which Your hands have established."*

As I mentioned earlier, when we receive the righteousness of God through faith in Jesus, we receive the inheritance of a daughter or son of God. The main benefit of this inheritance is the right to come boldly into God's presence. In Exodus, God is telling His people that He saved them into order for them to dwell *with* Him. As they choose to walk in relationship with Him, God makes some promises to them. Look at God's response to the people's worship:

> *"And He said, 'If you will give earnest heed to the voice of the Lord your God, and do what is right in His sight, and give ear to His commandments, and keep all His statutes, I will put none of the diseases on you which I have put on the Egyptians; for I, the Lord, am your healer.'"*

Exodus 15:26

If we look at this verse through the lens of the new covenant, we can know that God isn't asking us to perform all the little religious duties of the Mosaic law that the Israelites were given to perform. Instead, He's more interested in our hearts being in step with His will. As Romans 2:15 tells us, God has written His law on our hearts. The main commandments Jesus gives in the New Testament are to love God with all your heart, soul, mind, strength, and to love your neighbor as yourself. Choosing to forgive is doing both of these things at the same time. When we are unforgiving, it's like we are shoving God's forgiveness back into His face. If we are not willing to extend His grace, we are not cherishing His gift or His presence.

Notice how personal this principle is. It's all about relationship. It's when we consistently choose not to listen to the personal voice of the Holy Spirit telling us to forgive that we reject the benefit of His healing.

God told the Israelites that, if they would listen to His voice and obey Him, they would receive His healing power when they needed it. He would not allow any of the common diseases of that day to touch them. For any sickness or injury we experience, God has already offered us the solution. Yet, we reject that solution when we choose to live in disobedience.

Our obedience demonstrates the level at which we are willing to trust God. He is a perfectly loving Father. You can trust Him. If you are holding onto any unforgiveness or bitterness, let it go. Confess it, and ask God help you forgive.

You might be thinking, "I thought this principle was supposed to help me overcome worry. Living in fear of disobeying sounds more stressful than simply being unaware and disobeying anyway." If that's the case, I do want to clarify. God doesn't want us to walk around in the fear of making a mistake. Every time you or I mess up, God's grace and forgiveness are available. In fact, if we truly know Jesus, God has already forgiven us. When it comes to rejecting the benefit of God's grace, there's a big difference between making mistakes and living in unrepentant sin. Every believer makes mistakes. The question we need to ask ourselves is how do we respond to those mistakes? Are we attempting to hide our sin, or are we running to our Advocate, Jesus Christ? Hiding it or ignoring it is a sign of an unrepentant heart. Running to the Advocate is a sign that a person is leaning into their relationship with God.

The question we need to ask ourselves when we're living with unrepentant sin or unforgiveness is, do I love being close to my Savior or do I love being close to my sin? A close relationship with our Savior is going to bring benefits like peace, joy, healing, and wholeness. A close relationship with our sin is going to bring consequences, which end up producing a lot more worry in the long run.

If you know there is unforgiveness in your heart, don't let it hurt you emotionally, spiritually, or physically any longer. Confess it to Jesus, and if you need to, ask for forgiveness from the person you've directed your bitterness toward. It may be wiser not to talk to that person, or it may be too late to talk to them. But you can always talk to Jesus. He's reaching His hands out right now to take your bitterness and pain and give you the grace you need.

This leads me straight into the next principle. When we know that we've been living with an unrepentant heart, we need to confess it.

Principle: Confession
Benefit: Healing

Have you ever told a lie and then walked around worrying about when it would be uncovered? Sometimes people have to continue inventing more lies, trying to keep one lie from being discovered. This sort of situation can be an anxiety trap. It can weigh heavily on the mind.

The truth is that lies are not the only sins that cause anxiety. Every sin we commit and carry around hurts us. Psalm 38:3b and 32:3a state this clearly:

"There is no soundness in my flesh because of Your indignation; There is no health in my bones because of my sin."

"When I kept silent about my sin, my body wasted away..."

God created us in His image, and He cannot lie and does not sin at all. So, when we are carrying around unconfessed sin, holding onto it in our hearts, we are living in a way we were not designed to live. When you use a machine or tool in a way it's not supposed to be used, you add stress to that machine that can eventually

Our obedience demonstrates the level at which we are willing to trust God.

result in breakdown. Releasing the tension first involves admitting that you've been working the machine in the wrong way.

These two psalms also give us the key to releasing the stresses of living in a way we weren't designed to live. In Psalm 38:18 and 32:5b David says,

> *"For I confess my iniquity;*
> *I am full of anxiety because of my sin."*

> *"I said, 'I will confess my transgressions to the Lord';*
> *And You forgave the guilt of my sin."*

David knew the importance of confessing his sin to God, and if you read the Psalms you'll see that he does it a lot! This isn't a principle any believer is immune to, because we all make mistakes. Thankfully, God is always lovingly holding out His grace to those who turn to Him in truth.

Though the most important kind of confession is confession before God, there is also another form of confession in Scripture: confession to one another. James shows us that this form of confession can bring similar benefits.

> *"Therefore, confess your sins to one another, and pray for one another so that you may be healed. The effective prayer of a righteous man can accomplish much."*
>
> James 5:16

Even if you've repented of and confessed a sin to God, you may still need to confess that sin to another believer (someone you trust) in order to find complete freedom from that sin and its effects. Jesus says in John 3:21,

> *"But he who practices the truth comes to the Light, so that his deeds may be manifested as having been wrought in God."*

When we bring our mistakes into the light by confessing them to another believer, whether it's a spiritual mother or father, mentor, spouse, or friend, we are walking in faith. Remember that it's faith that allows us to accept God's grace and its wonderful benefits. If our sin is covered by the sacrifice of Christ on the cross, the only reason to hide our sin is because we want to appear better than we really are. When we do that, we are putting our trust in our own righteousness instead of the righteousness of Jesus. However, when we're willing to confess a sin—to admit when we've messed up—that sin's power over us is broken.

I would like to interject the idea that God does not require us to confess our sins to a pastor, teacher, or leader. He also does not command every believer to openly talk about all their past sins. Confessing our sins to God is always a good idea, but confessing our sins to another believer needs to be done in wisdom. Like every principle in God's word, this should be walked out relationally through communication with God. For example, there have been specific sinful mistakes I've made that I've confessed to God, yet I had a hard time letting them go emotionally because of the gravity of the effects of the sin. After praying about it, the Holy Spirit began to show me that I needed to confess it to a believer that I trusted in order to truly let it go.

The basis of this principle is simple: As children of the light, we should be willing to walk in the light. Disobedience is emotionally, mentally, spiritually, and physically self-destructive because it blocks us from experiencing the benefits of God's grace. The principle of confession removes the blockage so that His grace can flow freely and we can receive the healing we need. Yes, confession is a humbling experience. Yes, it hurts to talk about mistakes sometimes, but it is better than keeping them bound up inside.

When we're willing to confess a sin—to admit when we've messed up—that sin's power over us is broken.

My heart's plea to you is that you wouldn't bury or hold onto any unconfessed sin. Even if it's something you buried deep down years ago, make the choice not to carry it around any longer. There is a river of love and grace flowing for you at the foot of the cross. God's love is much bigger than any mistake you've ever made. Trust Him enough to be honest with Him. The benefits are worth it.

The Benefit of Revelation

One prerequisite to confessing our sin is to understand God's truth. How can we know that we've been living in disobedience if we don't know what God expects or desires from us? I believe some Christians are living in a constant state of anxiety because of wrong expectations. If we're living with wrong expectations about God's will or His plan, then the only way to fix those expectations is to seek out the truth.

Principle: Nearness
Benefit: Revelation

When we read the Bible, we read God's revealed truth to us. However, truth is more than just a set of rules or regulations. Truth is a Person (as we see in John 1). Knowing God's truth, and applying it, relies on us growing nearer to God through a real relationship with Jesus. Why? Because people pick up the Bible and interpret it in a variety of ways. To really know God's expectations and desires, we have to know Him. We have to be allowing the Holy Spirit to interpret the Bible for us.

This brings us directly back to the story of Mary sitting at Jesus' feet. Martha desired truth, but she didn't realize the importance of finding that truth in the person of Jesus the way Mary did. Mary was sitting at the feet of Jesus, and because of her nearness to Him, she could receive all the revelation she needed. When Martha finally gave up trying to do things her own way and approached Jesus for help, He also revealed His expectations to her as well.

You and I have a choice to make every time we read the Bible or pray. We can study God's word and ask Him for help out of duty or fear, or we can choose to read and pray out of a desire to know Him on a deeper level. When we are truly seeking Him for the simple benefit of being near to Him, the Holy Spirit not only begins to reveal His truth during our time reading the Bible, but He also begins revealing Himself to us during any and every part of our day.

How does this benefit help us to stop worrying about our health?
The answer requires us to separate revelation into its two functions.
Here is the first way revelation helps us to stop worrying:

I. Revelation helps us hide God's Word in our hearts

Worry and anxiety are the symptoms of an internal fear, and
fear in the life of a Christian is the result of a lie. Let's use the fear
of death as an example. If I'm afraid of dying as a Christian, I don't
need to hear mere friendly encouragement that perhaps dying won't
be that bad. I need a truth from God's word that will break the
lies I'm believing about death. I need revelation knowledge from
the Holy Spirit that will change the way I think. Also, there is a
difference between just knowing something and having something
revealed to you. I can read Philippians 1:21, in which Paul says, "For
to me, to live is Christ and to die is gain," and I can still be worried
about death. Lies are sometimes so deeply ingrained and embedded
in our hearts that God Himself has to uproot them and replace them
with His truth before we start thinking differently. The moment I
finally read Philippians 1:21 and the Holy Spirit personally reveals
the truth of that verse to me is when I begin to have peace about
my eventual physical death. It's when I hear God's perspective, and
accept it, that I begin to think along the same lines as Psalm 116:15.

> *"Precious in the sight of the Lord*
> *Is the death of His godly ones."*

This verse is saying, if you only knew how good heaven really
is, you wouldn't be afraid of death any longer. Here's another way of
saying it: If you're already walking in a close relationship with God,
then the sting of death has been removed because dying just means
you'll be that much closer to your Lord. Now, God does not, in any
way, give us the right to decide when we will die—that's still up
to Him. He does, however, want us to overcome our fear of death
through a revelation of the truth.

Bringing us back to my main point, if you and I want to
experience more of God's revelation in our lives, we need to be

dwelling in close proximity to Him. We need to be practicing the principle of nearness. Psalm 91 paints a clear picture of a person who doesn't have to worry about their health because of where they are in relation to God.

"For you have made the Lord, my refuge,
Even the Most High, your dwelling place.
No evil will befall you,
Nor will any plague come near your tent."

Psalm 91:9-10

Now look at God's promise to that person near the end of the chapter.

"Because he has loved Me, therefore I will deliver him;
I will set him securely on high, because he has known My name.
He will call upon Me, and I will answer him;
I will be with him in trouble;
I will rescue him and honor him.
With a long life I will satisfy him
And let him see My salvation."

Psalm 91:14-16

God says about the man or woman who loves and knows Him, "I will answer him." Skeptics often ask the question, "Why doesn't God answer the countless suffering people who cry out to them?" God's answer is simple: He answers those who are dwelling with Him. Why? Those who know Him personally and long to be in that intimate relationship with Him are the ones who are not rejecting the benefits of His grace.

One personal way in which I can say I've suffered to an extent in my life is in the area of sleep. Now, insomnia and sleep deprivation are not the worst circumstances you can walk through, and I understand that. However, it's an experience through which God has been able to teach me about the powerful principle of revelation.

It all started when I was in my late teens and early twenties, and if you've read my book, *My Mess*, you know I first started having sleeping problems because of habits and shame I picked up in college.

When I started a personal relationship with Jesus near the end of my sophomore year, I assumed I wouldn't struggle with getting adequate sleep anymore. To an extent, I was right. I definitely slept better than before, but the problem persisted. During my senior year of college, I tired myself out every day with cheerleading practice, and I slept like a baby. The year after graduating though, everything went downhill. There were times when I would not sleep at all for 72 hours, and that was during weekdays when I would have to be at work from 8 to 5. The more I struggled with sleeplessness, the more a single emotion emerged: anger.

It is possible to get angry at nothing, but most of the time when you're angry, something or someone is the recipient of that anger. For a long time I didn't want to admit it, but I was angry at God for keeping me awake when I should have been resting. I didn't realize it then, but I was making things much worse for myself by getting angry. For one thing, the anger made it even harder to fall asleep. On top of that, the anger stole my peace. The whole time, I thought the sleeplessness was causing the anxiety, but though it did add stress to my life, the major cause of anxiety was the fear surrounding the sleeplessness. I was worried and angry because I was afraid.

God did intervene on many occasions, and through some major life changes, my ability to sleep generally improved. However, a few shorts years later, I began to experience the same sleepless symptoms again.

Shortly before the sleeplessness returned, I had taken on my first ghost writing project. Having been tasked with writing the story of a believer who had experienced similar situations to my own, I began to open up about my problem. The person whose book I was writing had dealt with a much more severe version of insomnia, and yet they seemed to have peace in their heart. The more they shared their story with me, the more I began to understand that they had found peace, not outside of the pain but in the middle of the pain. God's unexplainable peace even acted as a catalyst for them to find victory over their symptoms.

Our emotional and mental health are in many ways just as important as our physical health. Good physical health might be of little benefit to us if we are an emotional or mental wreck. Many physical symptoms have even been linked to underlying emotional problems. Studies have been done showing that, if you're stressed out all the time, you are suppressing your immune system and have a much higher chance of becoming physically sick. The good news is that God doesn't just care about our physical health. He cares about our mental and emotional health, too. God cares about your feelings. He cares about your soul. He cares that we get enough rest—that we are able to recuperate.

The person whose book I was writing began to share some of the practical health steps they had taken to overcome sleeplessness, but they also gave me the key from God's word that made the difference. They had overcome insomnia through praying and speaking the truths of God's word over their mind before bed. Their life wasn't perfect—I won't pretend that it was, but the peace of God was present.

The more I listened, the more I realized that my unchecked anger about not being able to sleep blocked my ability to be emotionally healthy. The whole time, I thought my anger had been justified, and so why would I need to change? I thought, "I've been doing what God is asking me to do, so therefore I deserve good sleep." To let go of the anger, I had to get to the point where I remembered that I don't deserve any good thing. I don't deserve good sleep because of what I've done. I get to receive good sleep for the same reason I can receive any good benefit from God: because of what Jesus did for me on the cross.

Instead of getting angry about my problem, I began to thank God for His goodness. I also began to remind myself of God's truth every night before bed, quoting verses like:

"When you lie down, you will not be afraid;
When you lie down, your sleep will be sweet."

Proverbs 3:24

"It is vain for you to rise up early,
To sit up late,
To eat the bread of sorrows;
For so He gives His beloved sleep."

Psalm 127:2 (NKJV)

As I began to believe that the Lord gives sleep to those He loves, I was reminded of the way He showed His love to us. The Bible tells us that the cross was the demonstration of God's love. Learning to accept the grace of God before bed each night has changed the way I sleep. It has replaced my anxiety with peace. Yes, I still get angry sometimes—I'm not perfect, but God has brought me a long way through the power of His grace.

If you're in an emotional or mental battle, you may need to get counsel from someone who can see your situation through an outside perspective. When I listened to the counsel of someone wiser than me (who had also experienced similar health issues), I was able to accept some profoundly effective truths I had missed up to that point. Even when it feels impossible to listen to the counsel of others, we as believers always have the counsel of Jesus available to us. He went through the worst of hardships and pain, and yet He wasn't worried. Did He feel the effects of mental anguish and strain? Yes. He experienced real, raw emotions, but He did not allow those emotions to rule His world. Because He knew and lived by the truth of God, He lived a life of peace. In fact, He was so unfocused on His own situation that He spent most of His time teaching and healing others. Because of His death on the cross, that same healing is now extended to us.

Did you know that the word *worry* can be used in the form of a noun or a verb? I can say, "I worry a lot" or "I'm worrying about something" and use it as a verb in that context. Or I can say, "I'm feeling a heavy burden of worry right now," using it instead as a noun. Without realizing it, we often focus on the noun instead of the verb. When you use worry as a noun, the opposite of worry is *peace*, and that's what we search for the most. We say, "If I can just escape this worry and experience a moment of peace, I'll be okay." When you use it as a verb though, the opposite of worry is not peace, but *trust*. The bridge leading from anxiety to peace is a confident, unwavering trust in who God is and what He has done. When we understand the powerful revelation that the Holy Spirit wants to share with us concerning our issue, we can then say, "I choose to stop worrying and start trusting in the words of the Lord."

We'll never find peace if we don't learn to trust the Author of our peace. Here's the thing about trust though: You don't trust someone you don't know. Trusting God has less to do with how hard we are trying to trust Him, and it has more to do with how well we know Him. The more we get to know Him, the more we find that His character is trustworthy.

2. Revelation gives purpose to the pain

Many people use the phrase, "Pain only makes you stronger." This saying may have originated in the weight room where physical pain is often traded for an increase in strength. The problem with this statement is that it's not always true. Pain in and of itself doesn't strengthen us. When we're at the gym working out, some pains do indicate the process of growth, but sometimes pain is simply a symptom of something that's wrong. When your back is thrown out, you don't say, "I'm getting stronger!" and keep doing weighted presses, because you're just going to injure yourself even worse. It's the same in our Christian walk.

> **The bridge leading from anxiety to peace is a confident, unwavering trust in who God is and what He has done.**

The problem with always viewing pain as a spiritual strength exercise is that it can put the focus on us—on our innate ability to endure hardship. When we lean into our own strength to make it through the pain, it's like trying to lift that weighted exercise bar with a bad back. We're going to come out the other side, possibly feeling good about the fact that we pushed through but internally feeling the hurt of the lasting injury.

Pain is not there to make you a stronger individual. Like I said earlier, it can help to turn our eyes to God, but it's not meant to make us stronger. It's meant to make us rely more on God's strength. Sometimes it takes walking through a painful situation in order for us to realize how weak we are and just how much we really need God.

So, should that fact itself comfort us to continue walking through pain? Yes, to an extent, but God has also provided a way for us to find a much greater comfort in the midst of a painful process, and He offers us that comfort through revelation.

Remember, the two ways we can receive revelation from God is through His written word and through a specific word spoken by the Holy Spirit. So, the first place we should look if we want revelation about a certain illness is God's word.

Let me give you an example of what finding specific revelation in God's word might look like. I've heard many Christians say something like this, "The reason I'm sick is because God is punishing me for something I did years ago." The believer who says that needs a revelation about the love of God. Let's say they pick up their Bible and read 1 John 4:18, which says,

> *"There is no fear in love; but perfect love casts out fear, because fear involves punishment, and the one who fears is not perfected in love."*

They ponder this verse for a moment, and then they pray, asking for revelation about the meaning behind the verse. The Holy Spirit begins to speak to their heart, reminding them of the amazing grace of God they received when they believed in Jesus. Then, before they realize what's happening, they begin to have a simple conversation with the Holy Spirit in their heart.

"God, I know this verse is really meant for Christians who haven't messed up the way I did. I'm not like them. I'm afraid I won't ever deserve to be made well again. I deserve to be punished, and I know that's why You made me sick."

Yes, you do deserve to be punished, based on your own actions. But when you repented and believed in Jesus as your Savior, you traded what you deserved for what He deserved.

"Yes, I get that, but it doesn't seem right that I should get away without punishment."

You didn't. Jesus allowed Himself to be punished for you. Now there's no punishment left for you to receive.

"But, if that's true, then I shouldn't have anything to be afraid of now."

Exactly.

Through the help of the Holy Spirit, that person began to understand a spiritual truth in Scripture that directly affected the way they viewed their sickness. Through revelation, their mindset changed from "Maybe God is punishing me, and if that's the case, I don't have hope of healing," to "Jesus took my punishment upon Himself. He can also take away the sickness I'm currently facing." They open their Bible and keep reading. After a while, they come to Isaiah 19:20-22, which confirms what they learned.

> *"It will become a sign and a witness to the Lord of hosts in the land of Egypt; for they will cry to the Lord because of oppressors, and He will send them a Savior and a Champion, and He will deliver them. Thus the Lord will make Himself known to Egypt, and the Egyptians will know the Lord in that day. They will even worship with sacrifice and offering, and will make a vow to the Lord and perform it. The Lord will strike Egypt, striking but healing; so they will return to the Lord, and He will respond to them and will heal them."*

In this passage, the Lord does send the sickness. He does the striking. However, He sends the pain, not for the purpose of punishment, but instead for the purpose of nearness. He allows the Egyptians in this passage to walk through suffering in order to draw them back to Him.

Does God not punish people for sins? He does, and there are many instances in the Bible where God's wrath is seen in action, but His wrath is always against unbelievers—those who do not know Him—those who have rejected Him and His ways. God does not pour out His wrath on believers under the new covenant because that would be breaking the covenant, and God is not one that He should lie (see Numbers 23:19). Look at the beginning of the passage again. When it says, "He will send them a Savior and Champion," it's talking about Jesus. If you truly know Jesus, you don't have to fear punishment, because Jesus has already taken your punishment on the cross.

As a reminder, even though Jesus has taken our punishment, we can still limit the benefits we receive, like healing, through our disobedience. When we reject God's ways (His principles), we put up our hand against His benefits. The benefit of revelation allows us to specifically see the ways in which we are limiting His blessings, and it gives us the opportunity to repent and turn back to God.

When we face physical, emotional, or even mental suffering, we should pray for healing, but we should also pray for revelation. We should be asking God the questions, why has this been able to happen? Is this evidence that something inside my heart needs to change? Is this a sign that I'm rejecting God's grace in some way? The more we lean into God and the more we allow His word to sink into our hearts, the more answers we receive.

Now, I understand that the person in the example I used did not receive a specific answer to their problem. They didn't find out exactly why they were sick. When this happens, the best thing for us to do is to continue seeking God—to continue pressing in to hear from Him. The principle we're talking about is the principle of nearness, and the quickest way to stop hearing someone is to move out of range of their voice. There are a billion places on earth where you wouldn't be able to hear someone who is calling your name (without the help of technology, obviously). There's only one place where you would be able to hear them: within physical range of their voice. Similarly, if we want to hear God's voice clearly, we need to draw near to Him spiritually.

One Saturday morning, I started experiencing pains in my side. Continuing all day, the pains began to seriously worry me. So, Sunday morning at church, I cried out to God during worship. As I thanked Him for His goodness and grace, I also prayed for His help. To be honest, I was praying for more than just healing in my side. I was also praying about some major doubts and struggles I had been facing in my life and ministry that year. As I knelt there on the front row of the auditorium, I did everything I could to draw near to my Deliverer.

After the service, a woman who was visiting from another church approached me. Her name was Cindi Estep, and I recognized her from a ministry conference weekend I had attended in Louisiana. She said that she had been given a prophetic word for me and asked if it was okay that she shared it. I told her I would appreciate it. She related her message to me, and then she handed me a piece of notebook paper that summed up what she said. This is what was written on the paper:

"There are things that are coming to a head. There's an 'undoing' of sorts. This 'undoing' is of the Lord and will not destroy you. When it comes to a head, some infection is coming out, so healing can come. You will not be destroyed—just undone."

At first, I began to think that the "undoing" was the beginning of a physical healing that needed to take place. I wondered, could the pain in my side be the "infection" she referred to? Since I wasn't sure, I kept on praying.

Each day, the pain grew sharper and more unbearable. The increasing pain caused my anxiety to multiply. On top of that, I had been informed that same week that an error occurred with my family's health insurance account, and we would possibly be without coverage temporarily while we switched over to another plan. Because of branching out to work on my ministry more that year, our income had decreased, and I didn't feel like I had the money to pay for a doctor's visit out of pocket. The more I considered the facts, the more worried I became. Oddly enough, the more I worried, the more pain I felt.

Later that same week, I described my symptoms to a friend, and he said it sounded like a kidney stone. He had suffered through the pain of kidney stones before, and he gave me some practical advice that made me feel a little better. However, he and another friend both described the intense pain of passing a kidney stone, and that certainly didn't help my anxiety.

Then, I remembered the word I had received the previous Sunday. The more I prayed about it that week though, the more the Holy Spirit began to further reveal the truth to me. By the end of the week, I knew that the physical infection merely represented a deeper, spiritual issue I was battling. As I prayed and waited on the Lord, He began to speak the truth of the problem plainly. He told me that the "infection" inside of me was the spirit of pride. He explained that the physical difficulties were connected to a spiritual truth God was working out in my heart. On top of that, He told me to stop worrying about the pain.

As I thought about what the Holy Spirit had said, I remembered past experiences I had where His specific revelation had given me insight into His plan. I knew I could trust His goodness despite the pain, so I told Him I would stop worrying with His help.

The good news is that, when I stopped worrying about the potential kidney stones, the pain decreased. It didn't go away completely, but I was no longer in a state of flux. As I continued to wait upon the Lord and hand my worries over to Him, I also repented of my pride and began to ask Him to strip any unwholesome attitudes out of my heart. As I repented, I began to see a clear picture of the way I had been viewing my life. Because of the sacrifices I had made in order to minister to people online, I had developed a sense that God owed me. As I sought Him in humility that week, He reminded me that He didn't owe me anything. Everything He had given and would ever give me was a free gift based on the sacrifice of Jesus. As the pride left, so did the bitterness that had begun to crust over my heart due to disappointment. I could clearly see how the doubts and struggles I had been facing that year were connected to my pride.

Exactly one week after I had received the prophetic word from Cindi, the Holy Spirit spoke another word into my heart. I had gone to church by myself that morning, and as I drove from church to the grocery store to pick up a few items, I heard Him say, *It's about to pass.* I thanked Him for letting me know, and not long after that I began to feel the location of the pain moving. The stinging sensation that had stayed a little below my rib cage on one side of my body began to slowly move down closer to my hip and slide over. I drove to the store to do my shopping, I went home, and within an hour the pain was completely gone. God had helped me pass a kidney stone without feeling much pain at all.

I don't believe God gave me kidney stones to punish me. Instead, I believe God gave me the grace to live a life free of kidney stones, but I chose not to accept that grace by allowing a spirit of pride to rest in my heart. Now, I honestly don't know if the sin of pride and the pain of kidney stones are normally connected, but I do know that God walked me through the process of healing both at the same time. God was able to bring glory out of a physical ailment, the same way Jesus did with the man born blind. Yes, God could have spoken a word and instantly healed me of those stones, but He didn't. Instead, He healed me over the course of a week in order to also heal a much deeper hurt in my heart.

God didn't waste my pain. He saw it as an opportunity to demonstrate His glory. He knew that a potentially anxious situation would turn my attention to Him, and He was right. It wasn't anger or frustration that had motivated Him to heal me over a week's time. Love had been His motivation, and I am glad to know He loves me enough to draw me back to His side when I start wandering down my own destructive path.

The question we should ask ourselves is, when we experience pain, where do we turn? Does it cause us to set our eyes on Jesus, or do we look to other things?

Jesus says in John 15:7,

"If you abide in Me, and My words abide in you, ask whatever you wish, and it will be done for you."

If you believe what God's word says about your healing, the only thing standing between you and the benefit of divine health is your nearness to God. Jesus says that if we abide in Him (nearness to God) and His words abide in us (revelation from the Holy Spirit), then we can ask for and receive anything we need through faith.

Think about the account of the woman with the issue of blood in Mark 5. In this story, we see a woman who, upon hearing about Jesus and what He's able to do, believes that if He can do that for someone else, He can do it for her too. I encourage you to go read the whole story for yourself, but I'll give you the brief summary. She tracks Jesus down, follows Him through the street, pushes her way through a crowd of people, and reaches out to touch Him. She tells herself that, if she simply touches His cloak, she will be healed. Reaching out, she finds immediate freedom from her pain.

I believe the reason this woman received her healing was because she was willing to get close enough to Jesus to receive from Him. Some of us are praying for Jesus to heal us, but we're not willing to get close enough to our Savior to receive the grace He has already provided. Listen to Jesus' words about praying in faith in John 16:15 and 16:23.

"All things that the Father has are Mine; therefore I said that He takes of Mine and will disclose it to you."

"In that day you will not question Me about anything. Truly, truly, I say to you, if you ask the Father for anything in My name, He will give it to you."

When Jesus says in John 15:7 that we can ask for anything we wish and in John 16:23 that He will give us anything we ask for, He's not talking about a magic formula for getting our prayers answered. When He says we can ask for anything we wish, He makes the prerequisite that we are abiding in Him. If we're abiding in Him, our prayers are going to line up with God's will. So, we can paraphrase that verse to say, *When you know Me, you can ask for anything within God's will and I will give it to you.*

I think many Christians misunderstand what it means to pray in Jesus' name. Praying in His name doesn't mean saying, "in Jesus' name" at the end of a prayer. The devil could do that, and God wouldn't listen to him. Praying in Jesus' name means praying as His representative. Think about a political official sending a subordinate to deliver a message for them. If I came to you and said, the governor wants you to do this for them, but you knew I didn't work for the governor, you might laugh in my face. However, if you knew that I worked for the governor and was an official representative of theirs, you would show me more respect. Why? Because, when you represent someone, you carry the weight of their authority. Some of us are praying "in Jesus' name" but we don't carry the weight of Jesus' authority.

If you want your prayers to result in miraculous moves of God, you must be authorized to use Jesus' name. How do you become authorized? You know Him personally. You know Him intimately.

You trust fully in the righteousness of Jesus as your ticket into the courts of heaven. You allow His grace to empower change in your life. You stay in communication with Him. You listen to the conviction of the Holy Spirit, not just His comfort. You draw near to Him—all of Him—not just the parts you like.

> *"In that day you will ask in My name, and I do not say to you that I will request of the Father on your behalf; for the Father Himself loves you, because you have loved Me and have believed that I came forth from the Father."*

> John 16:26-27

Jesus boils the key to answered prayers down to whether we really know Him or not. He makes it personal once again. In this verse, Jesus describes the beautiful inheritance He won for us on the cross. Look at Paul's prayer over the Ephesian church in Ephesians 1:13-14a. He prays,

> *"In Him, you also, after listening to the message of truth, the gospel of your salvation—having also believed, you were sealed in Him with the Holy Spirit of promise, who is given as a pledge of our inheritance,"*

He is essentially saying that the Holy Spirit is God's down payment on our inheritance as believers. This means that every believer should expect to experience the Holy Spirit at work in their life. Paul continues in verse 17, praying,

> *"that the God of our Lord Jesus Christ, the Father of glory, may give to you a spirit of wisdom and of revelation in the knowledge of Him."*

Through the down payment (the Holy Spirit), we should also expect to receive revelation from God. In the next two verses, Paul takes it one step further in verses 18-19 and tells us to also expect miracles.

> *"I pray that the eyes of your heart may be enlightened, so that you will know what is the hope of His calling, what are the riches*

of the glory of His inheritance in the saints, and what is the surpassing greatness of His power toward us who believe. These are in accordance with the working of the strength of His might."

Through the working of the Holy Spirit, God pours His power onto those who know Him—those who draw near to Him through faith in Jesus. If you doubt whether God wants to heal you or not, my best encouragement to you is for you to start reading the gospels. Read them over and over until you see a clear picture of God's heart for healing. Then, I encourage you to read the writings of Paul over and over until you can see a clear picture of how we receive that healing today. Ask God to make it real to you. I've done my best to explain the truths behind healing to you in this chapter, but only the Holy Spirit can help you receive those truths in your heart.

Some people lean too far one direction when it comes to healing. They say that we can pray anything we want if we speak Jesus' name and see it happen. They ignore the truth that we need to be intimately acquainted with Him. Others believe God doesn't heal anymore at all. It's only when we allow the Bible to be the basis for our perspective that we can have a balanced view. One intricacy to the principles of divine health is this: Though we are promised the inheritance of Christ, and though God promises us some things here on earth, He doesn't give us the full inheritance this side of heaven. The full experience of our inheritance is something we won't see until we are with Him for eternity. One example of this truth is the fact that, even though we are saved, our physical bodies still grow old and die. When we are with Christ in eternity, we will receive new bodies that never grow old and never pass away. Because some of our inheritance is held back for now, there is pain in life. The good news is, by His grace, God offers us healing in Jesus' name.

The Benefit of Miracles

I know this chapter is egregiously long, but I can't move on to another topic without briefly discussing the principle of belief. I've covered the importance of revelation, but there's a simple and critical response God expects us to follow after we receive His revelation. He expects us to believe Him.

Principle: Belief
Benefit: Miracles

Two instances in Scripture where Jesus was left speechless (a creative way of describing it) are found in Mark 6:6 and Matthew 8:10. The first says, "He wondered at their unbelief," and the second instance says, "He marveled and said to those who were following, 'Truly I say to you, I have not found such great faith with anyone in Israel.'"

People said and did many things to try to intimidate or impress Jesus, but as far as I can see in Scripture, He rarely responded with surprise or fascination. Not many things made Him stop and stare. But here are two instances where He stood amazed, and they both have to do with belief.

God is amazed when we choose to believe His words with the faith of a child. Likewise, He is also amazed (in a sense of the word) when He generously gives us truth, signs, revelation, encouragement, counsel, and grace and we still wind up choosing to believe what we see in front of us over what He has said. Jesus makes this amazing statement in Mark 9:23b:

"...all things are possible to him who believes."

Some people don't like verses like this very much because of past experiences they've had of people praying for them, and I get that. I've heard several stories of people attending healing services or events and asking for prayer. After no recognizable change occurred, the person needing healing was yelled at for "not having enough faith." This phrase has been used and often abused to explain why someone didn't immediately receive healing, but please realize that God wasn't the one doing the abusing. If someone has ever told you don't have enough faith in a hurtful or condemning way, I'm very sorry. However, belief is still an area every Christian can improve in, myself included.

Please understand that I'm saying this out of love. None of us believe God perfectly every time. Only Jesus did that. Thankfully, He sent the Holy Spirit to help us abide by the truth. The more we allow God's Spirit to speak into our hearts, to remind us of the words of Jesus, and to lead us into all truth, the more we'll be naturally walking in belief.

As you read this phrase, I want you to ask the Holy Spirit to reveal any doubts left in your heart, and give Him permission to expel those doubts and begin to replace them with belief.

"Your faith has made you well."

This is a phrase Jesus speaks in the gospels to several different people directly after healing them. We need to be willing to ask ourselves this question: *Could Jesus say that same phrase to me? If He looked into my heart right now, would He see a person who is walking in faith?*

The good news is that God isn't asking us to grow our belief to a great size today. He's asking us to re-examine what belief we do have (no matter how small it is), and act on that. As we choose to take that first step in faith, God will help us to mature in our faith. A child's faith doesn't always look impressive to man, but it is pleasing to God. I encourage you to take a step of faith today. Read the Word and act on it. Choose to believe that Jesus is telling the truth. You will be amazed at the outcome.

The strength of a building relies heavily on the condition of its foundation. If your faith is wobbly, go back to the foundation. Remember what Jesus did for you on the cross. If you're battling a health problem externally, you need to remember that Jesus' entire body was marred beyond recognition on your behalf. If you're battling a health problem internally, you can remember that Jesus' internal organs eventually all shut down and died on your behalf. Three days later, life came back into His body. Learn to reinforce your faith on the foundation of His death and resurrection, and you will see miracles.

- 7 -

STOP WORRYING ABOUT MONEY

As I've started each chapter in this book, I've thought, "This is the area of life I worry about the most." Then I get to the next chapter and think, "Wait. Actually I worry more about this!" Though many different sources of worry can spring up in our lives, money may be the most prolific source of anxiety in our culture today. People who don't have money worry about attaining it. Some people that have money worry about how to use it or how to keep it. Almost everyone in between worries about all three issues. If this is something you struggle with, you need to know that God's plan for your finances is a plan of peace.

You don't have to worry about money, no matter how much you have or don't have. In this chapter, I'm going to show you the Biblical principles and benefits that justify that statement. I'm also going to do something a little different and share several money misconceptions that tend to cause worry.

When I talked about the benefit of rest in the chapter on work, I mentioned that I would share more about that benefit in this chapter. Some Christians would love to take a Sabbath rest, yet they can't see how it could be possible due to the constant strain on their finances. If you're living paycheck to paycheck, you may not have the luxury of taking time off, right? Even the thought of attempting to take time off may send you into a fluster of anxiety. Whether you relate to this, or whether you have money troubles of another kind, the basis to finding peace in the area of finances is to view money the way God does. When you view money from God's perspective, you treat it the way He intended it to be treated, and you thankfully no longer have to worry about it.

Consider the story of Jesus asleep in the boat in Mark 4. The disciples were worried sick due to an insane storm surging around them. Just for a moment though, imagine with me that the disciples were given God's perspective on the situation. Let's say they could clearly see that Jesus was the Son of God and that God had a purpose for Jesus to fulfill on earth that did not end at the bottom of the lake. If the disciples were able to look at the storm through God's eyes, then when Jesus was discovered sleeping in the stern, you know what they could have done? This probably sounds nuts, but they could have gone to sleep, too.

Imagine one of the disciples saying, "Hey guys, anyone know where my pajamas went? Jesus is sleeping, so I'm gonna take a little nap as well." The others would have thought he had lost his marbles. You and I would think the same thing, right? But as crazy as it sounds, here's why I believe it would have worked: There's no way that boat was going down with Jesus in it. You need to remember that worry reveals how much or how little we trust God. Jesus didn't worry about situations the way the disciples did because He looked at His life through His Father's eyes, and He trusted His Father with all His heart.

Some of us are waiting for the storm to cease before we start trusting God. But the key to finding peace isn't to see the waves settle down. We simply have to be paying attention to what our Savior is doing. Where is He leading us? What has He said? If He said we're going across the lake, then we're going across the lake. If He's saying, "Stop worrying about this money issue," listen to Him. If all else fails, God can carry the boat to shore while you're sleeping.

Principle: Priority
Benefit: Provision

The principle of priority applies to every area of life, not just money. The most important commandment in the Bible tells us to love God with everything we have—to seek, value, and obey Him first. If God expects us to put Him first in every area of life, our money is included. If you've heard any teaching on money before, you may have heard this principle specifically referred to as *the principle of first fruits*. Here is the principle simply stated: When we choose to prioritize God's ways, even over our finances, He promises to provide for our needs.

God makes it very clear that this principle isn't about balancing our desires with God's desires. This isn't a game where we are able to do things His way sometimes and do things our way at other times. In fact, Jesus says we're either all in with our money or we're not in at all. Look at this challenging statement in Matthew 6:24.

> *"No one can serve two masters; for either he will hate the one and love the other, or he will be devoted to one and despise the other. You cannot serve God and wealth."*

This isn't one of those verses that gets hung on the wall or tattooed on the back very often. However, despite how intense this verse sounds, it comes with good news. When money is our master, we are our own providers. When we make God our master, He becomes our provider.

We looked at the life of the rich young ruler earlier in this book, but I want to briefly inspect his character once more because of the priority he placed on his money. I used the story of the rich young ruler to talk about the assurance of salvation, but what I didn't share before was the fact that Jesus immediately connects an assurance of salvation with the assurance of provision. The story of the rich young ruler is often quoted from Mark 10:17-27, but what happens immediately after this is sometimes left out. Let's pick it up in verses 28-31.

> *"Peter began to say to Him, 'Behold, we have left everything and followed You.' Jesus said, 'Truly I say to you, there is no one who has left house or brothers or sisters or mother or father or children or farms, for My sake and for the gospel's sake, but that he will receive a hundred times as much now in the present age, houses and brothers and sisters and mothers and children and*

farms, along with persecutions; and in the age to come, eternal life. But many who are first will be last, and the last, first.'"

The rich young ruler doesn't get to hear this promise. He completely misses out—the poor guy. There's another bad dad joke. It's funny because he's not poor. He's actually rich—ha! Not funny? Just forget it.

My point is that this conversation takes place after he walks away. He may have worried about the type of life he would have to live if he gave all his possessions to the poor. He may have thought, "I can't be poor! I don't know how to live that way. I won't be able to afford my retro Air Jordans!" Whatever he was thinking, he misses out on Jesus' promise of provision. Peter obviously has some similar fears in his mind about money that he wants cleared up, and Jesus assures him that God cares about providing for His children.

Please note, Jesus doesn't promise Peter or us mind-blowing riches on earth, and He also doesn't promise that life will be void of hardship. He simply promises that God will bless those who have sacrificed their earthly treasures for the sake of the gospel. What the manifestation of those blessings really looks like and when they come is ultimately up to Him.

Some people take this passage too far and assume every believer needs to sell all their possessions and give everything away, but Jesus doesn't say that either. Jesus isn't asking every believer to give all their money away, and He's not asking us to disown our families. The reason I say this is because of the key to this passage found in the last verse. *Those who are last will be first.* He's actually talking about priority. When we prioritize what is valuable to God above what is valuable to us, He promises us a reward.

The rich young ruler worried about his salvation, but he worried about his riches even more. He could not see that the thing he *wanted* most was stopping him from receiving the thing he *needed* most. He feared the life he would have to live in order to obey Jesus. The reason some of us have so many money problems is because we're still choosing to prioritize our money the way the rich young ruler did.

Out of all the principles in this book, this may be the hardest to accept. But when we feel like a principle of God is hard to live up to, we need to remember that God does not expect us to live up to it in our own strength. One of the reasons Jesus sent the Holy Spirit is so that we can successfully walk in the nature of Christ. When we're walking in His nature and not our own, we aren't left to work it out by ourselves. He is working it out through us (insert the sounds of angelic choirs singing 'hallelujah!' here).

I have young children who often need help completing the tasks I ask them to complete. If I tell them to go clean their room and come back to check on them, I don't expect to see the whole room clean right away. They're young and I understand they need help. What I expect is to see them trusting that what I said was important. What often happens is, I'll find them cleaning, they'll see me walk in the room, and they'll say, "Daddy, can you help us?" I'll kneel down and start picking up toys alongside them. God is most concerned with seeing the principle of priority at work in our hearts. When our hearts are right—when we believe His words and choose to act on them—the Holy Spirit comes alongside us and begins picking up the pieces we have trouble with. If you struggle with the principle of priority, especially in the area of money, look up at your loving Father and ask Him for help.

If the disciples chose to believe Jesus that day, then they could have ceased to worry about money completely. That's the position God wants us to be in, too. He wants us to be free from the concerns of money so that we can focus on the work He is doing. Remember that Jesus' yoke is easy and His burden is light. The more we allow His burden to be placed on our shoulders, the more common burdens like finances fall away. Let me remind you of the beautiful truth found in Matthew 6:33.

> *"But seek first His kingdom and His righteousness, and all these things will be added to you."*

Keep in mind, Jesus hasn't promised that we'll always be secure on paper, but He has promised that we'll be secure in His presence. The rich young ruler was secure on paper, and he wasn't willing to give up that visible promise of security for the invisible promise Jesus could offer. You need to know, when you are seeking His kingdom first, your provision is already on paper in the courts of heaven. Even when you add up the numbers from your earthly bank account, if God's kingdom is truly your priority, God has a different set of numbers He is adding up on your behalf. It's not always going to come exactly when you prefer, and it's not always going to be the amount you want, but it will be what you need.

About five years into doing online ministry work, I began to pray about ways I could make a bigger impact. For several years, I had been slowly collecting clients in an effort to grow my freelance media business. Oddly enough, even after I reached a new level of income, I still worried about getting new clients and managing projects for my current clients.

A few months before the end of the year, I began to seek the Lord about what the next year would look like. The Holy Spirit asked me to branch out and start doing ministry work part-time. Years prior, I had started out working on ministry videos and books part-time, but that work didn't provide much income. After collecting about a dozen different clients who needed regular media work, I was making more and more each year, but I was also working less and less on the ministry. I knew I had a decision to make.

Jesus hasn't promised that we'll always be secure on paper, but He has promised that we'll be secure in His presence.

So, as the year came to a close, I began to respond in faith. I told most of my clients that I wouldn't be working for them anymore. When they asked me why, I replied, "I'm changing my career. I'm going into ministry." The following year, I began to see myself a little differently. Instead of viewing my ministry as another source of income, I began to see it as an income sacrifice. I had thought of myself as an entrepreneur, but now I saw myself more along the lines of a missionary. My wife and I agreed on the decision, and together we prepared for a drop in income.

As I settled into the "new job," I began to find that my anxieties about running a freelance business faded. Even my worries about making enough money seemed to disappear. I was making less money and worrying less too. How was that possible? The Lord began to show me that I had peace because I was following His lead and trusting that He would provide. And, as the year progressed, I also began to witness His provision in many, unanticipated ways.

If we're worried about our finances, we need to take a step back and ask our hearts this prying question: *If Jesus asked me to sell everything and give it to the poor, would I do it? Do I trust Him enough to prioritize His will over my financial security?*

The principle of priority is found throughout the entire Bible. One of the best ways to start shifting money priorities around is to study what God's word says about provision. You won't be disappointed when you do. Here is one encouraging Psalm that speaks about the provision of God for those who know Him.

> *"I have been young and now I am old,*
> *Yet I have not seen the righteous forsaken*
> *Or his descendants begging bread."*

Psalm 37:25

The Misconception About the Tithe

I'm saving my favorite money principle for last. Before I can share that principle with you, I need to talk about fairly common misconceptions some Christians have about money. Please don't get me wrong. I'm not talking about misconceptions in order to sound judgmental or condemning. I'm talking about these misconceptions because these are ideas I used to hold fast to, and they often made me anxious. When I began to think differently about these ideas, much of my money-related anxiety melted away.

The first misconception is the misconception about the tithe, and this may be the most controversial section in this entire book. I can feel those nervous sweats coming on already—no, I'm kidding. If you search online, you can find many strong, opposing views about the tithe, but my goal in writing this is not to be purposefully controversial. I'm not writing this to tell you I'm right and you are wrong. I'm simply going to share the ways in which God has altered my thinking about the tithe over the years and how it has helped me to live a more peaceful life.

So, here it goes. When I first got saved, I began to read through the Bible, and I've been reading through it on repeat ever since. I don't consider myself a Biblical scholar, but I do believe God speaks to me through His word. Many of the principles I've been taught by different pastors and Christian teachers over the years have been confirmed through God's word, but not all of them. Sometimes, I will measure a teaching against God's word and clearly see that it doesn't align. At other times, God's word will act as a refining fire, melting away the lies I've attempted to bond to the truth. The teaching of the tithe is one of those beliefs God has used His word to slowly change in my heart.

I do hope you won't jump to conclusions and close this book. If you tithe faithfully, my goal is not to get you to stop tithing. My goal is to simply get you to examine the motivation behind your giving. However, I may say some things you don't necessarily like, so please take my words with a grain of salt. Well, maybe a block of salt.

I'm not going to overwhelm you with a swarm of evidence that tithing is not for the New Testament church. However, one point I would like to make is this: There's not much evidence in the Bible to say that tithing is for today. Now, I'm not discounting the importance of the Old Testament, but I've searched and found that there's one main New Testament scripture you could use to say tithing is still a command we need to follow as believers under the new covenant. That is found in Matthew 23:23 and Luke 11:42. Jesus is speaking to the Pharisees, and in Matthew's book He says,

"Woe to you, scribes and Pharisees, hypocrites! For you tithe mint and dill and cumin, and have neglected the weightier provisions of the law: justice and mercy and faithfulness; but these are the things you should have done without neglecting the others."

The way you can tell this passage is divinely inspired is because Jesus is talking about spicy food. That's just a pro Bible study tip I felt like sharing, but let's get back to my point. The reason He mentions spices is because the Pharisees were so detail-oriented in following the law that they even made sure to tithe off of the smallest portions of their produce. Even if they were just growing a windowsill herb garden, they would cut portions off of it and pay a tithe.

It might seem like Jesus is paying them a tribute here for their diligence, but He's not. He's making a passionate plea for them to examine their priorities. Looking past their actions and into their hearts, He points out how they followed the letter of the law but not the Spirit of the law. He even goes so far as to say that the tithe wasn't as important as things like justice, mercy, and faithfulness. So, He's obviously not emphasizing the tithe in this passage, but instead He's using it to point out the Pharisee's inability to please God through the letter of the law alone.

I understand that many people point to this verse and say, "See, Jesus told the Pharisees they should be tithing. That means we should tithe too because Jesus didn't reject the tithe." However, we do need to keep in mind that Jesus was directly addressing the Pharisees, who had been living under the old covenant, and He also says, "You should have." The past tense language indicates that He could have easily been speaking to the Pharisees but not to new covenant believers.

Let me also remind you that some people today think Jesus rejected the principle of the Sabbath and not the principle of the tithe. Jesus didn't reject the principle of the Sabbath. He simply rejected the over-emphasis of the letter of the law concerning the Sabbath. He also pointed out the nature of change He would bring to the law through His death and resurrection. I believe the same applies here. Jesus is not rejecting the principle of first fruits, yet He is not necessarily saying the letter of the law surrounding tithing still applies either.

If you study the command of tithing in the law of Moses, you'll see that the modern concept of tithing within a large portion the Christian culture isn't actually what God considered tithing at all. Based on the tithing requirements within the Torah (the first five books of the Bible), I would be surprised to find that any modern churches actually teach the law correctly. Among many other specifics, God instructed the Israelites to proportion the tithes to the Levites and priests, and yet, there are no Levitical Priests under the new covenant. So, we have essentially picked out a part of the law we liked and rejected other parts entirely. The Bible warns us about this.

So, is the solution to study the law of tithing in the Old Testament and dive full in? I don't personally think so.

There is one often overlooked passage in the New Testament that seems like it should include tithing as a command, yet it doesn't. I'm talking about Acts 15. I encourage you to read the entire chapter, but I'm going to pull out a few key verses. The chapter starts from verse 1 with someone attempting to push the letter of the Mosaic law on those in the community of believers.

> *"Some men came down from Judea and began teaching the brethren, 'Unless you are circumcised according to the custom of Moses, you cannot be saved.'"*

Verses 5 and 6 repeat this problem and inform us of the apostles' response.

> *"But some of the sect of the Pharisees who had believed stood up, saying, 'It is necessary to circumcise them and to direct them to observe the Law of Moses.' The apostles and the elders came together to look into this matter."*

The problem here is simple. Some teachers and Pharisees were beginning to teach new converts that they needed to be following all the old covenant laws (the Mosaic law) in order to be saved. Listen to Peter's response. He takes the focus off of the letter of the law, and he places the focus on the Spirit.

> *"Brethren, you know that in the early days God made a choice among you, that by my mouth the Gentiles would hear the word of the gospel and believe. And God, who knows the heart, testified to them giving them the Holy Spirit, just as He also did to us; and He made no distinction between us and them, cleansing their hearts by faith. Now therefore why do you put God to the test by placing upon the neck of the disciples a yoke which neither our fathers nor we have been able to bear?"*

> Acts 15:7b-10

Peter is essentially saying, if the Gentiles were saved by faith the same way we Jews were, then why should we try to put a burden of "works" back on their shoulders? The Apostle James agrees with Peter's statement, and he adds in verse 19:

"Therefore it is my judgment that we do not trouble those who are turning to God from among the Gentiles, but that we write to them that they abstain from things contaminated by idols and from fornication and from what is strangled and from blood. For Moses from ancient generations has in every city those who preach him, since he is read in the synagogues every Sabbath."

James says, there are four basic rules we need to share with the Gentiles, and here they are: abstain from idols, abstain from fornication, and abstain from the eating of things strangled and from blood. A little further down, James' message is delivered to the Gentiles, and the messengers describe the decision in an interesting way. They say in verse 28,

"For it seemed good to the Holy Spirit and to us to lay upon you no greater burden than these essentials..."

This wasn't just something they came up with as a group. They didn't get signatures through an online poll. This decision was made with the help and agreement of the Holy Spirit. Once again, we see the importance of the Spirit of the law, not the letter of the law.

It would have made sense to many Christians today if the Apostles had said, *You need to be teaching Gentiles to do these five essential things: don't fornicate, don't worship idols, start tithing...* and so on. Some pastors do that nowadays. A new believer asks, "What do I need to do now that I'm a Christian," and the pastor responds, "You need to start giving ten percent of your money to this church or else God is going to curse your money." Here is my question (and please know that I'm saying this with a gracious heart): How is that not doing the exact thing the Apostles were trying to avoid? That sounds a lot like a burden to me.

Remember, Jesus did not reject the principle of first fruits. My heart is not to convince you to stop tithing. If you faithfully tithe to your local church, I'm proud of you. The misconception of the tithe really has to do with our motivation behind tithing. When we choose to tithe out of fear or obligation, the truth is that we are actually not fulfilling the principle of first fruits. *What? Really?* The principle of first fruits can be categorized under the principle of priority—putting God first in every area of life, including our money. Where is this stated the clearest in the New Testament? Jesus says in Matthew 22:37:

> *"... 'You shall love the Lord your God with all your heart, and with all your soul, and with all your mind.'"*

When we choose to tithe because we're afraid of our money being cursed, we are not loving God. We are in danger of only loving ourselves. Why? Because we're giving out of a desire to be financially prosperous instead of giving out of gratitude for what God has done for us. And when we choose to tithe only because we feel obligated by a preacher or specific teaching, we are also not loving God. We are bending under pressure.

The solution is simple, and the Apostles knew it. The reason they didn't have to give the new converts any more specific commands was because they understood the nature of the new covenant. As we've discussed before, the old covenant (under which the Mosaic law and the tithe were given) was a covenant of rules. The new covenant is a covenant of relationship. One covenant focuses on the letter of the law—doing exactly what's written. The other covenant focuses on the Spirit of the law—allowing God to write His laws on our hearts.

The apostles understood that, unless God was writing His laws on the believers' hearts, they could not successfully follow those laws. The same is true for us. Unless God writes the law of first fruits on your heart, you won't receive the full benefits of tithing. In fact, it's pointless for a non-believer to tithe at all. Our decision to give back to God must be firmly based in our relationship with Him through Jesus Christ. It's a love-based decision, not a duty-based decision.

> *"Each one must do just as he has purposed in his heart, not grudgingly or under compulsion, for God loves a cheerful giver."*
>
> 2 Corinthians 9:7

Jesus gives us a clear example of a man who tithed for the wrong reasons in Luke 18. He gives us an insiders look at a certain Pharisee's prayer in verses 11 and 12. The Pharisee prays,

"... 'God, I thank You that I am not like other people: swindlers, unjust, adulterers, or even like this tax collector. I fast twice a week; I pay tithes of all that I get.'"

At the end of this passage, Jesus reveals that this man was not justified in his actions. His fasting and tithing did him no good whatsoever because he had rejected the righteousness of God that is only available through faith. He faithfully tithed, but the motivation behind his giving did not please God.

How can we know that what we purpose to give in our hearts is pleasing to God? Here's a simple answer: We ask Him what He thinks. If you want to know answers to questions like these:

How much should I give?
Where should I give?
When should I give?

...then you need to have a humble, honest conversation with the Holy Spirit. The only way to make giving a relational thing is to allow Him to speak into that area of your life.

Please don't think that I'm trying to make excuses for not giving either. My wife and I have faithfully given to our local church and in other ways since we were first married. I won't tell you exactly how much I give, but I will say that it has consistently been over ten percent of our income. The only reason I'm telling you this is so that you can hopefully see my heart behind what I'm writing.

At one point in my life, I was giving out of obligation and greed. I thought I could work the tithing system so that God would be forced to make me wealthy. The reason I give now, though, is not because I'm afraid of a curse or because I'm trying to get rich. I give now because Jesus gave everything for me on the cross. I remember the day when I was able to look at Jesus' sacrifice and say, "God, you have given me so much. What do You want me to give You in return? It can be any amount, even everything that I have."

Before moving on, I want to share a little more about where I'm coming from when I talk about the issue of tithing. I grew up with a very legalistic mindset, and I tithed for years before I ever had a real relationship with God. I like to follow the rules (unless I'm playing a card game—then you'd better watch out), and I'm naturally prone to put a lot of stock in my behavior. I was a lot like that praying Pharisee. The day I finally understood God's grace, God began to reveal how, apart from Jesus, my "obedience" was nothing more than religious tradition. Because of this, my hope now is that others will find freedom from the burden of legalism the same way I did.

> **Unless God writes the law of first fruits on your heart, you won't receive the full benefits of tithing.**

My wife had a different experience growing up. She heard about and accepted God's grace from a young age, but she had difficulty actually obeying Him. Since early adulthood, God has been doing almost the opposite work in her than He has in me. He has been helping her to fully grasp the fear of the Lord and to understand the importance of walking in obedience. When I start to lean one direction too much, my wife balances me out and reminds me that both grace and obedience are important (she also reminds me not to cheat at cards).

Grace doesn't work apart from truth, and truth is impossible to obey without grace. The reason I'm sharing this with you is because there's an important aspect of grace that many Christians miss. Grace isn't just there to cover us when we sin. It's also there to empower us to be obedient to the truth. We receive God's grace for forgiveness when we believe in Jesus as our Lord and Savior. We receive God's grace for empowerment as we are abiding in Jesus daily. Jesus says in John 15:4,

> *"Abide in Me, and I in you. As the branch cannot bear fruit of itself unless it abides in the vine, so neither can you unless you abide in Me."*

190

If you know you've been tithing for the wrong reason, or maybe you're on the other side of the fence and you have a hard time giving to God at all, you need to know that you cannot follow the principle of first fruits apart from abiding in Christ.

Some people might ask, *Aren't all the principles in this book just another form of law-following legalism?* The answer is no. The principle of first fruits along with all the other principles listed in this book are all impossible to keep apart from walking in a real relationship with God. With each principle, I've attempted to show you not only how the principle reveals an expectation or desire of God, but also how each principle relies on a real connection with God. I hope you're able to look at these principles from a non-legalistic perspective. For example, you don't have to call the principle of priority by the same name as me. The Bible never says, "Follow the principle of priority." But my hope is that, when you read the Bible with the help of the Holy Spirit, you'll clearly see how He desires to be first in all areas of life.

God never changes, but He does use different methods to relate to His people under the new covenant than He did under the old covenant. Under the old covenant, living a life of obedience looked a lot more like following a list of rules. Now, through a personal connection with the Holy Spirit, it looks a lot more like a devoted friendship. Living a life of peace isn't based on us being proficient at obeying laws, commands, or even principles. It's based on us walking close to our Savior through fellowship with the Holy Spirit.

To help make this relatable to money, I want to give you an example from my own life. Like I said, I've had a habit of tithing for most of my life. However, that doesn't mean I've always put God first in the area of money. A few years into my marriage, I remember receiving a sudden shock. I rushed to the computer to check my bank account. Yep. Just as I thought. I had forgotten to pay my tithe after depositing my latest paycheck. I remembered some teaching I had heard about first fruits, and I began to fear that my money would be cursed that month. I had been taught that, giving God first fruits meant giving Him the first ten percent of my income, before paying for or purchasing anything else. I hadn't given Him the first ten percent that time. Scrolling down the transactions page of my online bank account, I could see how my wife and I had already made some purchases since depositing that check. One of the purchases was major.

I literally began to sweat. Then anger set in. How could God expect me to be so on top of my tithing all the time in a digital age where I don't even hold my money in my hand? I felt a burden on my shoulders, and the name of that burden in my mind was *the principle of first fruits*. After quickly paying my tithe, I decided to go for a walk to calm down. As I began to stroll past the row of parked cars behind our apartment complex, the Holy Spirit spoke very clearly into my heart.

He said, "The principle of first fruits has a lot more to do with what's first in your heart than it does with what's first on the calendar." Immediately, the burden lifted. The Holy Spirit was letting me know that He knew what I had already purposed in my heart. I had devoted a certain amount of my income to God, and bills, vacations, sudden losses, and unexpected payments were not going to stop me from giving what I had determined to give. What I had not realized was how legalistic I had made my choice to give. As I allowed the Holy Spirit to shift my way of thinking to align with His, I quit worrying about the principle of first fruits, and I began to live it out in freedom.

The Misconception About the Importance of Money

One major misconception I've seen scattered through the body of Christ is the misconception about the importance of money. Money is a common sermon subject, and for a good reason. The Bible talks about money a lot, and it's one thread of life that everyone shares. Jesus Himself even talked about money. However, there is a misconception in the Christian church that Jesus talked about money more than anything else. One repercussion of this misconception is that many Christians, myself included at times (wave your hands if you're not perfect), exalt money to a place God never intended it to be. Anytime we exalt money above its rightful place, we invite worry into our hearts.

Jesus makes a profound statement in Matthew 16:5-12. He and His disciples have just crossed over the Sea of Galilee, and the disciples have completely spaced out about lunch. They've forgotten to bring bread. You would think they would still be carrying some of the miracle bread Jesus gave to the people on the other side of the sea, for this was probably not long after Jesus had fed the four thousand men. I guess the disciples had snacked it away during the boat ride? Who knows? Jesus didn't ask them where that bread went, but if He had, I guess they could have just told Him Judas ate it. *Ah. That guy. Yes, he would do that.*

Despite their lack of bread, Jesus isn't really talking about food in verse 6 when He says:

> *"Watch out and beware of the leaven of the Pharisees and Sadducees."*

Leaven is an ingredient (like yeast) used in dough to make bread rise. Because of the miracle of making bread appear out of nowhere that Jesus had performed, and because they knew they would soon be hungry since they had no food, the disciples hear Jesus' warning and assume the focus of His statement is food. They assume He is talking about physical provision. And yet, when we consider the fact that Jesus had just been tested by the Pharisees a few moments prior to this, we can be sure that Jesus is simply using leaven in an illustrative way. His focus isn't on provision; it is on the destructive teachings of the Pharisees. When it's obvious to Him that His statement flies over the disciples' heads (like a lot of the things He said—those guys were a little dense), Jesus explains in verses 8b-12 saying,

> *"You men of little faith, why do you discuss among yourselves that you have no bread? Do you not yet understand or remember*

Anytime we exalt money above its rightful place, we invite worry into our hearts.

*the five loaves of the five thousand, and how many baskets full
you picked up?...How is it that you do not understand that I did
not speak to you concerning bread? But beware of the leaven of
the Pharisees and Sadducees."*

It goes on to say that this explanation revealed Jesus' real focus
to the disciples: He was using rising bread to create a picture in their
minds of a deeper, spiritual truth about the hypocrisy of some of the
religious leaders. The reason I'm discussing the meaning behind this
verse is so I can say this: If we're not careful, we can do the same thing
the disciples did. We can read the parables of Jesus, many of which
mention money, and we can assume Jesus is really talking about
money. In reality, most of the time He's actually just using money
(the same way He uses bread) to illustrate a deep spiritual truth.

Jesus is essentially saying to the disciples, *Haven't you figured
out that this isn't about provision yet? Haven't you figured out that it's
really about the kingdom of God?*

One reason some Christians worry about money is because
we haven't realized that Jesus was not as concerned about money as
we think He was. He was more concerned about the kingdom of
God. When we take His parables and only apply them to money,
we're missing the real truth behind those parables that Jesus wants
us to apply to our lives. My encouragement to you is this: When we
stop exalting money and begin to seek God's kingdom first, we get
to experience the same peace with which Jesus walked.

Though I'm saying all this, don't forget that when we're
seeking His kingdom first, He does promise to provide. Provision is
not Jesus' focus, but it is a benefit of knowing Him. When we focus
on what He is focusing on, we can trust that He will provide, even
if that means He has to cause miracle bread (or even better, miracle
enchiladas—praise God) to show up out of nowhere.

Here are a few examples of parables that I believe we can
twist the meaning of at times:

> *"The kingdom of heaven is like a treasure hidden in the field,
> which a man found and hid again; and from joy over it he goes
> and sells all that he has and buys that field."*

> Matthew 13:44

Jesus isn't teaching about real, physical treasure hidden in a field. He's not referring to a good business opportunity or a hot stock to invest in. He purely and plainly begins His parable by saying, "The kingdom of heaven is like…" to let us know that, what follows is simply a picture He is using to help us understand God's kingdom—to help us grab hold of a deeper spiritual truth. Bread and money are common. They are easy for people in every era to relate to. Jesus is simply making the concepts concerning God's kingdom easier for us to grasp.

The parable of the talents begins in a similar way. Look at Matthew 25:14-15.

"For it is just like a man about to go on a journey, who called his own slaves and entrusted his possessions to them. To one he gave five talents, to another, two, and to another, one, each according to his own ability; and he went on his journey."

Jesus starts this well-known parable by saying, "For it is just like…" The question we must ask here is: For *what* is just like? Directly before this parable is the parable of the ten virgins, which Jesus begins by saying,

"Then the kingdom of heaven will be comparable to ten virgins…"

Matthew 25:1a

Many preachers use the parable of talents as a basis for teaching on money. They teach that Jesus is trying to tell us that God wants us to grow our money while here on earth. And yet, when you look at the spiritual truth behind the parable, it's easy to see that Jesus is using this story to illustrate a deeper spiritual truth that really had little to do with money. He is using a story about something common like money to teach us about God's expectations involving our role in His kingdom here on earth. Jesus tells us that the kingdom of heaven is within people, and through this parable, He is teaching us not to wait until we get to heaven to invest in that kingdom. We should be using the gifts, talents, and resources God has given us here on earth to share the gospel and build up the body of Christ. That's what His kingdom is really about.

I'm not trying to say that money is a bad thing to have. I'm also not condemning good business practices and financial success. I'm trying to show you how some of us have traded Jesus' focus for our own focus. We've looked at His parables through the lens of greed, and it has impacted the way we've interpreted them, causing us to miss the real truth behind Jesus' words.

It seems like some Christians worry about money just as much as unbelievers, and God doesn't want His children to be stricken with worry. However, we'll never break free from the worries of money if we don't break free from the love of money.

I believe one of the reasons some people dwell on the money passages in the Bible so much is because adults must be concerned with money. There's no getting around it. Every adult is forced to learn how to earn, save, and spend money to some extent. Do you know who's not so concerned with money? Children. When I hand my young kids a five-dollar bill, I find it on the floor ten minutes later. It has probably been scribbled on or used to wipe snot away. I've explained the value of money to them, but their minds quickly get distracted by things they deem more important. The kingdom of God is never going to feel valuable to our flesh, and our flesh relates most easily to our learned, adult mind. Money feels valuable to our fleshly side because it's tangible. We've learned its value. When we have it, we can do good things like putting food on the table and buying the things we need. We can even use it to bless others. When we don't have enough of it, we suffer.

When we are seeking God's kingdom in a childlike way, our mindset is similar to the way my children see money; however, there is a slight difference. Seeking God's kingdom first doesn't mean we devalue money, but instead it means we understand the full value of the kingdom. The kingdom is something our flesh won't ever value. It's only through our spirit that we can truly see its worth. When we see the value of the kingdom, it draws our focus. Here's one way of saying it: To a spiritually-focused mind, money is literally not worth worrying about.

There was a young girl who worked harder than she had ever worked painting her parent's garage. It took her half of her summer to move all the junk out, clean the floor and walls, get her paint supplies ready, and then meticulously paint the walls. She wanted it to look perfect. After that, she did the same thing to the outside. When her parents looked at the garage several weeks after she had started, they were so impressed that they paid her even more than they had originally agreed upon. It was the most money the little girl had ever seen.

The next day, the mother watched the little girl empty her money box into her purse. Her older sister gave her a ride to the store so that she could spend her money. She came back without having purchased anything. She told her mother that she just hadn't found what she really wanted yet.

A few days after that, the little girl walked into the house carrying a dirty ole rock. Her parents said, "Don't bring that rock to the dinner table. Leave it outside." She told them about how she had met an old man in their neighborhood and how he had sold her this rock. "You paid money for a rock?" They couldn't believe it. "How much?" She told them that it cost all she had. You can imagine how

We'll never break free from the worries of money if we don't break free from the love of money.

furious her parents were, and they were determined to march her back to that old man and demand her money back.

What they did not foresee was the girl's response. She cried out, "No! I love this rock! Don't make me take my rock back. I earned that money myself and I wanted to spend it on this rock." Perplexed, the parents hesitantly allowed her to keep her rock. They couldn't understand why she would waste her money on something of so little value.

After that, the little girl went everywhere with her rock. It was almost like a doll to her. She loved that rock. Then one day, while she was skipping down the sidewalk, she lost hold of her rock. It flew out of her hands, and it burst open on the sidewalk. Inside her rock was found a priceless gem, worth more than she could have earned if she had painted garages for the rest of her life.

What the parents did not know was that, when the man had sold her the rock, he had told her of it's hidden value. Like a trusting child, she had believed him.

This is just a story, but it illustrates the way some of us view God's kingdom. We look at the money in our hands and consider it the most important. The kingdom of God holds no immediate value to our adult minds. It's like a dirty ole rock to our flesh. But within God's kingdom, there is a priceless treasure that can only be found when we seek it out with the heart of a child. The good news is, when we learn to value Jesus' kingdom the way He values it, not only do we discover the eternal worth attached to the kingdom, but our temporary money problems are taken care of too.

There are many more parables in which Jesus talks about money, and He nearly always uses money as an illustration to explain the kingdom. Don't just take my word for it, though. I encourage you to go read the money parables. Study them. Look at the context, and see for yourself.

Jesus clarifies His view of money in Matthew 6:19-21.

"Do not store up for yourselves treasures on earth, where moth and rust destroy, and where thieves break in and steal. But store up for yourselves treasures in heaven, where neither moth nor rust destroys, and where thieves do not break in or steal; for where your treasure is, there your heart will be also."

I'm not trying to be controversial. I'm especially not wanting to attack any pastors or teachers who have used Jesus' parables to teach practically on the subject of money. There are people who I've heard teach this way who I have a lot of respect for. It's not wrong to talk about the practical money-management principles within Jesus' teaching. Money is still an important, relevant topic that needs to be discussed within the church. However, if we want to understand Jesus' teachings to their full extent, we must be willing to acknowledge the actual focus of those teachings.

When we learn to stop exalting money to a higher place than God intended it to be, and when we choose to seek His kingdom first, we can stop responding to money problems with worry. We can begin to respond with a steady confidence that our loving Father is providing everything we need.

The Misconception About Our Dreams

If you're thinking, *I don't want to hear any more misconceptions. I want to hear about God's amazing provision,* just hold on a little longer. There's one more benefit, which I think is the greatest money benefit of all, that I'm still going to discuss. However, in writing this book, I'm doing my best to listen to the leading of the Holy Spirit. I know He has given me specific truths to talk about, and I can't skip this one in good conscience. The final misconception I'll cover is the misconception about our dreams.

Earlier in this book, I talked about the prophet Jonah and the story of him running from God in disobedience. Instead of delivering God's message of repentance and mercy to the people of Nineveh, he takes a boat in the other direction. Let's head out to sea once more with this wayward prophet as we start reading in Jonah 1:4.

> *"The Lord hurled a great wind on the sea and there was a great storm on the sea so that the ship was about to break up...But Jonah had gone below into the hold of the ship, lain down and fallen sound asleep."*

> *"Then the men became extremely frightened and they said to him, 'How could you do this?' For the men knew that he was fleeing from the presence of the Lord, because he had told them."*

Jonah 1:4 & 5b,10

When we catch up with our bro, Joe, we see that he's asleep below deck, and the desperate crew is scrambling to keep the ship from sinking during a violent storm. What they don't realize until Jonah tells them is that they're fighting a God-sent storm meant to get Jonah's attention. I used to assume this storm to be God's judgment upon Jonah, but when you read the full story, it actually looks a lot more like a storm of grace. God could have easily chosen to sink the ship, but the storm is His way of giving Jonah a second chance—a chance to turn back to Him.

I'm going to get creative for a second, so hang on tight. Maybe grab the ship railing or something? While the storm rages above deck, Jonah is dreaming, wholly unaware of the spiritual forces at work around him.

Some of us have done something similar to what the running prophet chooses to do. We've exalted the idea of fulfilling our dreams to a place where we've been willing to board a ship and head out to sea without consulting God. In His mercy, God has sent storms to warn us, but we're still dreaming away. We're still pursuing our dreams. I've watched some Christians chase their dreams for decades, only to wind up thwarted at every turn. Their lives resemble the persistent coyote, who's always chasing after the roadrunner but never catching it. Because they aren't willing to admit that God could have a different plan for their life than they do, they are ignoring the evidence that God Himself has blocked their path. His storm of mercy is constantly there telling them to turn around, but they keep pressing toward that dream.

The same way that I'm not trying to condemn money, I'm also not telling you that all dreams are bad. Many dreams are God-given. However, as good as dreams are, they can also be a detriment to our relationship with God and the fulfillment of our purpose if we seek them with the wrong motivation.

If there is a burden God has placed in my heart for His people, it is the burden of motivation. The reason I believe it's so critical is because God doesn't look at the outward appearance. He looks at the heart. His version of success looks different from ours. Here's what I mean: Jesus didn't ask us to live our lives as best we can for Him. He asked us to give our lives up for Him. That requires us to give God permission to replace our imperfect desires with His perfect desires.

Are you willing to allow God to shift your motivations to line up with His? If God presented most Christians with two buttons, one that said, "Give my life up for the sake of Jesus," and another that said, "Spend my life chasing after my dreams," most Christians would choose the button that led them toward Jesus. What we don't realize is that we are given that same choice every single day. You're not going to reach a single pivotal point of no-turning-back in your life where you can hear the angels singing and see the light of heaven pointing you down the right path. Giving up our lives for Christ's sake is not a one-time, monumental decision. You and I are making that decision every morning when we wake up. When our motivations are right—

when the love of Christ is abiding in our hearts through the help of the Holy Spirit—that's when we'll be consistently making the right decision. It's our motivation that leads our actions.

I know Jonah may not have been actually dreaming while asleep below deck. That's just a creative analogy. However, Jonah was chasing a dream-like fantasy when he stepped on that boat. He had made the assumption (consciously or not), that he could find a life worth living apart from obeying God. If he hadn't, he wouldn't have run away. We've all made that same assumption at one time or another. I can admit that I've been guilty of this, even after starting my ministry. I've ignored the storm and kept hoping God would make everything work out. It took me a while to learn that dreams are good, but they won't carry God's favor unless they are being dreamt within the context of His plans and in the vicinity of His presence.

God sends the storms because of His mercy. If you're walking through one right now, remember that His mercies are new every morning. Every time we wake up, we can receive His grace afresh. My encouragement to you today is to wake up from any dreaming outside of His plans. God created you for a reason, and He loves you. He loves you so much that He sent Jesus to die for you. Trust His plans, because He is trustworthy.

What if I feel like the dream I have is given to me from God, though? Sometimes, trust means being willing to wait for the right timing. When I was in middle school, I wanted to be in the Olympics. Practicing gymnastics every week, I dreamt that one day I would be skilled enough to compete at an international level. At the age of fourteen though, I gave up and I quit. When I began to follow Christ my sophomore year in college, I remembered the work I put into my gymnast training. I remembered my dreams. I literally cried over the fact that I felt like I had wasted my skill and ambition, but then the Holy Spirit began to encourage me that He could still use those talents. So, I started to pray that God would create an opportunity for me to use my skills. I also began to make plans to move to Hollywood and become a stunt-man, but the more I thought about that specific dream, the more I knew God was telling me it wasn't a good idea. I'm actually really glad I'm not jumping off of buildings for a living now.

At the end of my junior year in college, I walked into an all-girls meeting organized to discuss the potential of starting a cheerleading team at the university. The coach walked in, introduced herself, and then said, "First, I have to ask, what are *you* doing here?" She pointed directly at me, and I naturally blushed. About three dozen girls looked at me, probably wondering the same thing. Breaking out in an embarrassed sweat, I gathered my courage and responded, "I was wondering what the chances were of starting a guys team, too."

Because I showed up to that meeting, I got to play one year of college sports (unless you don't consider cheerleading a real sport, in which case, you might change your mind after trying to lift someone over your head and hold them there for five minutes). During the season, I got to tumble down the court regularly during basketball games. At the end of the year, I realized that I no longer felt like my years in gymnastics were wasted. More than that, I saw how God used that season to open up opportunities for His kingdom. Here's one example: I became friends with one of the young men on the cheer team, and through that friendship, I was able to witness to him and share the love of Jesus with him while he walked through the aftermath of some terrible mistakes.

I know this chapter is about money, but I told that story because I want to illustrate the fact that, God can use your dreams within the context of His plans if you're simply willing to surrender those dreams to him. Surrendering our dreams to Him means more than just praying about them, too. It means prioritizing His will in our hearts, and it also means being willing to wait patiently upon Him until we hear a specific word from the Holy Spirit about those dreams. Here's one way of saying it: God-given dreams can only truly be fulfilled by God Himself.

Oftentimes, the area of life in which we allow our dreams to lead us astray the most is the area of making money. One reason is because some of us believe that if we just had enough money, we could finally make the rest of our dreams come true too. The problem is, if we find our dreams apart from God, we aren't able to fully enjoy them. If we grasp our goal apart from God, we won't be able to hold onto it.

"Many plans are in a man's heart, but the counsel of the Lord will stand."

Proverbs 19:21

You and I can never really be happy if we never let go of the idea that money is the thing that is going to make us happy. Remember, Jesus said it's those who lose their life for His sake that truly find it.

If you've made plans that haven't worked out, I encourage you to embrace the mercy of the storm. Even if you've wound up in a state of disappointment, God can use the place you are right now for His glory. Many of us cry out to God when things don't go our way financially, but how often do we take the time to ask Him what He wants to show us through the trial?

Sometimes, hardship and disappointment can be the junctures God uses to turn our eyes toward Him. Our souls are composed of our mind, will, and emotions. Many of us dream about what we want (with our mind), diligently work to get it (with our will), and then get all bent out of shape when we lose it (with our emotions). We put so much hope into the object or idea we desire that our souls are left in despair when it goes away.

Do you remember what King David said when he found himself in a place of disappointment and despair? I quoted this at the start of this book, but I want to remind you of his beautifully honest words. In his desperation, he called out to God, saying,

"Why are you in despair, O my soul?
And why are you disturbed within me?
Hope in God, for I shall again praise Him,
The help of my countenance and my God."

Psalm 43:5

David was so distraught that he started talking to himself! Yet, he was reminding his mind, will, and emotions to put their hope in the only person who would never let them down. Money is going to eventually let you down, but God won't.

> **You and I can never really be happy if we never let go of the idea that money is the thing that is going to make us happy.**

When you feel like you're at the end of your rope—like there's no reason to keep hoping something good will happen, shift your hope. Turn your eyes to the one who Himself is good. We were made to experience God's love, kindness, and friendship. The reason you and I start putting our hope in money is because we're missing out on the fulfillment our Father wants to freely give us. There's nothing wrong with desiring good things, but don't put all your hope into them. Set your eyes on Him. Praise Him. Even when all your plans have gone awry, His counsel will stand.

The Benefit of Contentment

I know the previous section may have been hard to read. If it was, hopefully this section is more pleasant. You may also be asking the question, *How can I practically transfer my focus from money to God?* Because money is so central to daily life, this can be a difficult thing to do. I understand that feeling. That's why I saved what I consider the best money principle for last. God has outlined a clear path to finding contentment in His word: It's the principle of living with a generous heart.

Principle: Generosity
Benefit: Contentment

The flesh and the world will say, *The more you give, the less you have to enjoy.* God's word says, *The more you give with the right motives, the more you enjoy what you have.* Paul shares the secret to his lifestyle of contentment in Philippians 4:11b-13.

"I have learned to be content in whatever circumstances I am. I know how to get along with humble means, and I also know how to live in prosperity; in any and every circumstance I have learned the secret of being filled and going hungry, both of having abundance and suffering need. I can do all things through Him who strengthens me."

Now, you might be thinking, "Generosity isn't the key to contentment in this verse; the key is Jesus." You're absolutely right. There's a principle behind every principle in this book and it's simply this: You can do all things through Jesus Christ who gives you strength. Every one of God's principles are based in relationship. However, even though Paul connects his contentment directly to his relationship with Jesus Christ, he also takes it a step further. Immediately after this, he begins to talk about how the Philippian church has been financially generous with him, which reflects the way he has been generous in devoting his life to the preaching of the gospel. Look at what he says in verses 15 and 16.

"You yourselves also know, Philippians, that at the first preaching of the gospel, after I left Macedonia, no church shared with me in the matter of giving and receiving but you alone; for even in Thessalonica you sent a gift more than once for my needs."

Paul speaks about his own generous lifestyle, and then he assures the church that, while he was preaching the gospel, his needs were met (specifically by them). He flips the spotlight from himself to them when he goes on to explain the results of their generosity.

"Not that I seek the gift itself, but I seek for the profit which increases to your account. But I have received everything in full and have an abundance; I am amply supplied, having received from Epaphroditus what you have sent, a fragrant aroma, an acceptable sacrifice, well-pleasing to God. And my God will supply all your needs according to His riches in glory in Christ Jesus."

Philippians 4:17-19

The Philippians' generosity excites Paul, not because he is the recipient of their money, but because he knows what rewards they will receive for being generous for the sake of Christ. He makes them a simple promise, saying that God will provide everything they have need of.

Let me say it another way. When the Philippians chose to be generous, God took on the role of being their provider. With God as their provider, they didn't have to worry about the stresses and anxieties of themselves being the providers anymore. They could now rest. Paul had been leading up to something the whole time. He was using their own generosity as a prime example of what it's like to find contentment in Christ.

The reason many of us worry about money is because the mantle of provider is on our shoulders. We can't find contentment because there's always that nagging question in the back of our minds that asks, "What if there's not enough?" or "What if I made a poor financial choice?" or "What if I made a mistake in buying that second mini-fridge?" I'm not saying God wants you to be unwise with your money (so, yeah, the spare mini-fridge might be a bad idea). He just wants you to stop worrying about it, and that is able to happen when He takes responsibility over it. When you choose to respond to the gospel with a heart of generosity, God promises to take on the role of provider, and you can let those fears and worries fall into His hands.

One important distinction to make is the difference between simply giving money away and real, Biblical generosity. Anyone with money can seem generous, but not everyone who gives is going to receive the benefit of contentment. As I mentioned earlier, the key is found in our motivation. Why are we giving? In another verse, Paul strengthens the connection between generosity and a genuine relationship with Jesus.

> *"The point is this: whoever sows sparingly will also reap sparingly, and whoever sows bountifully will also reap bountifully. Each one must give as he has decided in his heart, not reluctantly or under compulsion, for God loves a cheerful giver."*
>
> 2 Corinthians 9:6-7 (ESV)

Paul's words echo the famous words of Christ: "give and it shall be given." Paul takes it a step further though as he examines the motivation behind giving. Our generosity should stem from the love of God that's been poured out in our hearts through the Holy Spirit. We get to receive that love because of what Jesus did for us on the cross. When we give based on what Jesus gave as He bled and died for us, we give out of love and gratitude, not duty. In fact, Paul says we shouldn't be giving out of obligation at all.

When I used to hear about giving with a cheerful heart, I would soon after attempt to add cheerfulness to my giving. Even though I had a creepy, fake smile on my face while I gave, I was still giving out of obligation. The answer is not to try to be cheerful. The answer is to go back to the source of why we do what we do.

The principle of generosity picks up where tithing left off. Though giving was commanded in the Old Testament through the tithe, the New Testament actually starts from a place of greater generosity. It gets past the letter and into the heart of the issue. The Old Testament looked forward to God saving His people. The New Testament looks back at the fulfillment of that promise. When you've taken hold of the truth of everything God has done for you through the cross, my personal belief is that you won't want to give less than what the letter demanded. I'm not saying you need to be there now. However, the more we allow the Lord to shift our desires and motivations, the more our hearts will begin to naturally overflow with the Spirit of the law, which is a Spirit of generosity. That's when giving truly becomes a freeing, joyful experience.

The year before I devoted myself to part-time ministry, my freelance video and design business hit its peak. A few new clients and some major projects combined to bring me into my most profitable year to date. My wife and I were enjoying the extra income, but a desire also rose inside us to be extra generous with the blessing God had given us. We weren't suddenly rich, but we had more than we were used to.

So, as the year progressed, the Holy Spirit began to ask me to give. On three separate occasions, He asked me to give what I considered extravagant cash gifts. We gave one gift to our local church and two other gifts to people in need. Each time we gave, I sensed my level of contentment growing. In fact, the more I gave, the more I wanted to give. I kept thinking about Jesus' willingness to give everything for me. I wanted to have a willing heart no matter how much God asked me to give.

As the next year started, we looked forward to the birth of our third daughter. My wife and I had gotten used to sharing a single car between the two of us, but it would be too small for a family of five. About a month before her due date, we put our savings toward the cost of a larger vehicle.

Then, right after buying the car, I received a sudden shock. Because of my self-employment status, I had been making quarterly tax payments to the IRS. Most normal employment situations allow workers to have their taxes taken directly out of their paychecks, but as a sole proprietor, I had to estimate my own taxes and keep up with the payments. Up to that year, I had always saved enough money to make those payments on time. However, I suddenly realized a quarterly payment was due in two weeks, and I couldn't pay it.

Besides purchasing a car, we were making monthly midwife payments, and we had run into several other unexpected costs prior to our daughter's birth. I felt foolish for not staying aware of the upcoming payment. Later on, I found out that a late estimated tax payment would probably only incur a moderate fee, but at the time I dreaded it due to my lack of experience. In my ignorance, I began to panic. I needed to make a $2,000 payment in exactly two weeks, and I didn't have the money.

I had two checks coming in that month. A check for hourly contract work would cover our monthly bills. A second check from a contract video project would cover our living expenses. Beyond that, I didn't expect any other income.

In my anxiety, I began thinking back to everything we had spent money on, trying to figure out where I went wrong. Because my wife and I are both very frugal, we hadn't wasted much money on unnecessary purchases. In fact, the largest recent expenditures, besides the car, were the three monetary gifts we had given that previous year. I looked at the tax payment due date on the calendar. I thought back to those gifts, and for a moment I began to regret my generosity.

The day after I found out that we owed $2,000 we didn't have, I complained in my mind to God. I essentially said, *Why did You let me give that money last year? It would have more than covered what I owe now.* The Holy Spirit didn't see things the same way. He began to show me that, even though I had given out of faith the previous year, I wasn't walking in faith now because I was regretting being generous. I quickly remembered that anything not done in faith is sin. So, I repented for my complaints and doubt, and I asked God to help me walk in faith.

That same day, my wife and I prayed together, and we asked God to provide. I told God that I believed He had asked me to give those gifts, and I told Him I did not regret honoring Him in that way. I was glad to have given the money. If Jesus gave everything for me, then in reality everything I possessed belonged to Him. I wanted to trust Him with what He had asked me to do.

Then, I took it a step further. I asked God to specifically give me $2,000 before the tax payment was due. Yes, it was a crazy prayer, but I prayed it while standing on God's truths about generosity and while choosing to trust God as my provider.

I prayed that same prayer every day, and after one week had passed, I completed the contract video project. Thankfully, it was immediately approved, and I quickly asked if they were ready for the invoice. The message I received back blew me away. They said something most clients would never say in a million years. They told me to go ahead and add an extra $2,000 to the invoice. I read the message three or four times. I could hardly believe it.

I kept thinking, "Add $2,000 to the price of the project after it's completed? Who does that?" Then it dawned on me who would do something like that: God would.

Proverbs 11:25 lets us taste the results of generosity when it says,

"The generous man will be prosperous,
And he who waters will himself be watered."

The original language used for the word prosperous actually implies that the generous person will have more than enough to eat. If you've ever been without food or water for a while, you know how difficult it is to be satisfied until those needs are met. When we catch hold of the principle of generosity, God promises to satisfy our deep longings. We finally are able to put that glass of refreshing water up to our lips, drink it in, and rest in contentment.

Adjusting the Giving Motivation

A prayer that you and I can't pray enough is this: *God give me a heart of generosity.* Giving a gift is not the same as having a heart of generosity. We sometimes want to run out and change our actions instead of taking the time to wait upon God, asking Him to change our hearts first. Generosity is a heart issue more than a hand issue. It's easy to focus on the work aspect of it—what we can do. But generosity starts with allowing God to change the way we see money. When it stops being about what we can do, and becomes all about what Jesus did for us, is when we're truly able to give with a cheerful heart.

I've mentioned two common motives for giving: fear and greed. As Christians, God doesn't want us to be motivated by either. Like I said before, my wife and I give over ten percent of our income back to God, but I give for a different reason than I used to. I used to tithe out of the hope that God would make me rich. I didn't know it at the time, but I was giving with a greedy heart (hence the creepy smile). Other times, I've tithed because I didn't want God to curse my finances. At those times, I gave out of a heart of fear.

Both greed and fear sell us short when it comes to living a generous life. Greed steals our rest and joy because it often causes us to work too hard to get more. Fear steals our rest and joy because it tells us that, no matter what we do, we'll never have enough. The devil is the author of both these lies, and the purpose behind his deception is to cause us to take our eyes off of Jesus. He wants to shift our focus so that we live with the wrong motivation.

Some of us have believed a simple lie about money, and it is working to destroy our chance at finding contentment. The lie is this: If we're not rich, we're doing something wrong as Christians. The truth is that God doesn't say He wants every believer to be rich the way we might define it. I know some preachers say this, but the Bible just doesn't teach that. It teaches contentment. It teaches provision. It even teaches blessing. However, as much as some of us would like it to be, the "prosperity gospel" isn't the real gospel. Yes, Psalm 35:27 does say that God "delights in the prosperity of His servant." But the key question is: Who are you serving? If you or I are following after God so that we can get rich, we're a servant to money, not God.

If God makes you rich, there's nothing wrong with that. But don't put your hope in wealth. Put your hope in Jesus. He can give you joy, rest, and contentment no matter what physical blessings you have or don't have.

Some of us are already blessed, but we're trading the real blessings God has given us in an attempt to obtain more monetary blessings. Our relationships with our family and friends are suffering because of how devoted we are to building wealth. Please don't confuse contentment with apathy either. I'm not making an excuse for laziness. Real contentment doesn't set a limit on future blessings; it simply allows us to enjoy what we have right now. When we are not content, always striving for a greater blessing, it's impossible to fully enjoy the ways in which God has already blessed us.

Many people will say, if you want to be content, you need to count your blessings more often. I don't believe that's necessarily true. As soon as we start to focus on our possessions, we often begin to compare what we have with what others have. It's part of our nature as humans. We start playing the comparison game. The answer isn't to measure our blessings. The answer is to measure the value of the cross. Keep allowing the Holy Spirit to remind you of the vastness of God's love which Jesus poured out for you on that hill.

I know talking about generosity can raise a lot of specific questions in people's minds. Here's a common one: *What if I don't have the ability to be generous because of a lack of finances?* I obviously can't specifically answer all the questions you may have, but I can tell you where to find the answers. To know how much God desires you to give, you've got to hear it straight from Him. God might not ask you to give all you have, but believe me, whatever He asks you to give will feel like a step of faith.

Even if you don't have much, you can give something out of faith, and the more clearly you hear the Holy Spirit leading you, the easier it will be to give. The same way He asks those who have plenty to walk with a heart of generosity, I believe God asks those who have almost nothing to still be generous. He desires all His children to live by faith. Greed and fear say, *There won't be enough to go around.* Faith says, *God can give me exactly what I need when I need it.*

In Luke 21, Jesus is observing the religious rulers and wealthy Jews giving out of their abundance. They throw in large purses full of money. To those standing around, it may seem like the leaders are being extremely generous, but Jesus knows their hearts. He knows that, deep down, their giving isn't an act of faith. Then, along comes a destitute widow. Jesus and His disciples watch her throw in two meager coins. Listen to Jesus' response to her gift.

> *"...Truly I say to you, this poor widow put in more than all of them; for they all out of their surplus put into the offering; but she out of her poverty put in all that she had to live on."*

Luke 21:3-4

Real contentment doesn't set a limit on future blessings; it simply allows us to enjoy what we have right now.

Can you imagine what it must have been like for that woman to let those two coins fall from her hands? Everything inside of her would have been saying "no," but she was looking to God in faith and saying "yes."

I'm not perfect when it comes to money, but my prayer is that God would bring me to a place where I am willing to lay down every possession I own for the sake of His kingdom. What I've learned is, the more I let God make me like that widow, the less I worry about money. Sure, it sounds silly. But that's the way God wants things to be in His kingdom. He wants us to become like children, and when we do, we can be content sitting in the lap of our Father.

If a spark of joy doesn't rise inside of you when you think about the generosity of the widow, I encourage you to start daydreaming about something better than money (and I'm not talking about cheesecake, either). Start dreaming about eternity. My hope every time I give is that, when I get to heaven, someone will say, "I'm here because your gift helped provide a way for me to hear the gospel."

I want to share in the joy and faith of the churches of Macedonia that Paul writes about in 2 Corinthians 8:1-2.

"Now, brethren, we wish to make known to you the grace of God which has been given in the churches of Macedonia, that in a great ordeal of affliction their abundance of joy and their deep poverty overflowed in the wealth of their liberality."

I encourage you to read the entire chapter, but these few verses paint a beautiful picture of people who had little and yet gave much. Even though they were in need, their joy in giving didn't stem from the idea that they might receive a financial return. They gave out of the overflow of God's love within their hearts.

I used to treat the money principles in God's word like a formula, but relationship is not based on a formula. All the principles in God's word are based on aspects of His character— they help us to know Him better. Your money is not simply a test of how good you are at following rules (though God does use it to test our hearts at times). It is first and foremost an opportunity to grow deeper in your relationship with God. Through our money, God is asking us the question, "Do you trust Me? Do you really believe I am who I say I am?"

We talked about limiting the benefit of grace through disobedience in the previous chapter. We can also limit the benefits of provision and contentment through greed. When we exalt money above God in our hearts, we put up our hand against God's blessing on our lives. This warning in 1 Timothy 6:6-11 speaks directly to this issue.

"But godliness actually is a means of great gain when accompanied by contentment. For we have brought nothing into the world, so we cannot take anything out of it either. If we have food and covering, with these we shall be content. But those who want to get rich fall into temptation and a snare and many foolish and harmful desires which plunge men into ruin and destruction. For the love of money is a root of all sorts of evil, and some by longing for it have wandered away from the faith and pierced themselves with many griefs. But flee from these things, you man of God, and pursue righteousness, godliness, faith, love, perseverance and gentleness."

The good news is that, when we prioritize God above money, He is then able to pour out the benefits of His grace He's been longing to give us the whole time. This isn't an easy transition, and it takes a lot of trust. But it's worth it. If money has a hold on you, I have a simple plea to make: Flee from these things child of God. God desires you to walk into the blessings of living a life of provision and contentment. When you're pursuing God first and trusting Him as your provider, you can release that grief of anxiety which has been trying to plunge you into ruin and destruction. When mixed together, godliness and contentment are great things to gain.

Walking Into the Promised Land

My goal throughout this chapter has not been to shame you, but rather, I pray that you are able to begin walking boldly into the promised land God has mapped out for you. Before we move on, I want to discuss some of the subtleties to successfully walking into the promised land in the area of your finances.

Caleb and Joshua are two people in the Old Testament often associated with a walk of faith. God called the Israelites to take the promised land, and while all the other spies doubted God's ability to lead them into victory over their enemies, Caleb and Joshua believed God. By faith, they made a good report of the land, pleading with their fellow Israelites to fight for what God had said was theirs. Though this is one of my favorite stories in the Bible, and though we can learn a lot from the faith of these two men, it's also possible to use stories like this in a way God never intended them to be used.

At one point, I envisioned financial success as my personal "promised land" that I thought God wanted me to take by faith. I thought, if I just have enough faith, I can claim the wealth my heart desires. At that time, I was missing two important truths.

The first truth I missed was the fact that Caleb and Joshua's faith was based on a specific promise from God to them. They weren't just believing really hard that their dreams would be fulfilled. They had heard from God, and they were simply believing what He had said. When you and I try to move forward in "faith," and that faith is only based in a strong personal desire, we are going to be acting in our own strength.

Some of us have a misconception about what faith is. It's easy to assume faith is equivalent with wanting something bad enough or focusing hard enough on a desire. Neither of those things are true Biblical faith. True faith is always rooted in what God has said. Walking in faith means believing and acting out His will. It has a lot more to do with what God wants than what we want.

A lot of us want to be Joshua and Caleb in the promised land, but we're not willing to act like Joshua and Caleb in the wilderness (and I'm not talking about going forty years without a shower). My point is: They weren't seeking after their own selfish desires. They were seeking after God Himself. We sometimes try to forge our way into this "promised land" mindset, but have we stopped and asked God what season we're actually in right now?

One reason "name it and claim it" teachings are popular in some circles is because they have the appearance of a faith-filled way of life. Speaking in faith is found all throughout Scripture, but we need to keep in mind that God never gives us control. He maintains control. He does give us authority through Jesus Christ, but that authority is only valid while we are acting under His authority. We can name our blessings and claim them all day long, but if we are operating outside of His authority, then we're on our own to make it happen. My encouragement to you is to seek God while in the wilderness and find out where He really wants to take you. Once God gives you a specific direction for your finances through His word and the voice of the Holy Spirit, then you can pray and even speak that in faith.

One thing we need to keep in mind is this: Joshua and Caleb, despite their faithfulness, could not shorten the length of time they were in the wilderness. Similarly, I believe God takes us through seasons of wilderness financially to teach us contentment. God is more concerned with us learning to be content than He is with us learning to prosper financially. God could hand us a million dollars tomorrow if He wanted to, but He can only make us content through our participation and willingness to be changed by Him. There are many discontented, wealthy people in the world. That's because riches can come in a variety of ways. Contentment can only come through abiding in Christ.

This leads me to the second truth I missed when I was trying to forge my way into a financial promised land. I missed the fact that God's version of the promised land looks different from mine. Money can bring temporary happiness, but greed ultimately steals our contentment. Without contentment, the happiness that money brings quickly fades. A greedy heart can help fill our financial bank account, but it pokes holes in our happiness bank account (that's not a real thing, but you get the idea). It's an endless cycle. We get what we want, we are temporarily happy, the happiness leaks out, we think more will make us happy, and then we gain more and find out it still doesn't satisfy. Contentment is the seal that stops the leak.

God's version of the promised land isn't necessarily a life overflowing with money. His version is a life overflowing with the fruit of the Spirit: love, joy, peace, patience, kindness, goodness, gentleness, faithfulness, and self-control. You and I both know there's only one way to enter this kind of promised land. Paul knew the secret, and he shares it with us in Philippians 4:11-13. I quoted the New American Standard Bible translation earlier in this chapter. I want you to read this verse one more time, yet this time I'm using the Contemporary English Version, which may be a little easier to apply.

I believe God takes us through seasons of wilderness financially to teach us contentment.

> *"I am not complaining about having too little. I have learned to be satisfied with whatever I have. I know what it is to be poor or to have plenty, and I have lived under all kinds of conditions. I know what it means to be full or to be hungry, to have too much or too little. Christ gives me the strength to face anything."*

This verse has been used to support many financial decisions and dreams, but we need to understand that Paul wasn't talking about investing. He was talking about knowing how to be content in any situation. Please also note that Paul isn't at all implying that we would normally be content when there's plenty. He's saying, we'll

216

never be content with a lot *or* a little unless we know what he knows about contentment. The key he reminds us of is simple: We can do all things through learning to abide in our Savior. He relied wholly on the friendship He had with the Sustainer of all life.

To be content, we've got to learn how to preach the gospel to ourselves in the good times and bad. More than that, we've got to learn how to hear the Holy Spirit preaching the gospel to us every day.

"Make sure that your character is free from the love of money, being content with what you have; for He Himself has said, 'I will never desert you, nor will I ever forsake you.'"

Hebrews 13:5

When God promises not to desert us, He's not talking about making sure we always have a sentimental memory to hold onto the day we got saved or the day we were baptized. He's talking about His presence abiding with us in the middle of the wilderness.

I told you about the Lord asking me to step out in faith and begin to dedicate myself to ministry part-time. After dismissing several of my clients, I prepared myself for a significant drop in income, and I also experienced a significant drop in anxiety, too. For a while, I enjoyed an overwhelming sense of relief.

I knew living with less than what I had been used to wouldn't always be easy, but I kept thinking about how little it compared to the suffering Jesus went through for me. God had done so much for me. A drop in income was nothing when I really thought about it. He was asking me to be generous with my time and resources, and I wanted to say "yes" with everything inside me. However, I also took solace in the idea that it would be a temporary financial setback. I assumed God would replace my income within a few month's time, and I told myself I could wait at least that long. A year later, I was still getting to the end of each month with just enough money to take care of my family. Because it was taking longer than I had expected to grow support for the ministry, I began to doubt.

Even though I constantly prayed about it, I still worried whether or not God was actually planning on providing. Month after month passed by, and He seemed to be taking His precious time. One night while I waited for Him during my quiet time, the

Holy Spirit spoke specifically to me in my spirit, saying, "Read the Bible. What you read tonight will answer your questions exactly. You won't know the future, but you'll have peace where you are."

Naturally, I got excited. Flipping open my Bible, I started reading in Exodus 16 where I had last left off. Verse 2 caught my attention.

> *"The whole congregation of the sons of Israel grumbled against Moses and Aaron in the wilderness."*

As I read this verse, I suddenly saw a clear picture of my own attitude. God had led me into a wilderness, and I had responded with discontentment. Because I didn't know where provision would come from, I had been grumbling in my heart. I had done what the Israelites did in the desert (except that I had been taking regular showers). Then I came to verse 4 and my perspective began to change.

> *"Then the Lord said to Moses, 'Behold, I will rain bread from heaven for you; and the people shall go out and gather a day's portion every day, that I may test them, whether or not they will walk in My instruction.'"*

Most people know that the Israelites walked through the desert for 40 years as a punishment for their disobedience. But did you know that God had already planned on sending them on nearly a 2-year march through the wilderness simply to test them?

Numbers chapter 9 tells about the beginning of the Israelites' second year in the wilderness. After constructing the tabernacle of God by His specifications, the presence of God fell upon the tabernacle as a cloud by day and a fire by night. Following that event, the Israelites wandered through the desert, not knowing where or why they were going. They simply stopped and set up camp when God's presence stopped, and then they moved when He moved. It wasn't until after this period of time that the spies went into the promised land and returned with an unfavorable report.

God's initial desire for sending His people into the wilderness, and one reason why they had to stay there so long, is clearly stated in Deuteronomy 8:2.

"You shall remember all the way which the Lord your God has led you in the wilderness these forty years, that He might humble you, testing you, to know what was in your heart, whether you would keep His commandments or not."

God sent His people through a wilderness time in order to test them. As I read Exodus 16 that night, I realized that God was testing me and my wife to see if we would, not only take a faith step in working on the ministry part-time, but also continue to take steps of faith on a daily basis through our personal wilderness. He was checking my heart to see if I would follow His presence through the desert or not. He was seeing if I would really trust Him to provide. Though I had failed to take it into consideration, God had actually already been providing the whole time. No, we didn't have any excess, but we had not gone hungry. Despite the decrease, our needs had been fully met, sometimes in unexpected, manna-like ways. What I was really complaining about was the fact that I couldn't see further than the next step. I couldn't see where the provision would come from next, and I had missed the fact that God had done that for a reason.

In verse 6 of Exodus chapter 16, we see the reason behind the test.

"So Moses and Aaron said to all the sons of Israel, 'At evening you will know that the Lord has brought you out of the land of Egypt.'"

God tests us to essentially ask us the question, *Is My salvation enough? Would you still be content if all I ever did for you was bring you up out of Egypt?*

God brought the Israelites out of the country called Egypt. God brings you and I out of a spiritual type of Egypt. The same way the Israelites were physical slaves, you and I were spiritual slaves to sin. Moses, though a real person in history, also acted as a shadow of the One who would eventually deliver the world from their sins. The question God was asking me that night was, "Is Jesus enough?" I believe He is.

As you read the following passage, I encourage you to concentrate on the principles and misconceptions I talked about in this chapter. See Jesus' desire for generosity, His focus on the kingdom, and His promise of provision.

> *"Do not store up for yourselves treasures on earth, where moth and rust destroy, and where thieves break in and steal. But store up for yourselves treasures in heaven, where neither moth nor rust destroys, and where thieves do not break in or steal; for where your treasure is, there your heart will be also. The eye is the lamp of the body; so then if your eye is clear, your whole body will be full of light. But if your eye is bad, your whole body will be full of darkness. If then the light that is in you is darkness, how great is the darkness! No one can serve two masters; for either he will hate the one and love the other, or he will be devoted to one and despise the other. You cannot serve God and wealth. For this reason I say to you, do not be worried about your life, as to what you will eat or what you will drink; nor for your body, as to what you will put on. Is not life more than food, and the body more than clothing? Look at the birds of the air, that they do not sow, nor reap nor gather into barns, and yet your heavenly Father feeds them. Are you not worth much more than they?"*

Matthew 6:19-26

God fulfills His promises, but His promises don't always look the way we want them to. Pure, unselfish, Biblical trust is where true peace comes from. God wants us to trust Him to deliver us, but He doesn't always deliver the way we want Him to. Walking in peace means learning to trust Him for whatever kind of deliverance He wants to give us. We must learn to trust in His eternal character above our temporary situation.

When our trust is in His words, His character, and His Spirit, we can confidently say, "Even if God doesn't deliver me now, He has already delivered me from sin, and He will deliver me into a better place for eternity." That's what it looks like for our hope to really be set in Jesus as our Deliverer. That's when we can truly stop worrying about our money and find lasting contentment.

- 8 -

STOP WORRYING
ABOUT
RELATIONSHIPS

If you looked at the level of my relationship-based worry over the course of my life and turned it into a graph, you would see a line that looked like a rollercoaster. As a young child, I didn't worry much about my relationships because I was naturally self-centered. A little later in my childhood, I began to worry about my parents' relationship due to overhearing their arguments. At that time, I thought my worry stemmed from my love for them. I didn't realize it, but my anxious concern still had a selfish motivation. I didn't want them to fight, and I wanted them to stay together. But I mostly wanted those things for my sake.

Upon entering high school, I gained some supposed "significance" by my academic and athletic accomplishments. With my newfound sense of importance, I no longer needed my parents to help me feel secure. As such, I stopped worrying about their relationship altogether. Then, when I developed a crush on a girl in my class (who became my lovely wife over a decade later), I started suffering from some of the common worries that follow romantic desire and rejection. However, by the time I reached college, I'd let my heart become so callus and bitter because of rejection, I no longer worried about romantic relationships. You could call me a little dramatic, maybe?

Halfway through college though, I found Jesus. I thought knowing God would help me not to worry about others, but I actually found myself worrying more! Where I had previously lacked real concern, I now genuinely cared about what happened to other people in a way I never had prior to that. The layers of selfishness began to peel away. I suddenly cared about the romantic interests I had hurt. I suddenly cared about the people I interacted with each day. I started to worry about whether my friends were saved or not. I started to worry that I would make the wrong relationship choices and that other people would suffer because of my actions.

I know I'm talking a lot about the problem right now. Literally just writing all this down has caused me to want to start worrying about it!

To be truthful, my relational experiences have been far from the worst, though. Some people's emotional rollercoaster of life looks like it was constructed by a team of trained apes who were working with a limited budget and without coffee. If you feel like that describes a relationship you've experienced, the good news is coming.

The reason I'm describing the areas in which I've worried about relationships is because I'm hoping to create a connection in your mind. I'm praying you will be able to recognize where in your life you tend to worry about other people and why.

I believe we often shelve our worries about people into the closet of "care" in our minds. We label our worries as healthy concerns when in reality they aren't always healthy. Love, commitment, genuine concern, and emotional connection are good, but worry isn't. As much as it promises to help, it's not helping. It's hurting.

You may actually be surprised how little I've talked about worry through the course of this book. The reason is because I know the danger of dwelling on the problem too much. The truth is that, when we spend all our time focusing on the problem, we inadvertently glorify it. My hope throughout this book and especially in this chapter is to get you to focus on Jesus. Only He deserves the glory, and only your relationship with Jesus can help you stop worrying about your relationships with others.

The reason I saved this chapter for last is because all the principles in God's word won't do you any good apart from a healthy relationship with Him. Though we often try to, we cannot reduce the Holy Spirit to a principle. Sure, He doesn't change, and His word remains true. Even if you feel disconnected from His presence, you can always rely on knowing the principle for a time, so the principles are necessary. But the goal should be His constant presence—intimacy with Him. When you are intimate with God through faith in Jesus Christ, the Bible says you're going to naturally obey the law the Holy Spirit has written on your heart. You'll be walking in the benefits of knowing Him, not because you're always focused on following commands or principles, but simply because you know Him.

So, yes, I'm going to cover a few more principles in this chapter, but my hope is that you'll take away more than principles from this book. My hope is that a deep hunger for God's presence and voice has stirred inside your heart. I'm praying that you've already connected with the Holy Spirit in a deeper way than ever before. My imploration to you is to stay connected.

Do you remember how I talked about our works not being what God is after? He's really after our belief—our hearts. Although work isn't what He's after, it does come into the picture. Martha was busy in the kitchen, working away to prepare everything for Jesus' stay. Sitting at the feet of Jesus, Mary had chosen to put the kitchen duties off till later. However, Mary would still have to work even while sitting there

Only your relationship with Jesus can help you stop worrying about your relationships with others.

at Jesus' feet. She would have to work at not getting distracted by other things. She would have to work at pursuing Him personally.

We cannot work hard enough to please God with our actions. It's our belief in Jesus that pleases Him. However, sometimes pushing the doubt out and grabbing hold of belief takes a little work. It takes a willingness to continue sitting at His feet. It takes a decision to keep following after Him on that wilderness road.

The amazing result of pursuing Christ is that, when our relationship with Him is right, it positively affects every other relationship. Jesus wants the love we share with Him to overflow out of our hearts and into the lives of every acquaintance, friend, family member, and spouse.

The Benefit of Courage

One major cause of anxiety in our relationships is our fear of what others think. We dread what people might say or do, and many of us make choices based on that fear. Maybe we're not honest with our spouses because we're afraid of them blowing up. Some of us won't talk about the gospel with our unsaved friends because we worry they won't like us anymore. We say "yes" to too many requests because we're scared of letting people down. If any of these examples sound the least bit familiar, you need to know that there is a Biblical secret to living a fearless life: An unhealthy fear of others will always be overcome by a healthy fear of the Lord.

> *"But the Lord your God you shall fear; and He will deliver you from the hand of all your enemies."*
>
> 2 Kings 17:39

Principle: The Fear of the Lord
Benefit: Courage

The fear of the Lord is a phrase I believe many people have used as an excuse not to get to know God in an intimate way. I get it, too. Why would you want to know someone you have to fear all the time? Throughout my childhood, there were adults I never really wanted to get to know because I feared them. But the truth is that cultivating a healthy fear of the Lord actually breaks the dividing walls down between you and Him. For this idea to make sense, we must have the proper definition of the fear of the Lord in mind. When the Bible talks about fearing God, it's not talking about fearing God the way you would fear a dangerous person. It's not talking about fear rooted in anxiety. Because of the subtlety behind the phrase, I want to give you three ground rules to help explain the Biblical meaning of the fear of the Lord.

The first ground rule of fearing God is to value His truth. This may be the easiest aspect of the fear of the Lord for most people to understand. Valuing God's truth means respecting and living by His standards. It means admitting, not just that God has a different way of doing things but that His way is ultimately the best way. We see the connection between healthy fear and truth in Psalm 86:11.

> *"Teach me Your way, O Lord; I will walk in Your truth; unite my heart to fear Your name."*

When the psalmist talks about fearing God's name, He is directly relating God's name to God's truth. Let me say it this way: Do you approach God with the understanding that His truth is the ultimate truth in the universe? If so, that is a sign that you fear God.

One of the signs that someone doesn't fear God is that they attempt to explain away specific truths from His word. For example: Some people in the Christian church have rejected the idea that hell exists simply because they don't like the idea of a loving God letting people go to hell. It doesn't fit within their idea of what God should be like; so they attempt to explain away the hundreds of verses about hell in Scripture, many spoken by Jesus Himself.

An unhealthy fear of others will always be overcome by a healthy fear of the Lord.

The problem with rejecting or ignoring parts of Scripture is that we have made our own standard the basis for truth instead of God's standard. God is loving, perfect, merciful, compassionate, and good. His word is also true. The hard-to-swallow truths in God's word do not fight against His character. They simply show us how little we really understand the depth of His character.

So, how can we start accepting hard truths that we don't understand? I can give you three answers. First, we must choose to accept God's words in faith. Many of the truths in the Bible won't make complete sense to our natural minds while we're on earth. Paul actually tells us that God's truths can only be understood through the help of the Spirit (see 1 Corinthians 2:14). If we really believe that, we must be okay with taking spiritual truths from God's word purely in faith, even if we don't fully understand them right now. Oftentimes, I've found that God asks me to be obedient before He explains the reason behind the request.

Second, we must choose to believe in God's character even when it's hard. God says that He is love. He also says that unbelievers will spend eternity apart from Him. When we trust in His character, we can say, "I don't understand how that works, but I still believe that God is love, so I know it ultimately does work." We must learn not to distrust God's character simply because we can't fully comprehend it.

Third, we have to learn how to take our unbelief straight to God. When we have a hard time believing a specific truth, we need to learn to be honest with God about it. The Holy Spirit can give us specific revelation and hope even when our natural minds have difficulty grasping a truth. The closer we are to Him, the more He will personally help us see the truth from His perspective.

My own misunderstanding of God's truth kept me from experiencing a real relationship with Him for years. I believed in God's perfect standard, but I didn't understand the grace of God available through Jesus. At that time I was only receiving partial truth, and my twisted perspective of God caused my fear of Him to develop into a severe dread.

To fear God, we must accept the truth of His standard and the truth of His grace at the same time. Because God is perfect, we must be righteous to know Him intimately. However, because our righteousness is based on God's grace and not our performance, we don't lose intimacy when we make a mistake. You can lose the good opinion of others in a heartbeat depending on what level of mistake you make, but you never have to be afraid of losing God's acceptance when you are walking in the truth of the gospel. That knowledge should cause courage to rise in your heart.

The second ground rule for walking in the fear of the Lord is to value His voice. This is where the fear of the Lord becomes personal. To value someone's voice, you must decide that what they say matters. Something I've said to my kids at times is: "I wouldn't have said it if it wasn't important." Let's look at something similar that God says through the prophet Samuel. (It's nice to know God can relate to my parenting struggles—oh, thank heavens!)

> *"Samuel said, 'Has the Lord as much delight*
> *in burnt offerings and sacrifices*
> *As in obeying the voice of the Lord?*
> *Behold, to obey is better than sacrifice,*
> *And to heed than the fat of rams.'"*

1 Samuel 15:22

This is where we see that valuing God's truth alone isn't enough. We must also value His voice. If you're wondering what the difference is, here's a weird example that should help. Let's pretend I believe the Bible proves the existence of aliens (I don't actually believe that, so calm down, heresy hunters). Pretend with me that I had been listening to a teaching about outer space, science fiction aliens being in the Bible. The teacher made such a compelling argument that they began to convince me. If I valued God's truth (which was the first ground rule), then I would go read the Bible and find out for myself what it says about this subject. Starting to skim through the pages of the Christian Standard Bible, let's say I came across Exodus 12:49, which says,

> *"The same law will apply to both the native and the alien who resides among you."*

Let's pretend I looked at that verse and said, "There! That proves that aliens exist." In my mind, I still valued God's truth because I was using Scripture to back up my belief. However, I would not be valuing His voice. If I was reading this while listening to the voice of the Holy Spirit, He would be gently pricking my heart, convicting me about misinterpreting this verse to fit my own beliefs.

This is a silly example. That word "alien" in this passage is obviously talking about foreigners, and if you read a few other translations or look at the original meaning of the words, you'll see that. But I believe we can do this in much subtler ways by reading the Bible in order to add "truth" to a belief we already hold instead of reading the Bible in order to shape our beliefs. Anyone can read the words of Scripture, but only those who are willing to hear from the Holy Spirit will be consistently interpreting it correctly.

I know that no one is perfect. I don't hear from the Holy Spirit perfectly every time. He speaks perfectly; I'm just not always listening. I'm still in process, and I need His grace just like anyone. However, a track record of correct interpretation requires us to value His voice.

As I've mentioned earlier in this book, the Holy Spirit also can speak to us about specific issues in our lives, such as giving us direction about a career path. Hearing from Him in that way also requires us to value His voice.

During my senior year of college, I started dating a young woman I liked and was good friends with. Though we had only dated for a short period of time, we started talking about marriage. She didn't want to keep dating me if we weren't intending to get married, so I gave into pressure and said that I was planning on marrying her. In my heart, I thought this was true, but I hadn't prayed about it. I hadn't prayed about dating her at all.

Soon after that, I came down with a sudden sickness. For two weeks, I lay in bed, battling a high fever off and on. Only leaving the house to collect my homework assignments or take a few tests, I began to feel exasperated that the sickness had hung around for so long. Finally, I began to ask God why I was sick. As I lay there, waiting on God, I began to hear the words the Holy Spirit had probably been trying to say to me for weeks. He said, "I want you to break up with her."

I remember fighting with Him after He said this. I couldn't break up with her. I wanted to be married, and I liked being with her. I didn't realize at the time that a lot of my motivation for getting into the relationship had been fear-based. I was afraid of not finding a wife by the time I graduated college. On top of that, I reminded God that I had already told her I wanted to marry her. I dreaded what she would say or do if I changed my mind.

Then, I began to think back over the few weeks prior. A slow but steady anxiousness had been growing in my heart, and I knew it stemmed from the relationship. God had shared the knowledge that I wasn't supposed to be dating her in my spirit, but I had been ignoring it. Trying to keep from admitting my mistake had worried me sick—literally.

Finally, I consented to do what God said. I asked her to come over. She sat down next to my sickbed and I told her we needed to break up. Her response scared me. I don't know if I've ever hurt someone so badly in my life. When I tried to explain, she didn't understand. However, I knew God had spoken.

The confirmation that I had listened to the voice of the Holy Spirit came almost immediately. Less than five minutes after she left my room, I sat up in bed, feeling completely well. I had been suffering only minutes before, and suddenly the feverish sickness vanished. I got up, took a shower, and went about my normal activities.

I would like to make a quick side note here. I don't believe God made me sick to punish me. As I talked about in the chapter on divine healing, Jesus already took the full punishment for our sins on the cross, and God is a just God. He will not lay a punishment upon believers that was already laid on Jesus. However, just because Jesus offers us forgiveness and its benefits, that doesn't mean we're always choosing to accept those benefits. When I chose not to value the voice of the Holy Spirit, I was putting up my hand against God's benefits. I was rejecting His peace and choosing to trade it for anxiety, and that anxiety built up until it made me a sick person.

I had prayed for healing, but God hadn't healed me. Instead, as I started listening to Him, He gave me a revelation (something else I talked about in the divine healing chapter) into the reason behind the sickness. As I began to value His voice, I received the knowledge about my situation I had needed the entire time. Not only that, but knowing He had spoken gave me the courage I needed to go through with a difficult breakup. Sure, I was afraid of how my girlfriend would react, but when I began to act in the fear of the Lord, I stopped allowing my fear of her to control me.

When we value the voice of God to the extent He deserves, it will almost be like we're afraid of not hearing what He has to say. We will fear (in a healthy way) moving forward without His input. The good news is that, when we get this principle down, we also receive the benefit. Courage comes when we receive a specific word from the Lord—either through the Holy Spirit's personal revelation of Scripture or through His still quiet voice in our hearts.

It seems like everyone has their own opinion about what decision you should make. Godly counsel can be good, but you don't have to allow the pressure of others to push you into making the wrong decisions. You can listen to and take into consideration the opinions of others, but you don't have to be controlled by those opinions. When you hear the Holy Spirit's voice, you have a firm truth to stand on despite how other people try to make you feel. Even when people call us crazy, if we're doing what God asked us to do, we can walk with courage because we know God is pleased. We can rest in delighting Him.

The year prior to writing this book, I began to receive this simple word from the Lord: "Clear your schedule." I didn't know why God wanted me to clear my schedule, and I didn't know exactly what that meant, but I knew that I was going to do it.

Around that same time though, I signed up to volunteer with our home church's youth group. I had volunteered in the same way in the past, and I signed up again because I felt like I wasn't helping out enough at church. Less than two weeks into volunteering, a constant anxiety began to grow inside of me. If I was volunteering out of my desire to serve the Lord, why was I worried about it? Then, the Holy Spirit reminded me of the word He had spoken, "I want you to clear your schedule." I tried to ignore it, but that just made the anxiety worse.

Finally, I had to admit the reason behind ignoring Him. I had valued the opinion of others more than I valued His voice. I knew other people expected me to serve, and I didn't want to let them down. I was giving the fear of people more influence over me than the fear of the Lord.

I had to go to the youth pastor, who happened to be my brother-in-law, and explain things. He completely understood my reasons. In fact, he supported them. For that next month, I still didn't understand why God wanted me to clear my schedule, but I tried to say "no" to any extra commitments. As the next year started, the Holy Spirit spoke to me again and told me that it was time to write this book. The idea for this book came years prior, but now I had the confidence and courage I needed to write. And, thanks to the leading of His voice, I had enough time in my schedule to write, too.

We see an example of the courage the Holy Spirit provides during the day of Pentecost in Acts.

"And when they had prayed, the place where they had gathered together was shaken, and they were all filled with the Holy Spirit and began to speak the word of God with boldness."

Acts 4:31

When the Holy Spirit speaks, you can move forward with a supernatural boldness. It's not just the Holy Spirit's voice that gives us courage, though. The third ground rule to fearing the Lord is to value His love. Look at how these two psalms speak about the fear of the Lord.

"The Lord favors those who fear Him, those who wait for His lovingkindness."

Psalm 147:11

"Oh let those who fear the Lord say, 'His lovingkindness is everlasting.'"

Psalm 118:4

Some people have a hard time accepting the fear of the Lord because they can't possibly see how we can fear God and love Him at the same time. *If God is supposed to be loving, why would He want us to be afraid of Him?*

Fearing and loving God is a little like falling in love. Before you fall in love, you don't have any idea what people mean by that phrase. When it happens though, you suddenly get it. It's different from what you thought it would be.

Fearing God is not a fear of punishment (a truth stated in 1 John 4:18). It's more like a fear of losing the one you love. When you truly love someone, you value them above all else. You would rather lose anything else than lose them. When you truly fear God, you love Him so much that you would rather lose anything else than lose the nearness you have with Him.

I need to make a critical distinction between a healthy fear and an unhealthy fear. A healthy fear of God is not a selfish fear. It doesn't ignore the possibility of personal hurt, but it also takes into consideration the other person in the relationship. A healthy fear of the Lord causes us to have a deep concern for protecting God's heart from our sin.

Keep in mind, I'm not talking about trying to hide sin from Him (because we can't and shouldn't try to), but instead I'm talking about repenting, turning away from it, and choosing to do things His way.

The reason valuing our loving relationship with God in this way gives us courage is because, when we draw near to Him, He also promises to draw near to us (see James 4:8). The more we reach out to connect with Him, the more love the Holy Spirit is able to pour out in our hearts.

It's not that God's love for us is reliant upon our love for Him. In fact, the opposite is true. He loved us long before any of us loved Him. But when we connect with Him, we are able to more fully experience the amazing love He has already given. When His love is filling our hearts, fear has no place. The same fears that others face, we won't even consider worth our time. Look at the amazing perspective a person who fears the Lord gets to live with:

> *"You are not to say, 'It is a conspiracy!'*
> *In regard to all that this people call a conspiracy,*
> *And you are not to fear what they fear or be in dread of it.*
> *It is the Lord of hosts whom you should regard as holy.*
> *And He shall be your fear,*
> *And He shall be your dread."*

Isaiah 8:12-13

When we have a healthy fear of God, we don't have to fear anything else. As Proverbs 28:1 says, we can be bold like a lion because of our righteousness in God's eyes. When we're not experiencing that courage, we need to examine where we think our righteousness is coming from. Are we trusting in our own works or are we trusting in Jesus' work on the cross? The best way we can learn to value God's love is to return to the cross. Remember how God poured His love out for you, and allow it to affect you every day. Don't limit the effect of His love on your heart. Embrace it.

In times of fear, some people quote courage-building verses like Joshua 1:9, Psalm 31:24, Romans 8:31, but just quoting verses like those doesn't guarantee we'll receive the courage we need. As amazing as those verses are, they won't be of much help if we're not practicing the fear of the Lord. Just because we're valuing God's help doesn't mean we're necessarily valuing His truth, voice, and love.

One way we reject the fear of the Lord without realizing it is by allowing non-believers too great an influence in our lives. We do this by listening to gossip or rumors from friends, but we can also do this by spending too much time soaking up the news media through the paper, television, or internet. The more credit and importance we give to the world's opinions, the more we take on their fears. The truth is, child of God, you are not meant to fear the same things the world fears. You don't have to worry about those things. God speaks this directly to His people in Isaiah 51:12.

> A healthy fear of the Lord causes us to have a deep concern for protecting God's heart from our sin.

"I, even I, am He who comforts you.
Who are you that you are afraid of man who dies
And of the son of man who is made like grass,"

The fear of the Lord is a lot better than some Christians assume. When we have a healthy fear of God, we walk in courage because His Spirit becomes the source of our comfort. The world is always talking about the trouble *out there*, but God wants to make you fearless within. Then, instead of being influenced by the fearful opinions of others, you get to influence people with the hope you have in Jesus. You get to live as a light shining in the darkness.

The Benefit of Peace

Comparison with other believers breeds more anxiety within the church walls and church body than possibly anything else. Have you ever allowed the blessings another Christian receives make you feel less-than-blessed? Instead of wearing a scripted-font t-shirt with the word *blessed* written across the front, some of us should be sporting some *not-as-blessed-as-them* apparel. Sorry for a lame play on words, but if the shirt fits, you know what it's like to suffer from the lie of comparison. Yes, comparison is a lie. It's a lie rooted in envy that can eat us up on the inside. We tell ourselves that the feeling is motivating us to do better or work harder, but it's really just stealing our peace.

Well, thankfully God has a cure for the curses of comparison, envy, jealousy, and strife. God's answer is found in Ephesians 4:1-3.

> *"Therefore I, the prisoner of the Lord, implore you to walk in a manner worthy of the calling with which you have been called, with all humility and gentleness, with patience, showing tolerance for one another in love, being diligent to preserve the unity of the Spirit in the bond of peace."*

Principle: Unity
Benefit: Peace With Believers

I remember my dad speaking to me and my siblings one night when we were young. He told us he wanted us to take care of each other when we grew up. I never forgot that phrase. I thought, "Why would he feel the need to tell us to take care of each other? Of course we are going to do that." Then it hit me. *There must be siblings who don't take care of each other. Maybe there are siblings who grow up and never speak to each other again.*

God created the family to work as a unit—together in unity. In a healthy sibling relationship, you don't walk around jealous or envious. You support and root for one another. You rejoice in their success and lift them back up when they fail. When we become believers in Jesus, we enter God's family. Romans 8:29 actually talks about Jesus being the firstborn among many brothers. When God calls us brothers and sisters in Christ, His intentions for us to walk in unity are clear.

To understand unity in the body of Christ, we must understand the phrase "preserve the unity of the Spirit in the bond of peace," which we just read in Ephesians 4. If you've ever heard someone preach on unity, you've probably heard about *the bond of peace*, but what is it exactly? Let's look at Paul's words a little earlier in the same book.

> *"remember that you were at that time separate from Christ, excluded from the commonwealth of Israel, and strangers to the covenants of promise, having no hope and without God in the world. But now in Christ Jesus you who formerly were far off have been brought near by the blood of Christ."*

Ephesians 2:12-13

Paul is specifically addressing the Gentiles (non-Jews) in this verse, and he is explaining the union of God's family that occurred when Jesus died on the cross. Before the cross, the Jews were God's chosen people to whom God had given His laws. In a sense, the Jews held the keys to pleasing God through the law of Moses. The Gentiles did not (though God still made ways for them to know Him). That's why Paul says they were strangers to the covenant and living without hope. When Jesus died on the cross, He offered the righteousness of God to anyone who believes in Him. Unless you have Jewish heritage, you are a Gentile like me. We were brought near to God through Jesus' death. We were able to enter God's family because of the blood that flowed out of Jesus' body. Paul continues to say,

> *"For He Himself is our peace, who made both groups into one and broke down the barrier of the dividing wall, by abolishing in His flesh the enmity, which is the Law of commandments contained in ordinances, so that in Himself He might make the two into one new man, thus establishing peace."*

Ephesians 2:14-15

The bond of peace is Paul's way of saying that the cross holds us together. Paul is specifically writing about peace between Jews and Gentiles, but these truths also directly apply to every person who believes. Paul even says that Jesus Himself is the peace between believers. In verse 18, he reaches what I consider the critical point in his argument.

> *"for through Him we both have our access in one Spirit to the Father."*

To enter God's presence, we are first required to be made clean. We need the blood of Jesus to wash our sins away before we can stand before God at peace with Him. When we are walking in disunity with another believer, even if they have wronged us, we are claiming to have more of a right to stand in God's presence than they. But the problem with this claim is that we all come into His family and His presence holding on to the same cross. We all have to admit, "Without the cross, I couldn't be here." In that moment, the Holy Spirit is able to remind us: *That believer you've been angry with, or that believer you've been unable to forgive, they came into My family the same way. They're holding on to the same cross you are.*

When we reject unity with another believer, we are ignoring the fact that Jesus is standing between us, grasping each of us by the hand.

I need to interject a few side notes. Just because you choose to walk in unity with another believer, that doesn't mean they are always going to walk in unity with you. You can't control their actions. You are only responsible for your own choices.

Also, it's important to realize that not every person who attends church is a true believer. Some preachers are wolves in sheep's clothing, as the Bible says. Some "Christians" are deceived, having rejected the truth of the gospel, and no matter how hard you try, you won't be able to walk in unity with them. This is another reason why personally hearing from the Holy Spirit is so important. The Holy Spirit can speak directly to us and give us wisdom about where other people are spiritually. However, just because you think you know someone isn't saved doesn't give you a right to be constantly angry at them or hold unforgiveness toward them. If someone doesn't know Jesus, we should immediately go into mission-field mode. Perhaps our willingness to forgive them, even when they don't deserve it, will reveal the love of Jesus to them in a way they've never seen before.

In fact, it's because of unbelievers that Satan exerts so much effort toward breaking the unity between believers. He knows that, the more unified we are, the more we will be able to shine the light of Christ to the world. He also knows that, the less unified we are, the more the world will have an excuse not to listen to us. Jesus says the world will know us by our love for one another (see John 13:15). If we aren't loving each other, then we're not being the witnesses God has called us to be.

So, if unity is so critical, then how can we practically improve in this area? This is where worry and anxiety actually help us. No, I'm not saying that worry and anxiety are good things. However, when we're paying attention to the source of our anxious thoughts, we can narrow down the real issue. Like I said, comparison is one of the most destructive forces against unity. The lie that comparison preaches often sounds like this: "Why do they get to have that new car? I've been faithful in my giving for years." It will say, "Why did the pastor ask them to serve in leadership? I'm more spiritually mature than they are." I could go on, but I bet you get the picture. When someone else has something that we want, we often get anxious about not having it. When we are willing to admit where those anxious thoughts are coming from, we can begin to deal with the real problem.

Jesus told a story about some people who had a similar problem with comparison. We know this parable is about believers because Jesus prefaced it by saying, "the kingdom of heaven is like." The parable of the laborers in the vineyard in Matthew 20:1-16 is one I encourage you to read, but I'm going to sum it up briefly.

In the story, a landowner went to town and hired people to work in his vineyard for the day, and he agreed to pay them a certain amount for their labor. He went back to town a few hours later, and upon finding more people to work in the vineyard, he agreed to pay them a day's wage. He hired even more people a few hours after that, and even more a few hours later. At the end of the day, he paid everyone the same wages.

The people who had worked all day long were furious. When they saw the others receiving the amount they had agreed to work for, they had at first assumed they would receive even more. It felt unfair to them to be paid the exact same amount for more work. Hear the landowner's words at the end of the parable:

> *"Is it not lawful for me to do what I wish with what is my own? Or is your eye envious because I am generous? So the last shall be first, and the first last."*

Matthew 20:15-16

When you think about the reason the men were angry, it's obvious they were envious. They wanted to be paid more per hour, like those who were hired towards the end of the day were. At the least, they would have preferred the comfort of only having to work for a few hours for the same pay. How often do we complain in a similar way, saying, "God, why do they get that blessing?" The real problem with the complaint is not in our desiring something, because it's not always wrong to desire things. The problem is that, when we desire something enviously, we essentially tell God that we're ungrateful for what He's already done for us.

It's important to keep in mind that the parable of the labors is not about how much work you are doing. It's more about your heart. The last laborers would have been speechless—extremely grateful for the undeserved blessing. The first laborers, even though they were blessed too, saw the work as a burden instead of a blessing. If they had not been hired at all, they might have stood out in the marketplace all day, dying of anxiety. They could have been thinking, "My family is going to starve because no one will hire me." They were blessed by the work they had been given, but they could not enjoy it because of their attitude. They were focused on what they were earning—what they deserved—and they had lost track of the fact that they really deserved nothing as they stood there in that marketplace.

As I mentioned in the previous chapter, Jesus often uses money in His parables to paint a picture of a spiritual truth. The payment in this parable doesn't represent a new car or a better job. It first and foremost represents the primary benefit of knowing God: salvation. On top of that, it could also represent crowns and rewards in eternity (and possibly on earth). Even if it represents other rewards too, it doesn't change the fact that our salvation outweighs any and every other benefit God gives us. When we allow the voice of comparison to cause disunity in our hearts, we are inadvertently letting God know that we are ungrateful for the gift of His grace.

Don't lose out on the joy of the gift. No matter how hard you've worked for the Lord, everything you have is still a gift. It's not deserved. Jesus earned your peace for you on the cross. The reward of walking into those heavenly gates, running up to Jesus, giving Him the biggest hug in the world, and elatedly leaping up and down before the Father (or whatever we'll do when we enter God's presence in eternity) is going to be so much greater than any blessing we could receive here on earth. When we allow envy, jealousy, or unforgiveness to enter our hearts, we are looking at our life through the wrong lens. We're missing God's perspective and allowing Satan to give us a perspective of division.

The reason I mention Satan is because he has a lot more to do with disunity among believers than we would like to think. Paul makes this clear later on in Ephesians when he tells us that our battle is not against flesh and blood (6:12). The battle you're in isn't really a battle with another believer. It's not a battle with your pastor. It's not a battle with your spouse. It's a battle against spiritual forces. It's easy to assume the source of our anxiety is another person, but though they may be involved, they are not the root cause. There is a spiritual enemy who is fighting, not just against you, but also against another believer you feel like you're at war with. Even if you haven't admitted it, you and that other believer are both fighting the same enemy.

When you're in a spiritual battle, you have to fight the battle from a spiritual perspective. The good news is that, through the cross, God has given us authority over the forces of evil at work against us.

> *"For though we walk in the flesh, we do not war according to the flesh, for the weapons of our warfare are not of the flesh, but divinely powerful for the destruction of fortresses. We are destroying speculations and every lofty thing raised up against the knowledge of God, and we are taking every thought captive to the obedience of Christ."*

2 Corinthians 10:3-5

239

Paul says that, to win the spiritual battle, we've got to address anything that raises itself up against the knowledge of God. We've got to trade the lies of fear, comparison, anger, jealousy, and envy for the truth. The truth will allow us to take captive our thoughts and walk in obedience to the will of our Savior, and it's His will that we live in unity.

So, to win spiritual battles, is there a specific truth we need to know? God's word is His revealed truth to us, but Jesus Himself is also called *the Truth*. Paul reminds us of Jesus' critical role in the transformation of believers at the end of Ephesians 2.

> *"...Christ Jesus Himself being the cornerstone, in whom the whole building, being fitted together, is growing into a holy temple in the Lord, in whom you also are being built together into a dwelling of God in the Spirit."*

No matter how hard you've worked for the Lord, everything you have is still a gift.

Our spirits walk in obedience when we are connecting with God's Spirit through Jesus. Jesus is the foundation on which everything else is built. He is the reason we can know God personally. By now, you've heard me say this about fifty times in this book. The reason I've said it so much is because, even though we know this deep down, Satan's main scheme is to draw our attention away from this truth. If He can't get us to reject the truth, he will try to get us to focus on a lie. He doesn't like seeing believers walking in peace and freedom. He likes to see us bound up, and so he comes up with every lie possible to distract us from the amazing truth of the gospel. My hope is that, when you're done reading this book, you won't get distracted any more. My prayer for you is that you would clearly see the importance of sitting at Jesus' feet the way Mary did—that you would fall so much in love with the person of Jesus that you wouldn't be able to go a day without spending time in His presence.

Paul says, the entire body of Christ should be constantly getting more and more unified as we learn to allow God's Spirit to dwell among us. In nearly every chapter he writes in the New Testament, Paul does the same thing I've been trying to do throughout this book. Have you ever noticed how often he talks about Jesus? He literally sounds like a madman who can't help repeating himself at times, but it's very purposeful. He constantly brings the Christian back to the simple truth of relationship.

Peace between believers is a benefit of knowing God. We make ourselves receptors of His benefits when we seek Him in faith, learn to sit at the feet of Jesus and wait, and allow Him to remind us of everything good He has done for us on the cross. In this way, our personal relationship with God directly affects our relationships with other believers.

Paul sums up the key to unity in Ephesians 4:20-27 and 32.

"But you did not learn Christ in this way, if indeed you have heard Him and have been taught in Him, just as truth is in Jesus, that, in reference to your former manner of life, you lay aside the old self, which is being corrupted in accordance with the lusts of deceit, and that you be renewed in the spirit of your mind, and put on the new self, which in the likeness of God has been created in righteousness and holiness of the truth. Therefore, laying aside falsehood, speak truth each one of you with his neighbor, for we are members of one another. Be angry, and yet do not sin; do not let the sun go down on your anger, and do not give the devil an opportunity."

"Be kind to one another, tender-hearted, forgiving each other, just as God in Christ also has forgiven you."

The Benefit of Intimacy

Two common intimacy-related causes of anxiety are loneliness and the fear of rejection. Because I've shared my personal struggle with loneliness through various online platforms, I've heard hundreds—maybe thousands—of people describe to me their battle with the same issue. A lot of times, loneliness comes with a metaphorical pack. I'm talking about a pack we carry on our shoulders that feels like a comfort for a while, but ends up being a burden. In this pack, we place things like anger, resentment, denial, criticism of others, unforgiveness, and even hatred. The problem is, though these things promise relief, they just make us more anxious.

If loneliness is an issue you've dealt with, or are still dealing with, you need to know that God can redeem your situation. He can fix the rift between you and others. He can bring you out of isolation.

I know what it's like to be alone. I haven't experienced it to the degree that many have, but I was alone long enough to know that: For the power of loneliness to be broken, the lies of the devil need to be reversed. So, for the sake of those who need to hear this, I'm going to say it again: God can change your situation. It may seem impossible to you, but Jesus said in Luke 18:27, "The things that are impossible with people are possible with God."

Fear of rejection, which is often linked to loneliness, is another cause of broken intimacy. Fear of being rejected by people can cause us to keep ourselves at arms' length from friends and family. Similarly, fear of being rejected by God can cause us to keep ourselves distanced from our Creator. Many times, we don't even know why there's a separation occurring. Fear of rejection likes to bury itself into our subconscious, hidden from view. It acts like wind on a kite. You don't see it, but it pushes you every which way. The same way God can heal the pain of loneliness, He can also strip the fear of rejection from our hearts. The solution for these intimacy-related issues is the next principle I want to discuss, and it's probably not what you might guess it to be.

Principle: Nakedness
Benefit: Intimacy

If you're laughing right now, please know that I'm about to attempt to explain what I mean by nakedness. My brother-in-law Chris might tell me that, by expounding upon this subject, I'm just going to dig myself a deeper hole. Sometimes you've just got to dig holes and get a little dirty, though. Okay, now I've made it awkward.

All joking aside, I'm using the term "nakedness," not to try to keep your attention, but simply because the Bible uses this same term on many occasions. Though bodily nakedness is involved in physical intimacy with another person, that's not the only situation I'm talking about here. It is however, where the illustration behind the principle of nakedness comes from. The nakedness I'm referring to consists of three parts: a physical nakedness in a marriage relationship, a spiritual nakedness in relationship with God, and an emotional nakedness in a friend relationship.

Nakedness is most often used in a negative way in Scripture, denoting humiliation, shame, and even judgement. However, it's not always a negative thing. When it's used in a positive light in Scripture, it can be broken down into two facets: purity (which I'm grouping with innocence) and vulnerability. I'm going to focus on both of these aspects during this section, showing how it

For the power of loneliness to be broken, the lies of the devil need to be reversed.

takes both purity and vulnerability in order to achieve true, Biblical intimacy. Thankfully, when we're living in a place of intimacy, the power of loneliness and the fear of rejection are broken.

The first place in Scripture nakedness occurs is within the story of Adam and Eve in the garden. Because they had no knowledge of evil, Adam and Eve skipped (if skipping was in style back then) through the garden butt-naked every morning. No shame, guilt, fear, or self-criticism existed in their minds. They were truly free to be exactly the way God had created them to be. However, the minute they lost their purity through committing the first human sin, they also lost their ability to be vulnerable. They covered themselves with fig leaves because they no longer wanted to be emotionally and physically vulnerable with each other, and they hid from God because they no longer wanted to be spiritually vulnerable with Him.

What resulted almost immediately after that? God removed them from the garden. They lost their intimacy with their Creator. God, however, had a plan. We see this in 1 Corinthians 15:45.

"So also it is written, 'The first man, Adam, became a living soul.' The last Adam became a life-giving spirit."

In the garden, the first Adam brought shame to the state of nakedness. Jesus Christ, who Paul refers to as the last Adam, made a way for our shame to be permanently removed. When I'm talking about nakedness, I'm not talking about feeling humiliated before God. I'm talking about, through faith in Jesus Christ, standing fully accepted before God with no shame or fear. For that to happen, we have to do two things: become pure by accepting the righteousness of Jesus as our own and become vulnerable when we sin. We accept Jesus' righteousness as our own when we choose to believe God's grace is enough, and we become vulnerable when we choose to admit our sin and repent.

If you're saved, it's easy to know these truths in our minds, but it's much harder to walk them out when we mess up. Getting vulnerable with God—choosing to expose our spiritual nakedness— is not a fun place to be. However, it is worth it.

Before I dive further into the blessing of spiritual intimacy though, I want to first look at God's desire and plan for us to experience physical intimacy.

Physical Nakedness

To walk in the benefit of Biblical intimacy, the first place we need to learn purity and vulnerability is in the area of physical nakedness. Yes, I'm talking about sex.

Human bodies did not create sex over a long period of time. Evolution didn't think up the design for our reproductive organs. God designed sex with the twofold purpose of giving us the ability to reproduce and providing us the pleasures of physical intimacy. Simply put: sex and sexuality were God's ideas. He meant for sex to be the physical expression of the deepest kind of intimacy a man and woman can have.

Satan and sin work to distort every good thing God created. Because sex was created by God, Satan attacks it all the time. I'm not saying he attacks it by attempting to withhold it from us. Instead, he attacks it by perverting it. He knows that, when you or I engage in sexual intimacy with another person outside of the bounds of God's standard, or when we engage in sexual sin alone, we lose out on the real joys and benefits of sexuality. Sure, sexual activity outside of marriage still generates a physical sensation of pleasure, but it simultaneously corrupts our ability to find true intimacy. When you use a machine in a way the inventor didn't create it be used, you often break it. The same is true with the way much of the culture uses sex. It has become broken from its original pattern and purpose, and its benefits have been very limited.

The full blessings of physical intimacy are only accessible when a man and woman have bound themselves to each other in a marital covenant ordained by God. There are many arguments I could make to back up this statement. I won't spend time discussing all of them, but here's one. When you're having sex outside of marriage, you're always trying to put your best foot forward. Your hope is to look your best to your partner because you want their acceptance. Alternatively, when a man and woman have been bound together under the union of marriage, they have vowed in the sight of God to accept each other no matter what. Wouldn't it be nice to know that the person you're seeking to find physical intimacy with is going to love you no matter what? If you knew this was true, you wouldn't fear rejection. You wouldn't worry about their judgments of your body. You would be able to rest easy in the knowledge that they long to embrace you just the way you are. That's what God designed marriage to be like.

The devil hates it when we receive the benefits of knowing God. He attempts to steal our promise of intimacy by telling us things like "you'll always be alone" or "you'll never be accepted." When we believe these lies, our guard comes down and we're suddenly willing to settle for less than God's best. Please, please, please hear me. Don't settle for less than God's best. God's best isn't the richest person you meet. It isn't the most sensually dressed person you meet. It isn't the person who is willing to meet your physical needs right now. God's best—the person who will bless you with the benefit of intimacy—is the person who has a real relationship with Jesus and is willing to enter a marriage covenant with you before God.

Satan attacks our potential for real intimacy by promising an alternative; his own version of intimacy. He promises intimacy through ungodly means. He tries to get us to trade our purity for intimacy now. You might be thinking, "It's too late for me to have purity anyway. I've already been sexually immoral." Let me pull the weight off your shoulders. None of us are pure on our own. We've all been sexually immoral in one way or another. What the devil is trying to attack by drawing us into sexual immorality is not our "perfect" record, but our hearts. None of us have a perfect record, but we all have hearts that God desires to be His. When our hearts are turned away from sin and toward Jesus, we get to receive and walk in His purity. Because of grace, we can find true spiritual intimacy with God right now, and we can experience the benefits of physical intimacy with a spouse at the right time.

Even if you're already married, I feel the need to say the same thing. Don't settle for less than God's best in your marriage. Satan has a slew of tricks he uses to steal our potential for God-designed intimacy. Satan uses things like pornography, adultery, lust, homosexual acts, and even ungodly emotional entanglements. The purpose of all these things is to direct our hearts away from Jesus—to get us to believe a lie instead of the truth. The truth is that, when we are choosing godly nakedness (purity and vulnerability within marriage), instead of the nakedness of the world, Jesus promises us the best kind of physical intimacy.

"For this reason a man shall leave his father and his mother, and be joined to his wife; and they shall become one flesh."

Genesis 2:24

Becoming one flesh with your spouse doesn't simply refer to a sexual partnership. It's a deeper, more loving concept than that. Paul gives us more insight into this verse immediately after quoting it in Ephesians 5.

"This mystery is great; but I am speaking with reference to Christ and the church. Nevertheless, each individual among you also is to love his own wife even as himself, and the wife must see to it that she respects her husband."

Ephesians 5:32-33

246

The intimacy between a husband and wife should model the intimacy between Christ and the church. Jesus laid down His life for the church. He left all His own desires at the wayside and carried the burdens of every believer on His shoulders. Real, Biblical intimacy means our entire marriage, even our sexuality, is a picture of this same selfless devotion and sacrifice. If you're not there yet, don't give up hope. We're all in process. Whether you're married or unmarried, God can begin to mold your heart into both believing His truth and walking in that truth. It simply takes you opening up to Him—getting spiritually intimate with Him—allowing His grace to make you pure and allowing yourself to be vulnerable with Him about your issues.

Spiritual Nakedness

The second kind of intimacy I want to cover is spiritual intimacy, and this is a result of our spiritual nakedness with God. I've already introduced this subject. The same way we can stand before a spouse pure and vulnerable, we can stand before God in complete righteousness and honesty. When we learn how to do this, we get to live in a restful place of beautiful intimacy with our Creator. This is a place where fears, worries, doubts, and anxious thoughts can't thrive. They're washed away by His love and the glory of His presence.

What keeps most people from getting spiritually naked before God is their own limiting of God's grace. Unfortunately, I don't believe there's anything I can say to get you to fully accept His grace. The only way to become spiritually naked with God is to begin to act on whatever faith you have at the moment. Whatever belief you have about the level of God's goodness, start acting on it. Start reading the Bible and looking for His grace, His mercy, and His love. It's when you begin to encounter Him in all His goodness and experience His endless love for you that you'll start trusting God enough to be consistently vulnerable with Him.

However, even though I believe this principle takes a personal seeking of God to fully grasp, I am going to do my best to describe it, too.

If you know Jesus as your Lord and Savior, there's nothing you've done and there's no aspect of who you are that will cause God to reject you. I can confidently say this because our acceptance with God is not based on our performance. It's based on what Jesus did for us on the cross.

I'm not saying that God approves of sinful areas in our lives. He doesn't. In His holiness, He lovingly molds His children into an image of Christ. But if we know Jesus, He accepts us despite our mistakes and struggles. Despite how long we've had that issue, He accepts us as His. Despite how often others have talked down to us or we've talked down to ourselves, God's Spirit is there to lift us up in a warm embrace.

The day Jesus was crucified, God the Father wanted desperately to reach down and lift up His Son. He saw His perfect child being mistreated, humiliated, tortured, and wrongly killed, and it would have been any loving parent's reaction to step in and help. But the reason God did nothing to help Jesus that day was because Jesus was trading His life for ours. Because Jesus faced ultimate, undeserved rejection, you and I get to receive ultimate, undeserved love and acceptance.

This is one reason why it's so critical that our daily walk with God be personal. When we're following God out of duty and in a formulaic manner, we may know in our minds that we're accepted, but we won't necessarily believe it in our hearts. Acceptance cannot simply be a doctrinal truth. It has to be experienced. You have to hear the Holy Spirit speaking the truth of God's acceptance to your heart.

If you've made it to this point in this book and you still haven't heard personally from the Holy Spirit, don't give up. Keep seeking Him. Keep taking your relationship with God to the next level. How do you take any relationship to the next level? You get vulnerable. I've had so many interactions with people where I can tell they are keeping all their real thoughts hidden under an emotional shell. The moment I choose to share something vulnerable with them is the moment they turn around and begin to share the struggles of their heart with me.

My encouragement to you is to continually be more and more vulnerable with the Holy Spirit. Tell Him what your fears are. Tell Him what your desires are. Tell Him how you feel. Best of all, be honest with Him when you sin. I know that may sound crazy, but remember that God isn't scared of your sin. Jesus already experienced the full punishment for your sin. When you say, "God, I messed up in this area today, and I'm sorry," He looks past your failure and sees into your heart. He sees the faith you are placing in Jesus Christ. He sees the trust it took for you to be honest and open with Him. Listen to me. Full acceptance and love are not found someday when you learn to do better. They're found the moment you choose to rest in God's amazing grace despite how you've done.

The year after I graduated college, I began to actively look for a wife. From asking coworkers out to signing up for Christian dating sites (one of those awkward things I included in this book against my better judgement…), I was trying my best to find a godly woman to marry. Yes, I could have pursued unbelieving friends who had expressed their interest in me. But even though I desired to be married, I also wanted God's best for me. At times, I would be tempted to go looking in places I knew I shouldn't, but when I would get alone with God and lay my desires at His feet, He would encourage me to wait. I was being vulnerable with Him, but I was also listening to His voice and allowing Him to help me walk in purity.

If you know Jesus as your Lord and Savior, there's nothing you've done and there's no aspect of who you are that will cause God to reject you.

No, I wasn't perfect. Not every thought I had could be considered righteous. However, I kept going into that living room (both the physical living room of my apartment and the metaphorical living room in Mary's house) and laying my failures and fears down at Jesus' feet. I would lay on my living room floor, day after day, crying out to God.

One day, as I lay there, I heard the Holy Spirit speak into my heart. He said, "You'll be married by the end of the year." I nearly laughed out loud as I replied, "God, I don't have any prospects." I knew it usually takes time to get to know someone before you can marry them. He said, "You'll meet her in October." It was probably mid-July to early August at that time. Despite how ridiculous the idea sounded, I chose to believe Him. I responded, "God, can you send her sooner? Can you speed it up a little?" My question thankfully did not come from a place of discontentment, but a place of gratefulness and hope. He said, "Yes."

That September, one month before God's original timeline, I visited a high school friend in my hometown. Four of us gathered that night: me, two guys from my high school class, and Leslie, the girl I had liked all through high school. If you've read my book, *My Mess*, you know the story there. I had seen her about once or twice per year since high school, and I didn't think anything would ever happen between us. However, as I looked at her that night, I couldn't help but wonder at how different she seemed. I kept thinking, "She feels so much like a new person. I can't understand it." We started dating that night, and a few days later I remembered what God had said about meeting my wife in the fall. I had thought God meant I would meet someone new, but instead I had met my future wife again for what seemed like the first time.

Because Jesus faced ultimate, undeserved rejection, you and I get to receive ultimate, undeserved love and acceptance.

In the excitement of beginning to date Leslie, I completely forgot the word God had spoken to me about being married by the end of the year. A few months later, we were already planning our wedding. There was one specific evening when Leslie and I were trying to determine if we should be married on January 1st of the next year or December 31st of that year. The two dates were only one day apart, so at first it didn't seem like it would make any difference. While we were discussing the wedding date, I suddenly remembered that God had told me I would be married that year. I knew which day to choose.

I said, "Let's get married on December 31st." Leslie and I held hands and said, "I do" in the living room of her parents' house (in which we somehow packed over 60 people) only a few short hours before the end of the year.

Yes, I did push my wedding date up 24 hours based on what God had told me, so you could potentially argue that I forced God's word to become true. However, I believe God allowed me to forget that word until the right time so that nothing would really be forced. Everything up to that point seemed to fall perfectly into place, as if God's loving hands had orchestrated every detail.

God had already planned how He would provide the physical intimacy (which is only one blessing of marriage, I'll admit) Leslie and I were both praying for, but it took me continuing to rest in that place of spiritual vulnerability and purity. It was through listening to His voice that I was able to wait for His blessing to come at the appointed time. I had been tempted to head down other roads prior to that, but I can see now that alternate routes would have only led me to a place of anxiety. Dating and marrying Leslie ended up being one of the most peaceful experiences of my life up to that point. God's peace and favor surrounded that time like a warm comforter on a cold night. Remember, I'm not saying I did everything right. I hadn't lived a perfect life up to that point. The peace, provision, and direction I received were all benefits of knowing God and walking in intimacy with Him. You can walk in that same peace. Through Jesus Christ, you can live in vulnerability and purity before your loving Creator.

Emotional Nakedness

Finally, I want to briefly discuss the idea of emotional nakedness. God's plan for most human beings involves physical intimacy, but His plan for all human beings involves spiritual and emotional intimacy. Emotional intimacy is one of those benefits I believe too many believers, especially Christian men, are missing out on.

Emotional nakedness is something that should exist between husband and wife, but it's also something that needs to happen between some believers as well. I understand that the word nakedness sounds odd in this case though, so I'm going to substitute the world *vulnerability* during this section.

There is an intimacy that exists between friends that cannot be found anywhere else in the world. A husband and wife who are great friends can experience this kind of intimacy, but just being married doesn't guarantee you have it. Look at the way Proverbs 18:24 describes the intimacy between some friends.

"A man of too many friends comes to ruin, but there is a friend who sticks closer than a brother."

When I was young, I couldn't possibly imagine being closer to someone than I was to my siblings and parents. However, the older I grew, the more I realized that life had been able to come between us. At one point, I agreed with my siblings about everything. I used to want to do everything with them. I still love all five of them immensely, but I've realized how deep and meaningful God created friendship outside of family to be, too. Being born into my family forced me to get to know my siblings. There's another level of intimacy that occurs when nothing makes you get close to someone, but instead you've made the conscious decision to pursue a friendship out of genuine, uncompelled desire to know them.

Usually the best friendships are built, or at least initiated around a common interest. What better uniting factor is there than the truth that the same Savior died for both you and me on the cross? The sad reality is that, in some cases, the quality of friendship found within the church is not any better, and sometimes worse, than that of the world. One contributing factor to this is the lack of vulnerability. Satan isn't just attacking our physical intimacy as believers. He's also attacking our emotional intimacy by convincing us that we have to have it all together all the time in Christian circles. The truth is, we don't.

I wouldn't suggest sharing your secrets with just anyone, but you and I were created to live in fellowship with other people. We need other believers who will listen and share with us within the bounds of a loving, trustworthy friendship.

Have you ever worried about something all by yourself—something no one else knew about? You weren't designed to carry those burdens alone. Paul told us to bear one another's burdens (see Galatians 6:2). Not even Jesus carried the knowledge of the cross alone. Sure, His disciples had a hard time catching on to what He was saying sometimes, but He still talked about it. Even in His last hours, He asked them to be there praying with Him. If the Son of God needed good friends, you and I do, too.

Proverbs 17:9 identifies one of the major signs that you've found a true friend.

> *"He who conceals a transgression seeks love, but he who repeats a matter separates intimate friends."*

A godly friend is one that understands that love covers a multitude of sins. They are a friend whom not only sometimes it still hurts to share with but also with whom vulnerability is not something you have to worry about. You know you've become intimate when you no longer fear healthy vulnerability with that person.

Now, there are people who will try to take advantage of vulnerability, and there are many instances where you should not be vulnerable with people. So please choose your close friends wisely. I'm not saying it's good to be emotionally intimate with everyone who is willing. The devil will try to pervert emotional connection as much as he can, so be aware. However, when the devil perverts something, it's because there is a healthy, beautiful, godly way of doing things that he doesn't want us to experience. God created friendship, and He meant it to be beautiful.

If you don't have any intimate friendships, I'm not trying to make you feel ashamed or condemned. This is one area I've struggled with personally, and at one point I wasn't able to admit that fact. When Leslie and I were first married, I would say things like, "I'm not good at making friends," or "I don't have any friends," and one day she looked at me in the eyes and replied, "That's a lie." Until that very moment, I believed it was the truth. What I didn't realize was, I had been listening to the lies of the one

If the Son of God needed good friends, you and I do, too.

who wanted to keep me lonely instead of listening to the truth of the One who created me for intimacy.

If you've struggled with loneliness or isolation, perhaps you've felt like Job at one point. He says in Job 19:14,

> *"My relatives have failed, and my intimate friends have forgotten me."*

Yet, even in the midst of Job's grief and heartache, he chooses to remember the One who would never forget Him. In verses 25-26 of the same chapter, he makes the amazing statement:

> *"As for me, I know that my Redeemer lives, and at the last He will take His stand on the earth. Even after my skin is destroyed, yet from my flesh I shall see God; Whom I myself shall behold."*

Even in His lonely, rejected state, Job remembers the personal connection He has with His Redeemer. He says, "…Whom I myself shall behold."

My greatest motivation in life is simple: One day in heaven, I'm going to take a walk with my Savior. I don't know what we'll talk about. We might talk about anything and everything. Maybe we'll just walk and enjoy each other's company. But when I think about all the blessings and treasures I could possibly receive, this one thing sits at the top of the list. I'm going to walk next to Jesus, the person who understands me and loves me more than anyone else in the universe, and I'm going to call Him my friend.

The truth is, you and I can walk in friendship with Jesus now. In fact, our intimate friendship with Jesus can be the catalyst that helps us make good friends and even be a good friend.

When you're being a good friend to someone, you're always giving them something: your advice, your time, your care, your help, your company, and many other things. I've been in that place where you're so isolated that you feel like you don't have anything left to give. You feel like you're trapped in an endless cycle of separation. Listen to me. If this is a battle you face, your friendship with Jesus can break that cycle. He always has something to give you, even when you feel like you have nothing to give Him. He never runs out of love. He never runs out of advice. He's never too busy for you. He never gets impatient with you. He never gives up on you. He never betrays you.

You have a friend in Jesus, and you don't have to wait for heaven to walk in that friendship. My encouragement to you is to connect with Him, no matter what it takes. He wants to hear your fears, your worries, your pains, and even your failures. And He wants to comfort you and speak to you through the voice of the Holy Spirit. Accept His purity as your own through faith, and trust Him enough to give Him your vulnerability. He is the friend who sticks closer than a brother.

Our intimate friendship with Jesus can be the catalyst that helps us make good friends and even be a good friend.

Jesus Himself describes His devotion to us as our perfect friend in John 15:13.

"Greater love has no one than this, that one lay down his life for his friends."

Fishing For People

The same way Jesus demonstrated His love for us on the cross, He desires us to demonstrate our love for Him by loving others. We can give that love in multitudes of ways, but the ultimate expression of God's love for another person is sharing the message of the gospel. Whether it's buying someone groceries, giving someone money, cleaning someone's house for them, or simply telling someone they matter, most loving acts only affect people temporarily. Acts of love can, however, be a platform through which we share the good news which will affect them for eternity.

Though we know Jesus desires us to witness, and though many of us wish we were better at witnessing, there is a problem stopping many of us from actually doing it: We worry about it too much. It makes us anxious, and the more we put it off or try to ignore it, the more anxious we become. Maybe you've settled on the idea that witnessing is always going to feel that way, and it's something we just have to bear up under and make ourselves do. But I want you to know that God doesn't intend for us to share the gospel under the weight of anxiety. You might not believe me at first, but He doesn't even want us to be motivated by fear of not doing it. He has such a better way in mind for us as His lights shining in this world.

As I mentioned earlier, many worries stem from the fact that we've missed God's perspective on the matter. If we could just see things through His eyes, we would relax. It's the same with sharing the gospel. When our perspective on witnessing doesn't line up with Scripture's view, the task is always going to be a source of worry.

One specific anxiety that some Christians carry is the worry that someone they love doesn't yet know Jesus. Since meeting Jesus myself, I had always cared about the salvation of my friends and family, but this worry multiplied suddenly upon having my first child. There are few loves like the love of a parent for their child, and many Christian parents have yet to see their children come to the Lord. I know several older couples who have been praying for years for their adult children to find Jesus.

My goal in writing about this isn't to agitate your stresses. Instead, it's to help you understand that God wants you to care about your friends and family, He wants you to love them, and He wants you to be proactive in leading them to Him, but He does not want you to be anxious about their salvation. I know this because of the simple truth Paul shares in Philippians 4:6-7.

> *"Be anxious for nothing, but in everything by prayer and supplication with thanksgiving let your requests be made known to God. And the peace of God, which surpasses all comprehension, will guard your hearts and your minds in Christ Jesus."*

In many ways, prayer is God's replacement for worry. When we would naturally worry about something, God says *pray*. Remember, prayer means you're talking to God, but it also means you're allowing the Holy Spirit to speak to you. Relationships require two-way communication. God promises that, when we do this, His peace will surround us like a shield. He also adds this caveat: The reassurance that God hears our prayers has nothing to do with our own merit, but it has everything to do with the position with God we've been given through Jesus Christ. When we go to God in prayer, we need to come boldly before Him, without fear or doubt, based on the amazing grace He has extended to us.

Many parents' first reaction to a child's problem is to act—to do something to fix it. I'm a parent, and I know that sometimes prayer feels like we're not doing enough, but it's essential. Through prayer and thanksgiving, God promises to strip the fear and worry away. He promises to give us peace.

Have you ever watched a television show or live performance where someone was nervous or anxious about performing an arduous task? Some game shows play off of this idea because they know they can get people to do or say crazy things under pressure. The truth is, if there weren't cameras or an audience watching, they would probably be less anxious and have a better chance at finishing the task. This is similar to our ability to witness as believers. If we're witnessing from a place of fear or anxiousness, we're not in a place where the Spirit of God can effectively lead us and give us the right words to say. God wants you and me to start from a place of peace so that we can hear His gentle voice speaking. Guess what? When God's peace surrounds you, that peace will itself shine like a light as it breaks through the darkness of the anxious world around you.

One mistake I've made when attempting to witness to someone is to get angry at them for not accepting the truth of the gospel. There have been times when I've wanted to shake someone and say, "Why can't you get this?" The problem is that my frustration often ruins my chances of being effective in that moment. People see frustration and anxiety everywhere, and they know how to respond in a similar manner. When they instead see the love, peace, and hope in your heart, it will stop them in their tracks.

Jesus said, "Follow Me" before He expected His disciples to become fishers of people. He knew that, for them to witness in the most effective way, they would have to be launching from a place of peace and relationship. It's when we abide in Christ that we're able to make an impact for His kingdom. It's when we can hear His voice clearly that we're able to best speak His words of life to others.

We now come to the practical principle that follows prayer. When we stay in prayer, we can launch our boat from a place of peace, but once the boat is launched, Jesus also hands us a net to throw into the water. This is where the desire to do something more than just praying is fulfilled.

The Benefit of Hope

The real reason the salvation of others can be such a galling source of worry is because it's an area we can feel hopeless and helpless in. When you really stop to think about it, you have to admit that we can't save anyone. No matter how hard we try, we can't make someone accept Jesus. But that doesn't mean we have to lose hope. The truth is, we first have to realize our limitations before we can begin to walk in the fullness of hope God provides.

Principle: Confessing Christ
Benefit: Hope

God doesn't leave us without hope when it comes to the salvation of a friend or loved one. He offers us real hope, and that hope comes through practicing the principle of confessing Christ. I'm going to tell you how this principle is connected to relationship right from the start. Confessing Christ isn't something we should do every moment we're with someone. If we're pestering someone about accepting Jesus and not taking their feelings into consideration, they won't want to be around us. If I had an unsaved friend who I always only shared the gospel with and never engaged in any other subject of conversation, they wouldn't be my friend very long. However, when we're walking in a daily relationship with God, the Holy Spirit will tell us when it's time to confess Him. He will even create opportunities for sharing the truth that we wouldn't have found on our own.

"Therefore everyone who confesses Me before men, I will also confess him before My Father who is in heaven."

Matthew 10:32

Jesus tells us that confessing Christ is so intricately connected to knowing God that, if we aren't confessing Him, our relationship with God will suffer. What this means is, our unwillingness to share Christ affects our internal peace. I'll say it another way: If you want to experience God's peace in a fresh new way, tell someone about what Jesus has done for you.

Confessing Jesus means being willing to talk about Him as if He's actually the Savior of your life. Look at it this way: If you have a real relationship with the God of the universe, isn't that something worth talking about? Jesus says, not only is it important, it's essential. Living out the principle of confessing Christ means being willing to acknowledge Him even when it's unpopular. This is often one of the easiest things to do in Christian circles (though some of us still struggle with it then, too), but it can be one of the most challenging principles to practice in front of unbelievers.

My hope is that you'll truly recognize the benefits associated with confessing Christ. I want you to grasp the idea that you are created for this—you're wired for it. When you're not doing it, something is missing. I don't want you to miss out on the blessing of hope God has for you.

The principle of confessing Christ produces hope in two ways. First, talking about Jesus reminds your own heart of the hope you have in Him. Second, it reveals that hope to those who have no hope themselves. They see an image of the glory you've received in Jesus. They are offered a drink from the well of His Spirit which overflows out of you. We see this hope of the gospel spelled out in Colossians 1:27, which says,

> *"...to whom God willed to make known what is the riches of the glory of this mystery among the Gentiles, which is Christ in you, the hope of glory."*

When Paul says "the mystery," he refers to the gospel. In fact, he takes it a step further and specifically mentions that the mystery really is Christ living within the believer. Here's another way of saying it: When an unsaved person sees you, they see a reflection of Jesus. You're not perfect on the outside, I know that. You don't even act perfect all the time, but your spirit has been made perfect through the blood of Christ. When they see Jesus in you, they see the only eternal hope they will ever find. Paul calls the mystery the hope of glory because the gospel is the foundation of our assured hope that we will experience God's glory throughout eternity.

One problem that arises is the fact that people don't always know what it is they've seen. I've had people ask me, "What's different about you? What is it that you've got?" In those moments, I have a choice to make. I can either share the hope I have in my heart, or I can keep it to myself. When we keep it to ourselves, people don't know that they've seen Jesus in us. I had one guy ask me if I was on drugs. He couldn't understand why I had so much peace and joy. I told Him that the only thing I had was Jesus. What's amazing is, when we share that hope with someone, we also experience it on a deeper level ourselves.

> *"but sanctify Christ as Lord in your hearts, always being ready to make a defense to everyone who asks you to give an account for the hope that is in you, yet with gentleness and reverence;"*
>
> 1 Peter 3:15

Paul had his own opportunity to worry about the salvation of others. He strongly desired for his fellow Jews to get saved, which he states in Romans 10:1.

> *"Brethren, my heart's desire and my prayer to God for them is for their salvation."*

So, what's his response to this desire? I'm sure he was tempted to worry about it, but instead he chooses to confess Jesus to them. He resolves his dilemma a little further down in verse 14.

"How then will they call on Him in whom they have not believed? How will they believe in Him whom they have not heard? And how will they hear without a preacher?"

This phrase has been circulated around the Christian church for decades: *Preach the Gospel at all times. When necessary, use words.* Now, if you've got this quote hanging on your bathroom mirror, please don't think I'm judging you. I'm not. There is a lot of truth behind the idea that our actions need to reveal Jesus to people just as much as our speech. However, the Bible makes it very clear that Jesus' idea of sharing the gospel involves, not just action, but also confession. Paul says, "How will they believe in Him whom they have not heard?"

Here's a specific example where this comes into play. I've made the mistake of assuming people are saved just because they go to church, attend a Christian school, work for a Christian organization, or talk about God among Christian friends. I never felt the need to preach Jesus to them. Later though, after finding out that they didn't really believe in Jesus as their Lord and Savior, I realized that it should have been obvious to me the whole time. They never talked about Jesus to me, and anytime I started to talk about what Jesus was doing in my life, they changed the subject.

In college, I had several close friends, and at first I assumed they were all saved. Then, when God got a hold of my life and I began to walk in the truth of the gospel and the freedom of the Holy Spirit, I began to talk about God's amazing grace with my friends. I didn't get too theologically detailed, and I didn't ask a lot of prying questions. I just began to tell them about what Jesus had done in my life as the Holy Spirit urged me to speak.

To my surprise, I had more than one friend look me in the eyes and say, "No one has ever explained it to me that way." They went on to tell me about how they didn't feel like they had a real relationship with God at all even though they had been in church their entire lives.

When you confess Jesus and what He's personally done for you to someone else, two things happen: You get to see their reaction and potentially discern where they are with the Lord, and you get to have hope in the seed you've planted in their life.

You may not be able to explain deep theological concepts to someone, but that's not what Jesus asks you to do anyway. If you know God has done something for you through the gospel, you can share that.

When we make the mistaken assumption that a child of ours is saved because they live in our Christian home or because they've heard about Jesus in church, we're in danger of letting ourselves off the hook from ever really personally sharing Jesus with them. We tell ourselves that the motivation behind that assumption is hope, but really it's fear. Subconsciously, we don't want to know if someone we love, especially a child, isn't really saved.

I'm not trying to make you feel bad. Really, I'm not. If you have grown children who still haven't accepted Christ, the last thing I want to do is put shame on you. I'm simply just trying to make a point. Real hope doesn't come from making an assumption. It comes through confessing Christ.

> *"These words, which I am commanding you today, shall be on your heart. You shall teach them diligently to your sons and shall talk of them when you sit in your house and when you walk by the way and when you lie down and when you rise up."*

Deuteronomy 6:6-7

The principle of confessing God's truth to the next generation is explicitly stated in this verse. Under the new covenant, the principle is the same, yet we get to confess the fulfillment of the law—Jesus Christ—not just the law by itself. When we keep our mouths shut based on an assumption, it makes us feel better in the moment, but it causes more worry in the long run.

I think we all do this in one way or another. Have you ever said to yourself, "They know Jesus; they just have a harder time showing it?" I have. The sad thing is it has not always been true. Please realize that I'm only saying this out of love, and I don't claim to be any better at this than anyone else. However, if we want to walk in hope, we do need to start being honest with ourselves. Making assumptions doesn't fix the issue, it just causes us to worry for a longer period of time. Assumption is a temporary fix, but confession gives us real hope for the future.

Because I have little children myself right now, I can recognize the temptation to want them to get baptized as soon as possible. But if my hope is set in seeing them get baptized, then I'm putting my hope in that physical act just as much as some parents place their hope in infant sprinkling. The physical act of baptism is useless if it's not fueled by that person's personal faith in Jesus. Baptism isn't a surety of someone's faith. Instead, it should be a response to faith. The way we know they've really gotten it is that we hear them confessing, not just repeating, the truth of Jesus back to us.

One other way we can receive surety is through a personal word from the Holy Spirit. Sometimes it takes hearing a confirmation from God that someone will be saved in order to stop worrying about their salvation. That's not an excuse to stop witnessing, but it can be a source of comfort during a time of waiting. Hearing a word of confirmation from the Holy Spirit can give us the ability to witness in faith, pray in hope, and leave the results up to God. Remember, you and I can plant and water, but God causes the growth (see 1 Corinthians 3:7). When we go to Him in prayer, He can reveal when that growth is going to happen. Until then, whether it's our children, a relative, or a friend, we should keep taking the opportunities, when the Holy Spirit leads us, to confess Jesus.

> *"Let us hold fast the confession of our hope without wavering, for He who promised is faithful;"*
>
> Hebrews 10:23

Your confession to someone else is an extension of the confession in your heart. With our hearts we believe, and with our mouths we confess (see Romans 10:10). Look at it like this: If you heard some amazing news in the morning, you would be telling people all day long. Why? Because that news had become the source of your joy, and that joy began to overflow. When we're walking in the truth of the gospel, the joy of the message will overflow out of our mouths.

After I started following Jesus in college, I began to worry about my older brother's salvation. I knew he may have been saved, but at that time it didn't seem as if he was living like a saved person. Because of his schooling and military job, I didn't see him often.

For a few years I kept my thoughts to myself, mostly talking to him about other things. After I graduated, he generously paid most of my way as we visited New Zealand together. As we drove around the Southern Island during those two weeks, our differing opinions began to cross blades until we finally got into an argument.

I picked the worst time possible to share with him about what God was doing in my life, and I said it in the wrong way, too. I was angry. I had gotten just angry enough to stop caring what he thought and actually confess Jesus the way the Holy Spirit had been telling me to. Afterwards, we forgave each other for the argument and became friends again. I knew I had said some things that I was supposed to say, but I wished I had said them in a better way. I had been too judgmental. I'm not perfect either.

However, despite my own failure, my hopes began to blossom. Every time I prayed after that, I prayed in hope, believing that God was working on my brother's heart the same way He was working on mine. Then, one evening the following year, he called me and we spoke over the phone. Well, I should say *he* spoke over the phone. He did most of the talking. It's a good thing too, because I wouldn't have been able to talk much through the tears. He was preaching the gospel to me. He was preaching the righteousness of God by grace through faith.

I had gotten my assurance. My hopes had been fulfilled. I thought, "Why did he want to call and tell me these things? He knows I know this." Then it hit me. He knew how much I cared that he knew it, too. He knew it was important to me because I had confessed it to him.

I'm not saying my brother wasn't saved prior to that. I don't know. I'm not even saying I was better than him. I know I wasn't. My point is that, through confessing Christ, I found hope, and through prayer and trust, that hope led to a joyful assurance.

The problem I encountered when attempting to confess Jesus with my brother is a common problem. As I mentioned at the start of this section, though many Christians desire to be better witnesses, there's one thing stopping us: We worry about it too much. We worry about how people will react. We worry about what they'll think. We fear people talking about us behind our backs. We get nervous about how or when to speak. The final principle I want to cover gives us the solution to this problem. If you want to confess Jesus and yet you just don't know how to start, you can sigh a sigh of relief; because here's your answer.

The Benefit of Relief

As I said, witnessing is the ultimate way we can share God's love with someone. It's not always the first way, and it's not always the right way depending on the circumstance, but it's ultimately the best way. For example, if you came across a person stuck in a pit and crying out for help, you shouldn't yell, "Hey down there! Do you know Jesus?" The first priority in that moment should be to pull them out of their physical pit, and then God will give you an opportunity to offer them freedom from their spiritual pit after that.

One problem with attempting to witness is that, in our natural state, we are limited in our ability to love people. We get judgmental, angry, over-passionate, fearful, and anxious. We eventually run out of love. The only way to become the witnesses God desires us to be is to allow Him to transform us from the inside out through His love working inside our hearts. God is love, and we are not. He's much better at it than we are. The solution is to begin to love people through the lens of His love.

Look at Paul's description of love in 1 Corinthians 13:4-7.

> *"Love is patient, love is kind and is not jealous; love does not brag and is not arrogant, does not act unbecomingly; it does not seek its own, is not provoked, does not take into account a wrong suffered, does not rejoice in unrighteousness, but rejoices with the truth; bears all things, believes all things, hopes all things, endures all things."*

How many of us can say we've witnessed in this way? The truth is, on our own, it's impossible. To try to love someone with this kind of love is nothing short of an impossible burden. It's something we aren't strong enough to carry. If we want the stress and anxiety of the burden to fall off us, we've got to first let the burden itself fall off. Our love will dry up, but God's love will not. Simply put: Let Him carry the burden. He can handle it.

With His love flowing through us, we can love others with a strength that goes far beyond our human capability. That's when we don't have to rely on our own strength anymore. We can relax. We can find relief knowing that God is the one doing the heavy lifting.

Principle: His Burden (Yoke)
Benefit: Relief

You've probably heard Matthew 4:19 before, but I want to point out the way Jesus chooses to word this famous statement:

"And He said to them, 'Follow Me, and I will make you fishers of men.'"

I mentioned this briefly earlier, but notice how Jesus doesn't say, "Fish for men and I'll tell you if you're doing it right or not." He first says, "Follow Me," and then He says, "and I will make you fishers of men." Before we can be the witnesses God has commissioned us to be, we must become the followers Jesus has called us to be. Our success on the mission field is directly related to our connection with His Spirit. The question we need to ask ourselves is: Did I just start witnessing because it's something I'm supposed to do, or am I doing it because it's something Jesus has placed inside of me during my times of intimacy with Him?

Let's look at the way Jesus words it in Matthew 11:28-30.

"Come to Me, all who are weary and heavy-laden, and I will give you rest. Take My yoke upon you and learn from Me, for I am gentle and humble in heart, and you will find rest for your souls. For My yoke is easy and My burden is light."

In both Matthew chapter 10 and 11, Jesus talks almost exclusively about witnessing. He first tells His disciples to go to the lost sheep of Israel. Then, he speaks warnings and encouragement to every believer who witnesses. After that, he speaks about the witness of John the Baptist, and then he moves on to His own witness and the witness of the miracles He had performed. Finally, he ends by saying, "Take My yoke upon you." He's talking about the burden of witnessing.

I'll be honest; Jesus' words do sound a little contradictory at first. However, the only reason they sound strange is because some of us are reading this with our carnal minds. Paul tells us in 1 Corinthians 2:16 that as believers, we have the mind of Christ. Through the help of the Holy Spirit, we don't have to look at Scripture through the lens of carnality. We can look at it with the understanding the Holy Spirit freely gives us. Here's what I'm saying: Jesus is talking about a supernatural principle that doesn't work unless we accept that it's supernatural in nature. It's not bound to the laws of the natural world.

In most cases, accepting more of a burden means the job will be harder to do. Carrying more weight during a hike makes it more difficult to make it up the mountain. Yet, Jesus says when we take His burden, we find rest. Jesus knew this concept wouldn't make sense to our natural minds, and He clues us in to this fact in verse 25 when He says, "I praise You, Father, Lord of heaven and earth, that You have hidden these things from the wise and intelligent and have revealed them to infants." This should lead us to a single conclusion: To accept the principle of His burden, we've got to believe it with a childlike faith. The good news is, when we accept it, it changes everything.

Have you ever worried about running out of gas on the highway? I've stretched the limits of my fuel tank a little too far sometimes, choosing to ignore the "low fuel" light for about an hour or so. What can I say? I like to live on the edge. Most of us though, when we start worrying about running out of gas, we fuel up. The gasoline actually adds weight—a greater burden—to the vehicle, and yet it causes us to go a lot farther than we would without it. In fact, without fuel, we eventually stop altogether.

If you didn't understand how fuel worked, you might assume adding the weight of gasoline to your vehicle would make the trip more difficult. It's the same with the weight of Jesus' burden. When we choose to pick it up, it gives us the life we need to continue doing what God has called us to do. So, since I'm using the illustration of fuel, let's look at the actual fueling element God gives us.

"We love, because He first loved us. If someone says, 'I love God,' and hates his brother, he is a liar; for the one who does not love his brother whom he has seen, cannot love God whom he has not seen."

1 John 4:19-20

The reason Jesus' burden gives us strength is because it comes with the fuel of God's love. God's love, when it is fully received, compels us to love one another. The greatest way we can love someone is to share the gospel with them, so the simple act of carrying God's love with you will make you a natural witness.

This is how you know if you have Jesus' burden or not: His burden is healthy. It doesn't cause worry or anxiety. In fact, it alleviates those problems. However, the opposite is also true. An unhealthy burden does cause us to worry more. The motivation behind the burden makes all the difference. An unhealthy burden will be fueled by fear and shame, and it will lead you to act in your own strength. That's when you'll eventually feel like you're running on fumes. A healthy burden for the lost will be fueled by God's love and empowered by the Holy Spirit. It will be a restful, relief-filled process through which you always have enough strength to keep going.

So, how do we take up His burden? We must continue to look intently into the truth of the gospel ourselves, no matter how long we've been saved. Imagine for a second the way Jesus may have looked at the criminal who hung next to Him on the cross. The man said, "Remember me when You come in Your kingdom." Despite the intense torture He was undergoing, I can see Jesus looking at that man with all the love in the world as He accepted Him into His eternal family. Jesus said, "Truly I say to you, today you shall be with Me in Paradise." Jesus could have just nodded at the guy. He could have just forgiven him and said nothing. But He didn't. I believe He wanted the man to know that, even though he may have lived a life of pain, disappointment, and wrong choices, he had nothing to worry about anymore. Forever after that, he would be resting in the loving presence of His compassionate Savior. Think about the weight that must have lifted off that man's shoulders when He heard Jesus' kind words of life. If you and I want to walk in the relief Jesus provides, we need to abide in the hope-filled belief that Jesus didn't just suffer and die for people like that man. He died for us, too. We needed it just as much.

When we're resting in that relief—in that state of undeserved love—our natural response will be to share that love with others. When we accept Jesus' heart of compassion as our own, we can't help but reach out to those who are lost.

> *"In this is love, not that we loved God, but that He loved us and sent His Son to be the propitiation for our sins. Beloved, if God so loved us, we also ought to love one another. No one has seen God at any time; if we love one another, God abides in us, and His love is perfected in us. By this we know that we abide in Him and He in us, because He has given us of His Spirit."*

> 1 John 4:10-13

The phrase "we also ought to love one another" is Jesus' burden spelled out plainly. It's not a burden we take on to earn something. It's a burden we take on because Jesus gave everything for us. Learning to receive God's love and then turning around and redistributing it to others should be a natural process in our relationship with God.

One thing we need to keep in mind is when we choose to hold back that love from others, we are actually hindering our relationship with God. It says, "If we love one another, God abides in us." Here's what the devil will try to do with that statement: He will try to twist it and make it about your works. He will attempt to get you to think that you have to try harder to love others. It's not about you trying harder. It's about you fully accepting the burden of love Jesus Himself is holding out to you. When His love is flowing to you, it also flows through you and out to others.

In that same passage, we also see that our ability to love others is directly connected to our fellowship with the Holy Spirit. Once again, God makes it personal. When you're hearing from the Holy Spirit, He gives you the right words to say to someone when you feel like there's nothing good to say. He gives you ideas for new ways to share the love of God. He reminds you of the Scriptures you need when you're witnessing to someone. He enables you to love people the way they need to be loved instead of just the way you prefer to love them. He's even constantly replenishing the love you give out.

"...the love of God has been poured out within our hearts through the Holy Spirit who was given to us."

Romans 5:5b

When you stop at a gas station during a long trip, you take a small detour off the highway. Sometimes you have to drive into a town to find a station. The same way, when we feel spiritually dry, we need to take a detour off our normal path. We need to seek out the Holy Spirit. We need to spend some time in God's presence, allowing Him to refuel us, to give us the relief we need during the journey. We need to go into that living room and sit at Jesus' feet.

If you're reading this and you know you need to pick up Jesus' yoke—His burden for the lost—I want you to pray with me. Pray out loud if you need to. Pray in faith that God is not only going to give you a burden for the lost but that He's also going to give you the relief you need.

Jesus, You loved me with a perfect love when You died on the cross, paying the penalty for all my sin. I can't ever begin to repay You, but I know that's not what You're asking. You're asking for my heart, and I want to give it. Will You please take the burdens off my shoulders that I've been thinking are important. Replace them with Your yoke. Give me Your burden, and empower me to take the message of the gospel to those who need to hear it. Your love is incredible. It has changed my life. Don't let it stop with me, Jesus. Use me as a vessel through which You spread Your love to the nations. Holy Spirit, remind me of God's amazing love every day, and keep drawing me back to You. I haven't done this perfectly, but I believe Your grace is enough for me right now. And I believe You can change me. Thank you Lord Jesus that one day I'll be resting with You in Your heavenly kingdom. I love You, my Savior. Amen.

If you prayed with me, I want you to know that God is going to start relieving your burdens. When you take on Jesus' burden for people, He takes away all the burdens people have placed on you. He takes away the burdens you were born with. He takes away the burdens you have placed on yourself. Where did those burdens go? He lets them fall on His own shoulders as He hung on the cross.

270

When we allow Him to lift the weight off, we can finally find relief. We can finally stop worrying.

So that you know I'm not exaggerating, let's quickly examine the language Jesus uses in Matthew 11:30. He says, "For My yoke is easy and My burden is light." The greek word translated "easy" here is *chréstos*, which literally means *good*. However, it also carries the meaning of something being better, gentle, pleasant, or gracious in nature. Jesus is essentially saying two things here: *My way is pleasant, and it's also a better way than your own.*

The other descriptor Jesus uses is the word "light," which comes from the greek word *elaphros*. The meaning behind the word *elaphros* is *easy to bear*, and it's used to show that something is not burdensome.

Don't you see? The world, the devil, and even our own minds offer us one way to live this life. Jesus offers us a better way. On the day Jesus visited Mary and Martha, Martha chose her own way, and it left her in a state of helpless anxiety. Mary chose the better way. Jesus' words in Luke 10:42 translated into the Contemporary English Version read like this: "Mary has chosen *what is best*, and it will not be taken away from her."

> **When you take on Jesus' burden for people, He takes away all the burdens people have placed on you.**

Are you choosing what is best? Maybe this question is more applicable: Do you *believe* Jesus' way is better? Just as importantly, are you believing it every day? If there's one thing God wants us to hold onto more than anything else, it's our belief in His words. That's why Jesus is able to say in John 6:29, "This is the work of God, that you believe in Him whom He has sent." God is after our hearts, and the language of our hearts is faith. Put your trust completely and uncompromisingly in Him. Give Him your heart. Choose the one thing that's necessary, and let the worries and cares of this life fall away. All the peace and favor you need are found at the feet of Jesus.

- 9 -

CONCLUSION

I want to quickly cover two things in this short conclusion chapter. First, I want to say that, if some of the principles in this book have made you feel like you're doing things wrong, you need to know that God has grace for you today. Maybe you think you've wasted time. Maybe your heart has been seeking something other than God. The good news of Jesus Christ is *yours* today. He's still doing His redemptive work. God isn't done with you. If you need to, reach out to God right now and receive His amazing grace all over again.

The cross isn't just behind us. It's in front of us, too. You may have been saved years ago, and you may have made mistakes since then. But today is still the day of salvation.

> *"Thus says the Lord, 'In a favorable time I have answered You, and in a day of salvation I have helped You; and I will keep You and give You for a covenant of the people, To restore the land, to make them inherit the desolate heritages;"*
>
> Isaiah 49:8

Three things happen when we choose to make today the day of salvation. First, God hears us. We experience His nearness and His voice. Second, God helps us. He provides for our needs and gives us strength to walk through every trial and hardship. Third, God changes us. He takes what little we have left, even if we feel like it's been wasted, and He makes it beautiful and useful for His kingdom.

The second thing I want to briefly address is this question that may be sitting in your mind: *What if I feel like I should be receiving the benefits of God's grace, and yet it seems like I'm not? What if I'm trying to follow the principles of God, and yet I'm not seeing the promises?*

In Psalm 77, Asaph asks a similar question. He says in verses 1-2,

> *"My voice rises to God, and I will cry aloud;*
> *My voice rises to God, and He will hear me.*
> *In the day of my trouble I sought the Lord;*
> *In the night my hand was stretched out without weariness;*
> *My soul refused to be comforted."*

Asaph's soul is so troubled that it refuses to accept any comfort. In his desperation, we find him seeking God with all his heart, crying out for an answer. In verses 8-9, he asks some startling questions about God's goodness.

> *"Has His lovingkindness ceased forever?*
> *Has His promise come to an end forever?*
> *Has God forgotten to be gracious,*
> *Or has He in anger withdrawn His compassion?"*

Asaph deals directly with the doubt in his mind. He doesn't try to hide it, but he brings it straight out into the light. Have you ever asked this question: Why does it seem like God isn't keeping His promises? If you haven't yet, at some point you will. When you do, remember to do what Asaph does in this psalm. Take your doubts to God and lay them down at His feet. Be honest with Him. Though it may feel like God has forgotten to be gracious, He hasn't. He still keeps His promises, and the best place to find that out is at His feet.

Then, I would also do what Asaph does as he begins to close out his prayer. He reminds himself of what God has already done. Verses 11-12 say,

> *"I shall remember the deeds of the Lord;*
> *Surely I will remember Your wonders of old.*
> *I will meditate on all Your work*
> *And muse on Your deeds."*

What deeds does he refer to? Well, for him, the greatest example of God's love, power, provision, and grace occurred when God delivered the people of Israel out of Egypt.

"You have by Your power redeemed Your people,
The sons of Jacob and Joseph."

"The sound of Your thunder was in the whirlwind;
The lightnings lit up the world;
The earth trembled and shook.
Your way was in the sea
And Your paths in the mighty waters,
And Your footprints may not be known.
You led Your people like a flock
By the hand of Moses and Aaron."

Psalm 77:15, 18-20

Asaph reminds himself just how good God's deliverance really is. God's deliverance is still just as good today. Remember, God's deliverance for His people out of Egypt was just a shadow of the deliverance Jesus would win for us on the cross.

On the day of His death, Jesus asked a similar question to Asaph. He cried out to God, saying, "Why have you forsaken Me?" When life feels unfair to us, we can look at the unfair treatment Jesus took for us. The reason God forsook Jesus there on the cross was so that He would never have to forsake we who believe in His Son.

Even at our lowest moments, we can always look back at what Jesus did for us and see the fulfillment of God's promises. The love He poured out for us can lead us to come into His presence with a prayer sort of like Asaph's:

Dear God, I don't feel Your hand at work right now, but I know Jesus' hands felt the nails for me. I don't see Your provision yet, but I know Jesus' death provided life for me. I'm carrying a burden right now, but I know Jesus carried the burden of the world on His shoulders for me. My body is still aching right now, but I know Jesus' body was torn apart for me. My heart is still hurting right now, but I know Jesus' heart burst open for me.

Jesus, help me to find You in my right now. It's worth it all as long as I get to sit with You and listen. Heal the pain, Lord. Redeem the time, Savior. Fix the things I can't fix, my King. Keep making me a new creation in You. You're my everything. You're the reason I can walk in peace and favor. Take my burdens, take my fears, take my worries, and give me You.

THE AUTHOR

Troy Black lives with his wife, Leslie, in East Texas. He likes board games, playing sports, reading, and going for long walks. Troy and Leslie have three daughters named Mirabelle, Iona, and Lauralee.

Troy and Leslie have a strong passion for spreading the gospel and the truth of God's word. It is their desire to see those who are lost come to salvation in Christ Jesus and for the Christian church to experience abundant life through the work of the Holy Spirit.

Other books by Troy Black include *My Mess: Believe it or not, a story about grace* and *30 Days of Inspiration and Hope: Daily Devotionals for Your Christian Walk.*

KEEP IN TOUCH

TroyBlackVideos.com
Facebook.com/AuthorTroyBlack
Youtube.com/InspireChristianBook

Made in the USA
Monee, IL
14 July 2022

99678413R00154